Food Legislation of the UK

A concise guide

Third edition

D. J. Jukes BSc, MSc, PhD, MIFST

Lecturer in Food Technology
Department of Food Science and Technology
University of Reading

Butterworth-Heinemann Ltd
Linacre House, Jordan Hill, Oxford OX2 8DP

OXFORD LONDON BOSTON
MUNICH NEW DELHI SINGAPORE SYDNEY
TOKYO TORONTO WELLINGTON

First published 1984
Second edition 1987
Third edition 1993
Revised reprint 1994

British Library Cataloguing in Publication Data
Jukes, D.J.
Food Legislation of the UK: Concise
Guide. – 3Rev.ed
I. Title
344.1044232

ISBN 0 7506 1175 8

Library of Congress Cataloguing in Publication Data
Jukes, D.J.
Food Legislation of the UK: a concise guide/D.J. Jukes. – 3rd ed.
p. cm.
Includes index.
ISBN 0 7506 1175 8
1. Food law and legislation – Great Britain. I. Title
KD3453.J85 1993
344.41'04232-dc20 93–8569
[344.1044232] CIP

Printed and bound in Great Britain by
Biddles Ltd, Guildford and King's Lynn

Contents

For my wife Helen and our daughters Camilla, Polly, Verity and Kezia

Important

Readers should note that this Guide is not a legal document and, whilst every care has been taken in its preparation, no responsibility can be accepted for problems arising from its use.

Acknowledgements

The inspiration for this Guide came from the original work of David Pearson whose *Concise Guide to UK Food Legislation* was published in May 1976.

I would welcome comments from readers on the content, presentation and relevance of any of the topics covered (or left out).

David Jukes
Lecturer in Food Technology
Department of Food Science and Technology
Food Studies Building
University of Reading
Whiteknights
Reading RG6 2AP

Introduction 1

This Guide has been designed to cover the legislative controls under which food technologists have to work in the United Kingdom. The much smaller original document was prepared to provide students of the then National College of Food Technology at Reading University with sufficient detail of the legal standards they would need when working as technologists in industry. It has grown considerably since then, as this third published edition demonstrates. Its publication illustrates that a wide range of people require information on the laws and regulations applied to food and food processing.

The selection of regulations for inclusion has been difficult and readers should note that the Guide does not provide a comprehensive list of all the regulations affecting food and food production. In particular, a distinction has been drawn between the requirements for food products, which are mostly covered, and the requirements for agricultural produce, which are not. Thus for example, grading standards for vegetables and eggs are not included. A further distinction is made between food regulations of interest to the industry as a whole, and those complex regulations affecting one particular section. As an example of this, the EC Wine Regulations have not been included. Regulations affecting all industry and not specifically food production are also not included.

It should be noted that the Guide is based on the Regulations for England and Wales. Whilst most of the Regulations for Scotland apply the same standards, certain details may be different. Appendix 1 should be consulted for further details. A similar situation affects the Regulations for Northern Ireland.

As with any attempt to simplify legal matters, it is likely that in the process certain requirements or exemptions will have been dropped. It is important that readers appreciate that the Guide is not a legal document and that for full details of the legal requirements the Acts and Regulations must be consulted.

Legislation is constantly changing. This Guide gives the legal requirements at the time of writing. Any changes that occur prior to printing but after the preparation of the main text will be included in Appendix 6. It is therefore suggested that readers check Appendix 6 prior to using the Guide.

2 UK food law

In the United Kingdom, as elsewhere, legislation controlling food has two principal aims – the protection of the health of the consumer and the prevention of fraud. In addition there is legislation which has an economic motive (tariffs, taxes, quotas, etc.) which provide economic benefits to an industry but which do not usually involve the technologist. The two principal aims are achieved in the UK by a combination of primary legislation (the Acts) and more detailed secondary legislative measures (the regulations or orders). The Acts usually contain general prohibitions, which, when interpreted and enforced by the courts, provide general consumer protection. The scientific and technical requirements of food production require more detailed controls. The Acts therefore also contain the authorisation for Ministers, subject to specified parliamentary approval, to issue detailed regulations. It is these which form the main bulk of this book.

While this book is meant as a guide to the technical requirements of legislation, it is necessary to put it into the context of the legislative structure in the UK. It is therefore important to discuss briefly some of the more important aspects of the application of food law in the UK.

Primary legislation

In England and Wales, the primary legislative powers are now contained in the 'Food Safety Act 1990'. This new Act updated the primary legislation for England, Wales and Scotland. For Northern Ireland, very similar controls are contained in the 'Food Safety (Northern Ireland) Order 1991'. Only very brief details of the Act are given in this book and readers are strongly urged to obtain an actual copy of the Act.

The Act states that food should not be 'rendered injurious to health' and should comply with certain specified 'food safety requirements'. General consumer protection is contained in a section which requires food to be of the 'nature or substance or quality demanded by the purchaser' and another which makes it an offence for food to be falsely described or to have a misleading label. There are numerous provisions providing for more detailed controls to be applied by regulations and these can cover a wide range of topics: composition, labelling, processing, packaging, hygiene, microbiological standards, novel foods etc.

Enforcement powers are detailed and enable enforcement officers to enter premises to inspect the business to ensure compliance with the various controls. If they suspect a failure to comply, food can be seized, instructions can be issued to improve the premises ('improvement notices') and, in extreme cases, the business can be prevented from operating ('emergency prohibition notice') pending a court hearing.

Failure to comply with the provisions of the Act is a criminal offence and courts have significant penalty powers. An opportunity is provided for a food business to defend itself by using certain statutory defences provided by the Act. In particular, provision is made for a defence if the person charged can show that they 'took all reasonable precautions and exercised all due diligence'. However, this requires the presentation of sufficient information to convince the court that the requirements have been met. It is not an easy defence to operate. For example, what is 'reasonable ' will vary from one business to another depending on the size of the operation and the potential hazards of the products.

A number of other Acts apply to food products and therefore require consideration. In particular the 'Weights and Measures Act 1985' (a consolidation of previous Acts) has many provisions which apply to food. Other Acts have to be considered and are listed in Section 3.3. Special mention should be made of the 'Food and Environment Protection Act 1985' which contains provisions enabling the prohibition of food sales where health hazards may exist and for the control of pesticides (and their residues). This had been a gap in the previous legislation.

Regulations

The vast majority of the detailed technical requirements for food products are contained in the regulations issued by Ministers and laid before Parliament. In most cases the regulations are passed unless Parliament specifically votes against them. In other cases draft regulations may have to be presented to Parliament a number of days before the actual regulations are published and, in a few cases, Parliament has to positively approve the regulations. Prior to the Food Safety Act 1990, since there were three separate Acts covering the UK there had to be three separate sets of regulations issued on any particular subject. For most products this does not present any difficulty since the technical requirements are identical and only certain administrative provisions may differ. However, for historical reasons the legislation on milk for Scotland has evolved slightly differently and certain technical standards are different from those specified for England and Wales. Provisions for food hygiene which include certain registration requirements also differ. The situation has now been improved to the extent that England, Wales and Scotland now can have a combined Regulation. Details are given in Appendix 1 of those regulations which are similar and those which contain some differences in detail.

Depending upon the requirements of the primary legislation, some of the secondary powers are issued as 'Orders' rather than 'Regulations'. For England, Wales and Scotland these are all published as Statutory Instruments (SI) with a reference number indicating the year of publication and the number assigned to the particular SI. The equivalent regulations for Northern Ireland are generally issued in a separate series known as the 'Statutory Rules of Northern Ireland'. Due to the difficult legislative position in Northern Ireland, certain measures (including primary legislation) are being published as Statutory Instruments. It is therefore important to check which series is involved when quoting a reference number.

Development of regulations

Before issuing regulations, Ministers are usually required to consult with those organisations which may be affected by them. Thus, when a Minister proposes to make a regulation, a press notice is issued and the proposed regulation is sent for comment to manufacturers, retailers, consumer groups and a number of professional bodies representing technologists, enforcement officers, councils, etc. Only when this consultation is complete will the Minister decide on the final form of the regulations.

For matters which require more extensive or formal scientific consideration a number of independent committees have been established to advise the Ministers. The principal one for food is the Food Advisory Committee (FAC) which was constituted in 1983 by combining two previous committees (the Food Standards Committee (FSC) and the Food Additives and Contaminants Committee (FACC)). When requested to study a particular topic, the FAC invites comment from interested parties and often asks other committees to give advice on certain specialised subjects. The publication of a report by the committee is often used as the basis for future regulations. A full list of published reports is given in Appendix 2.

Compositional standards

One of the methods used to prevent consumer fraud is to ensure that products described by a particular name conform to certain standards. When standards are set for a particular name then that name is known as a 'reserved description' and can only be used for products conforming to the set standard. When someone buys that product the legislation ensures that the consumer is buying a set standard and hence a satisfactory product.

Compositional standards were originally permitted by the Food and Drugs Act of 1938 but the stimulus for such standards was provided by the need for controls during wartime rationing. Many of these were continued after the war and additional compositional standards were added. Some rather obscure products were included in this category (mustard, curry powder and tomato ketchup for example) as well as some of the staples of the British diet (flour, bread and sausages). During the 1950s and 1960s compositional controls were considered the most useful way of providing consumer protection.

Soon after the UK joined the European Common Market in 1973 further regulations were issued covering compositional standards for a number of products (cocoa and chocolate, sugar products, fruit juices and nectars) some of which had never previously had a UK standard. However, more recently the emphasis has been to restrict the number of compositional standards to a number of basic products and enable manufacturers to produce a broad spectrum of goods. Consumer protection is maintained by more stringent labelling requirements. This trend is demonstrated by the revocation, in 1990, of the legal standards for mustard, curry powder and tomato ketchup.

Additives

The use of most additives in food products is controlled by regulations which adopt the ‘positive list’ system. Under this system only those additives positively listed in the regulations which perform the function (antioxidant, colour, etc.) defined by the regulations are permitted for food use. Provision is made in the definitions to cover the case of additives having a number of different functions. When it is considered necessary to restrict the use of a particular additive, the regulations also contain provisions which limit the foods in which the additive may be used, and the levels of usage.

All additives are subjected to a number of evaluations prior to being positively listed. Within the UK, the initial assessment is on the basis of any technical need for the additive and is conducted by the FAC. If they are satisfied that the additive does serve a useful purpose, then they ask the advice of other committees and in particular the Committee on Toxicity of Chemicals in Food, Consumer Products and the Environment (COT). These committees examine all the evidence relating to the toxicological evaluation of the additives before advising on their safety for food use.

All major categories of additives are controlled by specific regulations and most minor categories have been incorporated into the ‘Miscellaneous Additives in Food Regulations’. The most recent controls, those on flavourings, were applied in 1992. In this case, given the great number of chemicals involved, a ‘positive list’ has not been established and the

Regulations contain a 'negative list' which places restrictions on a few substances known to be hazardous.

Contaminants

The controls on specific contaminants in the UK are of a limited nature. Government policy has been to monitor and, when necessary, agree a voluntary policy of eliminating contamination at source rather than establishing numerous different levels for different contaminants in different foods. Only where a hazard has been sufficiently great or where the contaminant is widespread have controls been introduced. Thus, maximum arsenic, lead and tin levels have been introduced by regulation and, very recently, maximum aflatoxin levels on nuts and nut products sold to the ultimate consumer have been imposed.

The control of pesticide residues has also been by a monitoring process. Detailed regulations have now been issued in line with EC requirements and using the powers in the 'Food and Environment Protection Act'.

It is important to note that prosecutions can be brought under the Food Safety Act on the basis that a product is injurious to health and that, in establishing this fact, non-statutory limits (internationally recommended limits for example) can be used as evidence in the court. It is then up to the court to decide whether to accept the evidence as valid.

Processing and packaging

Under this category are included certain specific regulations inappropriate elsewhere. Examples include irradiation, permitted since January 1991, and controls on quick-frozen foodstuffs (implementing an EC Directive). Controls on packaging materials have also been established to prevent any harmful substances becoming incorporated into food.

Labelling

Labelling requirements for food products can be very complex. Certain products have their own regulations which incorporate labelling provisions. Most food products though are subject to the 'Food Labelling Regulations 1984' (as amended). Any changes to these regulations can have quite major consequences for the whole food industry. The current regulations have been fully effective for several years now but major amendments have been made in the last four years. The changes introduced by the 1984 Regulations and the amendments have provided consumers with much detailed information. Further amendments are thought likely in the near future and the opportunity may be taken to introduce a new consolidated set of Regulations.

Hygiene and health

The maintenance of satisfactory hygienic practices is ensured by the various food hygiene regulations. While these are the most used regulations in terms of food prosecutions, the vast majority of cases are against small retailers, restaurants and catering establishments. The regulations have certain specific requirements but in most cases they establish the general principles and it is for the enforcement authorities and the courts to interpret the requirements.

Associated with hygiene are the various regulations governing public health with regard to milk handling, poultry and meat inspection and the various import controls to prevent the spread of certain specific animal and human health hazards. The possibility of the spread of disease from country to country has always been a risk. Even within the UK powers exist to control food movements and, in particular, Northern Ireland has certain powers to restrict the import of food from the mainland of England, Wales and Scotland. These controls have been relaxed but it is wise to check the current position with the Northern Ireland authorities.

Where it has been considered important to prevent the spread of disease by incorporating a heat treatment step in the processing of food, standards have been incorporated in regulations. Thus a number of different heat treatments are permitted for milk so as to eliminate pathogenic organisms. Other products with similar controls are milk-based drinks, cream, liquid egg and ice-cream. Where appropriate, these are covered in this book in association with the relevant compositional standards.

Microbiological standards for food products are another area in which the UK has believed that statutory limits are usually inappropriate. As with contaminants, the emphasis has been on monitoring and ensuring hygienic practices rather than establishing limits for specific products. However, many European countries do have such statutory standards and it is possible that the UK will eventually have more. It is worth noting that both the 'Natural Mineral Waters Regulations' and the 'Milk (Special Designation) Regulations' do incorporate certain microbiological limits.

Weights and measures

Although the subject of weights and measures legislation is vast and mostly beyond the scope of this book, there are two aspects which do regularly affect the food technologist. These are the controls on specified weights (prescribed weights) which restrict pack sizes on a number of food products to certain set weights and the 'Packaged Goods Regulations' which apply an average weight system to most food products. Weights and measures legislation is the responsibility of the Department of Trade and Industry.

Enforcement structure

Enforcement of food legislation in the UK has, since its start in the late nineteenth century, been the responsibility of local authorities. Each local authority employs trained personnel to ensure that a wide range of Acts and Regulations (including food) are enforced. The two major types of trained officers involved in food work are the Environmental Health Officer (EHO) and the Trading Standards Officer (TSO). Veterinary supervision is also required in certain areas where animals enter the food system (e.g. inspection at time of slaughter).

Environmental health officers usually have responsibility for enforcing those aspects of food law which have a hygiene or health basis. Their main area of work is therefore the enforcement of the food hygiene regulations and the controls on unfit food contained in the Food Safety Act. Trading standards officers are involved in the enforcement of a wide range of controls on all types of trading. Thus for food they usually have authority relating to composition and labelling. Qualified Trading Standards Officers are also the inspectors for the weights and measures legislation.

The structure of local government in the UK is very varied and thus the administration of food law varies throughout the country. For the non-metropolitan parts of England and Wales, trading standards are allocated to the county councils while the environmental health controls are allocated to the district councils (there being a number of districts in each county). In the metropolitan areas, where there are no counties, both responsibilities are covered by the metropolitan district councils (or for London, the borough councils). For Scotland, trading standards are covered by the regional councils and environmental health by the districts. In Scotland there is an important difference in that since April 1983 responsibility for food composition and labelling has been a district matter (and hence enforced by Environmental Health Officers). For Northern Ireland, food law administration is the responsibility of a number of Group Public Health Committees. Imported food arriving in the UK is usually inspected initially by officers employed by the Port Health Authority, although inspection may be delayed until the food arrives at its destination. Assisting in the work of the enforcement officers is the public analyst who is usually appointed by the county council to provide official analysis of sampling taken by the officers. Their analysis, usually chemical or physical, is then used as the prime evidence in any prosecution relating to composition of food. Microbiological examination of food is undertaken by food examiners who are required to be qualified to certain minimum standards.

The concept of microbiological 'examination' was introduced for the first time in the Food Safety Act 1990.

With the very varied structure of local government and the enforcement of legislation at a local level there has always been scope for a different degree of enforcement around the country. Thus, even if a food label has been agreed by one trading standards department, those in another part of the country could still object to it. The need for uniform interpretation and application of the law is therefore important. To help achieve this trading standards departments and environmental health departments are all represented on a national body – the Local Authorities Co-ordinating Body on Food and Trading Standards (LACOTS). This organization provides a valuable forum for discussion among TSOs and EHOs and hence helps to ensure that the law is applied in a uniform way. In particular they have established a system where most companies only have to deal with one local authority (the 'home authority') and any complaints are referred to that authority for investigation. It must be stressed though that it is possible for any trading standards department to bring a prosecution against any product sold in its area and it is for the courts to decide what the law actually requires.

The need for stronger central guidance on the execution, by enforcement officers, of their responsibilities was accepted when the Food Safety Act was passed. Section 40 of the Act provides the Minister with the authority to issue codes of recommended practice. Several have now been issued and are listed in Appendix 3.

Prior to the formation of LACOTS another body had attempted to introduce certain nationally agreed standards in the form of codes of practice. The Local Authorities Joint Advisory Committee on Food Standards (LAJAC) produced a number of codes which are listed in Appendix 3. While LACOTS does not actually develop codes, it has accepted a number (also listed in Appendix 3) as being useful and circulated them to its members. These codes have no legal status but they do provide a guide which can be considered as evidence by a court in any prosecution.

The European dimension

Since 1973, the UK has been a member of the European Communities (EC) and has therefore also been applying legislation agreed among the EC member states. European legislation is aimed at creating a common market in goods so that products produced anywhere in the Community can circulate within it unrestricted by both tariff and non-tariff barriers.

EC legislation applied to food usually takes two forms – the Regulation and the Directive. The Regulation is usually applied to primary agricultural products and is applicable to all member states at the same time. The vast majority relate to the Common Agricultural Policy and are involved with standards for intervention goods, tariffs applied to goods entering the Community and various production quotas. They are mostly beyond the scope of this book. The Directive has been widely used to try to create a market free of non-tariff barriers. Thus, differences in technical standards contained in national legislation hinder the movement of goods between member states. By agreeing common standards, these barriers are removed. Directives require implementation by each member state before they become law. Thus a large number of the UK regulations listed in this book contain standards agreed at a European level. A list of the main European legislation on food products is given in Appendix 4.

With the completion of the 'internal market' programme of the EC at the end of 1992, many more Regulations and Directives have been adopted. Some of these have been incorporated into UK legislation. Some have still to be adopted within the EC – progress on agreeing the new controls on additives has been particularly difficult. Many changes are still likely before a true internal market will exist. There remains constant pressure for new and amended controls. Technologists, and others, must remain vigilant in a constantly changing control system.

Acts 3

3.1 Food Safety Act 1990

3.1

Note: This Act is generally applicable to England, Wales and Scotland. For Northern Ireland, see:

Food Safety (Northern Ireland) Order (1991/762)

Details are given of those Sections which are particularly relevant to food processing.

Part I Preliminary

Section 1 Meaning of 'food' and other basic expressions

Definition of 'food':

1) In this Act 'food' includes
   a) drink;
   b) articles and substances of no nutritional value which are used for human consumption;
   c) chewing gum and other products of a like nature and use; and
   d) articles and substances used as ingredients in the preparation of food or anything falling within this subsection.
2) In this Act 'food' does not include
   a) live animals or birds, or live fish which are not used for human consumption while they are alive;
   b) fodder or feeding stuffs for animals, birds or fish;
   c) controlled drugs within the meaning of the Misuse of Drugs Act 1971; or
   d) subject to such exceptions as may be specified in an order made by Ministers: (i) medicinal products within the meaning of the Medicines Act 1968 in respect of which product licences within the meaning of that Act are for the time being in force; or (ii) other articles or substances in respect of which such licences are for the time being in force in pursuance of orders under section 104 or 105 of that Act (application of Act to other articles and substances).

Also included are definitions of 'business', 'commercial operation', 'contact material', 'food business', 'food premises', 'food source' and 'premises'.

3.1 Section 2 Extended meaning of 'sale' etc.

This section states that the supply of food, otherwise than on sale, in the course of a business shall be deemed to be a sale. Offering food as a prize or reward or if it is given away in connection with any entertainment to which the public are admitted or in an advertisement is regarded as exposing for public sale.

Section 3 Presumptions that food is intended for human consumption

The sale of food commonly used for human consumption shall be presumed to be a sale for human consumption until the contrary is proved. Any food commonly used for human consumption and found on a premises used for the preparation, storage or sale of that food, and, any article or substance commonly used in the manufacture of food for human consumption which is found on such premises, shall be presumed (until the contrary is proved) to be intended for food use.

Section 4 Ministers having functions under the Act

Section 5 Food authorities and authorised officers

Section 6 Enforcement of Act

Part II Main provisions

Section 7 Rendering food injurious to health

Any person who renders food injurious to health by means of

a) adding any article or substance to the food;
b) using any article or substance as an ingredient in the preparation of the food;
c) abstracting any constituent from the food; and
d) subjecting the food to any other process or treatment, with intent that it shall be sold for human consumption, shall be guilty of an offence.

Provision is made for any cumulative effects of consumption in ordinary quantities. Injury includes any impairment, whether permanent or temporary.

Section 8 Selling food not complying with food safety requirements

It is an offence to sell, offer to sell, deposit for the purpose of sale, etc., any food which fails to comply with food safety requirements. Food fails to comply with food safety requirements if:

a) it has been rendered injurious to health;
b) it is unfit for human consumption; or
c) it is so contaminated (whether by extraneous matter or otherwise) that it would not be reasonable to expect it to be used for human consumption in that state.

Additional provisions provide for a batch, lot or consignment to be regarded as failing (until the contrary is proved) if a part of it fails.

Section 9 Inspection and seizure of suspected food

Authorised officers are permitted to inspect at all reasonable times any food intended for human consumption which has been sold or is in the possession of a person for the purpose of sale or preparation for sale.

Additional provisions provide for powers to prevent the movement of food or to seize food if an officer considers that the food fails to comply with food safety requirements, or if it appears that the food is likely to cause food poisoning or any disease communicable to human beings.

Section 10 Improvement notices

If an officer has reasonable grounds for believing that the proprietor of a food business is failing to comply with certain regulations (those which require, prohibit or regulate the use of any process or treatment in the preparation of food, or which secure the observance of hygienic conditions and practices in connection with commercial operations with respect to food or food sources) he may serve an 'improvement notice' on the proprietor. The notice will state:

a) the grounds for believing a failure to comply;
b) the matters which constitute the failure;
c) the measures necessary to comply; and
d) a time by which the measures should be taken (not less than 14 days).

Section 11 Prohibition orders

Two types of 'prohibition order' can be imposed.

1) If a court convicts a proprietor for an offence under certain regulations (identical to those listed in Section 10) and it is satisfied that there is risk of injury to health (the 'health risk condition') by:
   a) the use of any process or treatment;
   b) the construction of any premises or use of equipment; or
   c) the state or condition of any premises or equipment,

   then, it can make an order prohibiting, as appropriate, the use of the process, treatment, premises or equipment.
2) If a court convicts a proprietor for an offence under certain regulations (identical to those listed in Section 10) and it thinks it proper, then, it can make an order prohibiting the proprietor participating in the management of any specified food business.

Section 12 Emergency prohibition notices and orders

If an officer is satisfied that the 'health risk condition' (see section 11) is fulfilled and that there is imminent risk of injury to health, then he may serve an 'emergency prohibition notice' on the proprietor prohibiting, as appropriate, the use of a process, treatment, premises or equipment. Application must be made within 3 days to a court for the notice to be made into an 'emergency prohibition order'.

Section 13 Emergency control orders

If it appears to the Minister that the carrying out of commercial operations with respect to food, food sources or contact materials (of any class or description) involves or may involve imminent risk of injury to health, he may issue an 'emergency control order' prohibiting the carrying out of such operations with respect to food, food sources or contact materials (of that class or description).

3.1 Section 14 Selling food not of the nature or substance or quality demanded

Any person who sells to the purchaser's prejudice any food which is not of the nature or substance or quality demanded by the purchaser shall be guilty of an offence.

Section 15 Falsely describing or presenting food

Any person who gives or displays food with a label (whether or not attached to or printed on the wrapper or container) which

a) falsely describes the food; or
b) is likely to mislead as to the nature or substance or quality of the food, shall be guilty of an offence.

A similar provision applies to publishing an advertisement. Any person who sells any food the presentation of which is likely to mislead as to the nature or substance or quality of the food shall be guilty of an offence.

Sections 16–19 Regulations

These sections contain the provisions which allow Ministers to issue necessary regulations for a very wide range of purposes.

Section 16 provides the power for most common situations;
Section 17 provides additional powers for any EC obligation;
Section 18 allows for the control of novel foods or food sources or the use of genetically modified food sources; and
Section 19 allows for the registration or licensing of food premises.

Sections 20–22 Defences

Section 20 provides that, where the commission of an offence by any person is due to an act or default of some other person, that other person shall be guilty of the offence.

Section 21 provides a defence for a person charged with an offence to prove that he took all reasonable precautions and exercised all due diligence to avoid the commission of the offence by himself or by a person under his control. Additional subsections of 21 provide for certain conditions under which a person is deemed to have satisfied this requirement.

Section 22 provides a publisher with a defence if he publishes an advertisement in the ordinary course of business and the advertisement is contrary to provisions of the Act.

Sections 23–26 Miscellaneous and supplemental

Part III Administration and enforcement

Section 27 Appointment of public analysts
Section 28 Provision of facilities for examinations
Section 29 Procurement of samples
Section 30 Analysis etc. of samples
Section 31 Regulation of sampling and analysis etc.
Section 32 Powers of entry
Section 33 Obstruction etc. of officers

Section 34 Time limit for prosecutions
Section 35 Punishment of offences
Section 36 Offences by bodies corporate
Sections 37–39 Appeals

Part IV Miscellaneous and supplemental
Section 40 Power to issue codes of practice
For the guidance of food authorities, the Minister may issue codes of recommended practice as regards the execution and enforcement of this Act and of regulations and orders made under it. Food authorities shall have regard to the provisions of the codes and shall comply with any direction which is given by the Minister and requires them to take any specified step in order to comply with the code.
Section 41 Power to require returns
Section 42 Default powers
Section 43 Continuance of registration or licence on death
Section 44 Protection of officers acting in good faith
Sections 45–47 Financial provisions
Sections 48–50 Instruments and documents
Sections 51–52 Amendments of other Acts
Section 53 General interpretation
Some additional definitions are given in this section
Section 54 Application to Crown
Sections 55–56 Water supply
Section 57 Scilly Isles and Channel Islands
Section 58 Territorial waters and the continental shelf
Section 59 Amendments, transitional provisions, savings and repeals
Section 60 Short title, commencement and extent

3.2 Weights and Measures Act 1985

Note: The majority of this Act only applies to England, Wales and Scotland. For Northern Ireland, similar controls are contained in:
Weights and Measures (Northern Ireland) Order 1981 (1981/231)
The titles of the individual Parts are given below along with fuller details of those Sections having particular relevance to food.

Part I Units and standards of measurement
Section 1 Units of Measurement
For measurement of mass, the pound or kilogram shall be the unit to which any measurement is made and the pound shall be exactly 0.45359237kg.

Part II Weighing and measuring for trade

3.2 *Part III Public weighing or measuring equipment*

Part IV Regulation of transactions in goods

Section 22 Orders relating to transactions in particular goods

Orders may be made with respect to any specified goods to ensure that they are packed or sold in specified quantities, marked in specified ways or satisfy any other circumstance detailed in the Section.

Section 25 Offences in transactions in particular goods

Section 28 Short weight

Any person who, in selling or purporting to sell any goods by weight or other measurement or by number, delivers or causes to be delivered to the buyer

a) a lesser quantity than that purported to be sold, or

b) a lesser quantity than corresponds with the price charged,

shall be guilty of an offence.

Sections 33–37 Defences

1) Requirements necessary for a defence of warranty are given.
2) It shall be a defence for the person charged to prove that he took all reasonable precautions and exercised all due diligence.
3) If the loss occurred after packing, it is a defence if it can be shown that the loss occurred due to factors for which reasonable allowance was made.
4) For food (not prepacked) which loses weight by evaporation or drainage, if product is light, it shall be a defence to have taken due care and precaution to minimize the loss.
5) If the offence is of excess weight, it shall be a defence to prove that the excess was necessary to avoid a deficiency.
6) A person shall not be charged based on a single article unless, when available, a reasonable number of articles are also tested, and the court
   a) must consider the average weight of tested articles,
   b) if the proceedings are for a single article, shall disregard any inconsiderable deficiency or excess,
   c) have regard generally to the circumstances of the case.

Part V Packaged goods

Sections 47–48 Duties of packers or importers as to quantity and marking.

States the requirements of an 'average weight' system and allows for Regulations to prescribe methods for the selection and testing of packages. Allows for the publishing of a code of practical guidance. States requirements for marking of packages with weight and name and address or mark to enable inspector to ascertain packer or person who arranged for the packages to be made.

Sections 55–62 Co-ordination of control

These sections established a 'National Metrological Co-ordinating Unit' with certain duties and powers. The unit has now been abolished and most of the duties and powers have been taken over by the Secretary of State.

The duties include:

a) To review the operation of this part of the Act.
b) To provide information on the operation of this part of the Act.
c) To give advice to local authorities on the discharge of their duties.
d) To collaborate with similar bodies abroad on matters connected with the unit.
e) To make and maintain a record of the names and addresses of
   i) packers and importers with the kinds of packages they make up or import and the marks they use,
   ii) makers of measuring container bottles and the marks they use.

The Secretary of State has powers to require local authorities to conduct checks on certain packages and provide information.

Part VI Administration

Section 69 Local Weights and Measures Authorities

The Local Weights and Measures Authorities shall be the councils of the non-metropolitan counties, metropolitan districts and London boroughs.

Section 72 Appointment of inspectors

Each local weights and measures authority shall appoint a chief inspector of weights and measures and other inspectors of weights and measures.

Section 73 Certificate of qualification to act as inspector

Part VII General

Section 92 Spelling of 'gram', etc.

Permits the use of 'gramme' or '-gramme' as an alternative to 'gram' or '-gram'.

3.3 Miscellaneous acts

Prevention of Damage by Pests Act 1949

Note: Not applicable to Northern Ireland.

This Act provides for the control of pests which are infesting food premises. Infestation is defined as 'the presence of rats, mice, insects or mites in numbers or under conditions which involve an immediate or potential risk of substantial loss of or damage to food'. The following Sections have particular relevance to food processors.

Part I Rats and mice

Part II Infestation of food

Section 13 Obligation of certain undertakers to give notice of occurrence of infestation

Every person whose business consists of or includes the manufacture, storage, transport or sale of food shall notify the Minister if he is aware of any infestation present in

a) any premises, vehicle or equipment used for the above purposes,or
b) any food in his possession or other goods likely to be in contact with food.

Similar obligations apply to people handling containers intended for food use.

Regulations may be issued to relax the requirements of this Section (see below).

Section 14 Powers to give directions

Directions may be given to prohibit or restrict

a) the use for food of premises, vehicles or equipment, and
b) the delivery, acceptance, retention or removal of food, which is or is likely to be infested.

Part III Supplemental

Section 22 Powers of Entry

Any duly authorised person may enter any land to ascertain whether there is any failure to comply with the Act or Directions issued under the Act.

The following Regulation has been issued under Section 13 of the Act: The Prevention of Damage by Pests (Infestation of Food) Regulations 1950 (1950/416)

These Regulations relax the requirements of notification for infestation by insects and mites where:

a) the premises are used wholly or mainly for certain specified processes using certain specified imported foods,
b) the food is oil seeds being moved from one extracting mill to another for the purpose of oil extraction,
c) the food is fresh fruit or green vegetables, fresh home-killed meat, or fish other than cured or processed.

The Regulations should be consulted for full details.

Trade Descriptions Act 1968

Note: Applicable to all UK

Section 1 Prohibition of false trade description

Any person who, in the course of a trade or business,

a) applies a false trade description to any goods; or
b) supplies or offers to supply any goods to which a false trade description is applied; shall, subject to the provisions of the Act, be guilty of an offence.

Section 2 Trade description

1) A trade description is an indication, direct or indirect, and by whatever means given, of any of the following matters with respect to goods or parts of goods, that is to say:
   a) quantity, size or gauge;
   b) method of manufacture, production, processing or reconditioning;
   c) composition;
   d) fitness for purpose, strength, performance, behaviour or accuracy;
   e) any physical characteristics not included in the preceding paragraphs;
   f) testing by any person and results thereof;
   g) approval by any person or conformity with a type approved by any person;
   h) place or date of manufacture, production, processing or reconditioning;
   i) person by whom manufactured, produced, processed or reconditioned;
   j) other history, including previous ownership.

The application of a legally required name under Regulations under the Food Safety Act 1990 is not a trade description.

Section 3 False trade description

1) A false trade description is a trade description which is false to a material degree.
2) A trade description which, though not false, is misleading, that is to say, likely to be taken for such an indication of any of the matters specified in Section 2 of the Act would be false to a material degree, shall be deemed to be a false trade description.
3) Anything which, though not a trade description, is likely to be taken for an indication of any of those matters and, as such an indication, would be false to a material degree, shall be deemed to be a false trade description.
4) A false indication, or anything likely to be taken as an indication which would be false, that any goods comply with a standard specified or recognized by any person or implied by the approval of any person shall be deemed to be a false trade description, if there is no such person or no standard so specified, recognised or implied.

Section 4 Applying a false trade description

Section 5 Trade descriptions used in advertisements

Section 16 Prohibition of importation of goods bearing false indication of origin

Section 24 Defence of mistake, accident, etc.

3.3

International Carriage of Perishable Foodstuffs Act 1976

This Act enables the UK to accede to the Agreement on the International Carriage of Perishable Foodstuffs (the 'ATP'). A minor amendment, not relevant to food, was made by The International Carriage of Perishable Foodstuffs Act 1976 (Amendment) Order 1983 (1983/1123).

The Act enables Regulations to be made governing all aspects of the carriage of perishable foodstuffs.

For relevant details of the Regulations, see Section 4.5.

Animal Health Act 1981

Note: Applicable to England, Wales and Scotland.
For Northern Ireland, similar controls are contained in:
Diseases of Animals (Northern Ireland) Order 1981 (1981/1115)
This Act consolidated several previous Acts and, in particular, The Diseases of Animals Act 1950.
Section 1 provides the Minister with powers to make Orders for the purpose of preventing the spreading of disease.
Section 10 specifically provides for Orders for the purpose of preventing the introduction or spreading of disease into or within Great Britain through the importation of:
animals and carcases; carcases of poultry and eggs; and other things (whether animate or inanimate) by or by means of which it appears that any disease might be carried or transmitted.
For relevant details of the Orders, see Section 4.5.

Food and Environment Protection Act 1985

Note: Applicable to all UK.
This Act covers three main areas: powers to make emergency orders when escaped substances may have contaminated food; matters related to dumping at sea; and the control of pesticides previously subject to voluntary controls.

Part I Contamination of food
Section 1 If there is an escape of substances likely to create a hazard to human health through human consumption of food and the food may be in an area of the UK, ministers may make an emergency order. The order may prohibit certain specified things including preparation, processing and movement of food. The first such order was made in June 1986 to prohibit the movement or slaughter of sheep from parts of Cumbria and North Wales following the escape of radioactivity from Chernobyl, USSR (see SI 1986/1027).

Part II Deposits in the sea

Part III pesticides, etc.

Section 16 Control of Pesticides, etc. Permits Regulations to be made on all aspects of pesticide control including specifying how much pesticide or pesticide residue may be left in any crop, food or feeding stuff and provides for seizure and destruction if the limits are exceeded.

Part IV General and supplementary

4 Food regulations and orders

4.1 4.1 A–Z food standards

Bread

Regulation: Bread and Flour Regulations 1984 (1984/1304)
Amendment: Potassium Bromate (Prohibition as a Flour Improver) Regulations 1990 (1990/399)

Definition

Bread a food of any size, shape or form which is usually known as bread, and consists of a dough made from flour and water, with or without other ingredients, which has been fermented by yeast or otherwise leavened and subsequently baked or partly baked; but does not include buns, bunloaves, chapatis, chollas, pitta bread, potato bread or bread specially prepared for coeliac sufferers.

Reserved descriptions

(Names to be used for bread or doughs and dry mixes intended to make bread)

Description	*Requirement*
1) Where all the flour is derived from wheat, the name of the bread shall include the following words (1,2):	
'Wholemeal'	All flour used is wholemeal.
'Brown'	Has a crude fibre content (from wheat) of min 0.6% (bread dry matter) and includes flour other than wholemeal.
'Wheat germ'	Has an added processed wheat germ content of min 10% (bread dry matter).
'White'	All bread other than wholemeal, brown or wheat germ.
'Soda'	Bread made using sodium hydrogen carbonate.
2) Where the flour is derived from any cereal the following shall be used (1):	
'Wholemeal'	Made from the whole product derived from any cereal.

(*continued*)

Description	*Requirement*
3) Miscellaneous descriptions	
'Aerated'	Bread, other than soda bread, in which a major method of leavening is by the incorporation of air, carbon dioxide or nitrogen (or any mixture) into the dough either chemically or mechanically.
'Part-baked' or 'Partly Baked'	Bread requiring further cooking prior to consumption.

Notes:
(1) No account shall be taken of any rice flour used (max 2% of flour used) or any barley malt flour (small quantities for technological purposes).
(2) Not applicable to 'malt bread' or 'malt loaf'.

The following ingredients may be used without their presence being indicated in the name of the bread if used in small quantities for technological purposes or up to the maximum specified:

a) Any bread (except wholemeal for which the presence of these ingredients shall be indicated) – milk and milk products, liquid or dried egg, wheat germ, rice flour (max 20 g/kg), cracked oat grains, oatmeal, oat flakes.
b) Any bread – soya bean flour (max 50 g/kg for brown bread, max 20 g/kg other bread), salt, vinegar, oils and fats, malt extract, malt flour, any soluble carbohydrate sweetening matter, prepared wheat gluten, poppy seeds, sesame seeds, caraway seeds, cracked wheat, cracked or kibbled malted wheat, flaked malted wheat, kibbled malted rye, cracked or kibbled malted barley, starch other than modified starch (max 225 mg/kg).

The name 'wheatmeal' is not to be used to describe any bread.

Permitted additional ingredients of bread and flour
(Where no maximum quantity is given, the use must be in accordance with good manufacturing practice):

Additive	*Types of flour and bread in which additive may be used*	*Maximum quantity* (mg/kg of flour unless specified)
E150 Caramel	Wholemeal; brown flour. Wholemeal bread; brown bread; malt bread	
E170 Calcium carbonate	All flour except wholemeal. All bread	2000

4.1

(*continued*)

Additive	*Types of flour and bread in which additive may be used*	*Maximum quantity* (mg/kg of flour unless specified)
E220 Sulphur dioxide E223 Sodium metabisulphite	Flour, except wholemeal, for biscuit or pastry manufacture	Max E220 and E223 200 (calculalted as sulphur dioxide)
E260 Acetic acid E262 Sodium hydrogen diacetate E270 Lactic acid	All bread	
E280 Propionic acid E281 Sodium propionate E282 Calcium propionate E283 Potassium propionate	All bread	Total of E280-E283 Max. 3000 (calculated as propionic acid)
E290 Carbon dioxide	Aerated bread; all pre-packed bread	
E300 L-Ascorbic acid	All flour except wholemeal. All bread	200
E322 Lecithins	All bread	
E330 Citric acid E333 *tri*Calcium citrate	Rye bread	
E336 *mono*Potassium L-(+)-tartrate E341 Calcium tetrahydrogen diorthophosphate	Self-raising flour; flour for bun or scone manufacture. All bread	
E341 *tri*Calcium diorthophosphate	All flour except wholemeal. All bread	600
E450(a) *di*Sodium dihydrogen diphosphate	Self-raising flour; flour for bun or scone manufacture. All bread.	
E460 *alpha*-Cellulose E466 Carboxymethyl-cellulose sodium salt	Bread for which a slimming claim is made.	
E471 Mono- and diglycerides of fatty acids E472(b) Lactic acid esters of E471 E472(c) Citric acid esters of E471 E472(e) Mono- and diacetyltartaric acid esters of E471	All bread	

(*continued*)

Additive	*Types of flour and bread in which additive may be used*	*Maximum quantity* (mg/kg of flour unless specified)
E481 Sodium stearoyl-2-lactylate E482 Calcium stearoyl-2-lactylate	All bread	Total of E481/E482 max 5000 (based on bread weight)
E483 Stearyl tartrate	All bread	
500 Sodium hydrogen carbonate	Self-raising flour; flour for bun or scone manufacture. Soda bread	
510 Ammonium chloride	All bread	
516 Calcium sulphate	All flour except wholemeal. All bread.	4000
541 Sodium aluminium phosphate, acidic	Self-raising flour; flour for bun or scone manufacture. Soda bread	
575 D-Glucono-1,5-lactone	Self-raising flour; flour for bun or scone manufacture. Soda bread	
920 L-Cysteine hydrochloride	(a) All flour for biscuit manufacture except wholemeal or flour which has E220 or E223 added.	300
	(b) Other flour except wholemeal. All bread except wholemeal	75
925 Chlorine	All flour for cake manufacture except wholemeal	2500
926 Chlorine dioxide	All flour except wholemeal. All bread except wholemeal	30
927 Azodicarbonamide	All flour except wholemeal. All bread except wholemeal	45
Ammonium dihydrogen orthophosphate *di*Ammonium hydrogen orthophosphate Ammonium sulphate	All bread	
α-Amylases Proteinases	All flour. All bread	

4.1

(continued)

Additive	*Types of flour and bread in which additive may be used*	*Maximum quantity* (mg/kg of flour unless specified)
Nitrogen	Aerated bread	
Benzoyl peroxide	All flour except wholemeal All bread except wholemeal	50

General points

1) In addition to the above list, additives contained in ingredients of bread are also permitted unless:
   a) it was a constituent of flour used, or
   b) it serves a significant technological function in its preparation, or
   c) it serves a significant technological function in the finished product.
2) The use of an additive in bread as a flour improver must be indicated in an ingredients' list or, when the bread has no ingredients' list, on a suitable label, ticket or notice.
3) Where a dough or dry mix which is intended to be made into bread is being labelled, the name shall include the name of the type of bread and any additional words specified above.

Butter

Regulation: Butter Regulations 1966 (1966/1074)
Amendments: Colouring Matter in Food Regulations 1973 (1973/1340)
Food Labelling Regulations 1980 (1980/1849)

Definitions

Butter the fatty substance derived exclusively from cow's milk, the pH of which may have been adjusted with alkali carbonate, and may contain the following:
annatto, α-, β- and γ-carotene, synthetic β-carotene, or turmeric (subject to Colouring Matter in Food Regulations), and salt or lactic acid cultures; and includes whey butter.

Butter standards

a) minimum milk fat: 80%
b) maximum solids other than fat: 2%
c) maximum moisture: 16%

However, butter may contain less than 80% (but not less than 78% milk fat) if the amount by which the milk fat % falls below 80% does not exceed the amount by which the % of salt in the butter exceeds 3% and the butter is labelled 'salted butter'.

Labelling

The word 'butter' may only be used to describe butter which meets the above standards, except it may be used:

a) to describe any dehydrated butter, butter fat or butter oil (meeting the compositional standards for butter above) which is used as an ingredient of a food;
b) in such a context as to indicate clearly that butter was used as an ingredient in the food;
c) in such a context as to indicate clearly that the word 'butter' does not refer to the presence of butter as defined above.

If the butter contains no added salt it shall be labelled 'unsalted butter'; if it contains added salt (meeting the requirement above) it shall be labelled 'salted butter'.

Caseins and caseinates

Regulation: Caseins and Caseinates Regulations 1985 (1985/2026)
Amendment: Casein and Caseinates (Amendment) Regulations 1989 (1989/2321)

Definitions

Casein the principal protein constituent of milk, washed and dried, insoluble in water and obtained from skimmed milk by precipitation by the addition of acid, or by microbial acidification, or by using rennet or by using other milk-coagulating enzymes, without prejudice to the possibility of prior ion exchange processes and concentration processes, and where skimmed milk is cows' milk reduced only in fat content.

Caseinate a product obtained by drying casein treated with neutralizing agents.

Casein product edible acid casein, edible casein or any edible caseinate.

Reserved descriptions

Edible acid casein: edible casein conforming to the standards below and precipitated using lactic acid (E270), hydrochloric acid (507), sulphuric acid (513), citric acid (E330), acetic acid (E260), orthophosphoric acid (E338), whey, bacterial cultures producing lactic acid.

Edible rennet casein: edible casein conforming to the standards below and precipitated using rennet, other milk-coagulating enzymes.

Edible caseinates: caseinates conforming to the standards below obtained from edible caseins using hydroxides/carbonates/phosphates/citrates of sodium/potassium/calcium/ammonium/magnesium of edible quality.

General points

1) Casein products must be labelled with the reserved description and, in the case of caseinates (or mixtures of caseinates), an indication of the cation or cations.

4.1

	Edible acid casein	*Edible rennet casein*	*Edible caseinates*
Moisture (max)	10%	10%	8%
Milk protein (min) (1)	90%	84%	
Milk protein casein (min) (1)			88%
Milk fat (max) (1)	2.25%	2%	2%
Titratable acidity (max)	0.27 (2)		
pH value			6.0–8.0
Ash (P_2O_5 included)	2.5% max	7.5% min	
Anhydrous lactose (max)	1%	1%	1%
Sediment content (max) (3)	22.5 mg	22.5 mg	22.5 mg
Lead (max)	1 mg/kg	1 mg/kg	1 mg/kg
Extraneous matter in 25 g (4)	nil	nil	nil
Odour	(5)	(5)	(6)
Appearance	(7)	(7)	(7)
Solubility			(8)

Notes:
(1) Calculated on the dried extract
(2) ml of decinormal sodium hydroxide solution per g
(3) Burnt particles in 25 g
(4) Such as wood or metal particles, hairs or insect fragments
(5) No foreign odours
(6) No more than very slight foreign flavours and odours
(7) Colour ranging from white to creamy white; the product must not contain any lumps that would not break up under slight pressure
(8) Almost entirely soluble in distilled water, except for the calcium caseinate

2) Casein products sold as mixtures must be labelled as 'mixture of' followed by the relevant reserved descriptions (weight descending order).
3) Mixtures containing caseinates must be labelled with the protein content calculated on the dried extract expressed as % of the total weight of product as sold.
4) Any casein or caseinate used in the preparation of a casein product must be subjected to heat treatment at least equivalent to pasteurization unless the casein product is itself subject to heat treatment during its preparation.

Cheese

Regulation: Cheese Regulations 1970 (1970/94)
Amendments: Cheese (Amendment) Regulations 1974 (1974/1122)
Emulsifiers and Stabilizers in Food Regulations 1975 (1975/1486)
Colouring Matter in Food (Amendment) Regulations 1976 (1976/2086)
Food Labelling Regulations 1980 (1980/1849)
Cheese (Amendment) Regulations 1984 (1984/649)

Definitions

Cheese the fresh or matured product (excluding whey cheese) obtained by coagulating the following: milk, cream, skimmed milk, partly skimmed milk, concentrated skimmed milk, reconstituted dried milk and buttermilk, and partially draining the whey resulting.

Whey cheese the fresh or matured product obtained by concentrating (and moulding) or coagulating whey, with or without the addition of milk and milk fat.

Processed cheese cheese which has been subject to a process of melting and mixing with or without the addition of emulsifying salts.

Cheese spread (food) cheese which has been subject to a process of melting and mixing with milk products other than cheese, with or without the addition of emulsifying salts.

Soft cheese cheese which is readily deformed by moderate pressure (excluding whey and processed cheese and cheese spread but including cream and curd cheese).

Hard cheese cheese other than soft cheese, whey cheese, processed cheese or cheese spread.

Emulsifying salts ammonium, sodium, potassium or calcium salts of citric and orthophosphoric acid; sodium, potassium or calcium salts of diphosphoric acid; [i]penta[r]sodium triphosphate; [i]penta[r]potassium triphosphate; ammonium, sodium, potassium and calcium polyphosphates; the sodium, potassium or potassium sodium salts of tartaric acid.

Compositional requirements

Cheese types	*Milk fat in the dry matter* (%)	*Milk fat* (%)	*Maximum water* (%)
Full fat hard cheese (1)	min 48		48
Medium fat hard cheese (1)	10-48		48
Skimmed milk hard cheese (1)	max 10		48
Full fat soft cheese		min 20	60
Medium fat soft cheese		10-20	70
Low fat soft cheese		2-10	80
Skimmed milk soft cheese		max 2	80
Cream cheese		min 45	
Double cream cheese		min 65	
Full fat whey cheese	min 33		
Whey cheese	10-33		
Skimmed whey cheese	max 10		
Full fat processed cheese (1)	min 48		48
Medium fat processed cheese (1)	10-48		48
Skimmed milk processed cheese (1)	max 10		48
Cheese spread/food		min 20	60

Note:

(1) As an alternative to the description given, the label may include either of the following declarations:

(a) 'X% fat in dry matter' and 'Y% moisture', or

(b) 'Z% fat'

where X = min % milk fat content in dry matter, Y = max % water content and Z = min% milk fat content

4.1 For hard cheese, soft cheese (including cream cheese) or processed cheese, where the cheese conforms to one of the following varieties, the name of the cheese type given in the above table may be omitted from the description of the cheese (except processed cheese must be preceded by the word 'processed'):

Cheese varieties	*Minimum milk fat in the dry matter* (%)	*Maximum water* (%)
Cheddar	48	39(1)
Blue Stilton	48	42
Derby	48	42
Leicester	48	42
Cheshire	48	44
Dunlop	48	44
Gloucester	48	44
Double Gloucester	48	44
Caerphilly	48	46
Wensleydale	48	46
White Stilton	48	46
Lancashire	48	48
Edam	40	46
Loaf Edam	40	46
Baby Edam	40	47
Baby Loaf Edam	40	47
Gouda	48	43
Baby Gouda	48	45
Danablu	50	47
Danbo	45	46
Havarti	45	50
Samsoe	45	44
Emmental (Emmentaler)	45	40
Gruyere (Greyerzer/Gruviera)	45	38
Tilsiter (Tilsit/Tylzycki)	45	47
Limburger	50	50
Saint Paulin	40	56
Svecia	45	41
Provolone	45	47

Note: (1) May be 43% for processed Cheddar cheese

Permitted ingredients

1) Hard cheese

   Sodium chloride, starter, enzyme preparation for coagulating milk for cheesemaking, certain miscellaneous additives (calcium chloride anhydrous, calcium chloride, calcium hydroxide), certain colours (E160(a), E160(b), E160(e), and E161(g)) or the synthetic equivalent of the colouring principle.

2) Rind of hard cheese

   Any permitted colouring matter except aluminium, silver, gold or methyl violet.

3) Soft cheeses and whey cheeses
As in 1) plus flavourings, starches (modified or not), certain emulsifiers and stabilizers (E400, E401, E404, E407, E410, E412, E413, E414 and E415) and certain miscellaneous additives (E260, E270, E330, E338, 507 and 575).

4) Processed cheese and cheese spread
As in 3) plus
a) enzyme preparation for the acceleration of ripening,
b) the stabiliser E466,
c) emulsifying salts,
d) certain additional colours or the synthetic equivalent of the colouring principle (E100, E101, E140, E141, E160(c), paprika, turmeric, or the pure colouring principle of paprika and turmeric),
e) gelatin.

5) Hard sage cheese
As in 1) plus sage and the green colours in 4) d) above.

6) Soft sage cheese
As in 3) plus sage and the green colours in 4) d) above.

7) Sage cheese spread
As in 4) plus sage.

8) Mozzarella cheese
May contain the colour E171

9) Blue veined cheese, Feta cheese and Provolone cheese
May contain the colours E140 and E141.

10) Sliced or grated hard cheese and sliced or grated processed cheese
The following as anti-caking agents: emulsifiers and stabilizers (E460 and E322 (the latter used in combination with soya bean oil)) and miscellaneous additives (551 and 554). Total weight of these additives to be max 1% of cheese weight.

11) Feta, Provolone, Pecorino and Romano cheese
May contain lipases from animal sources for flavour production.

12) All cheese
Any ingredient mentioned in the definition of the cheese given above, mould characteristic of the cheese variety, water and preservatives permitted by the Preservatives in Food Regulations.

General point
The description 'blue-veined' may be included where *penicillium* moulds have produced blue-green veining.

Chocolate products

Regulation: Cocoa and Chocolate Products Regulations 1976 (1976/541)
Amendments: Emulsifiers and Stabilizers in Food Regulations 1980 (1980/1833)

4.1 Miscellaneous Additives in Food Regulations 1980 (1980/1834)
Food Labelling Regulations 1980 (1980/1849)
Cocoa and Chocolate Products (Amendment) Regulations 1982 (1982/17)
Food Labelling Regulations 1984 (1984/1305)

Definitions

Chocolate product any product whose reserved description is given below but does not include any product specially prepared for diabetics or to which a slimming claim is lawfully applied and which has been specially prepared in connection with that claim by the addition of any ingredient other than an edible substance (as defined in the Regulations).

Chocolate any product obtained from cocoa nib, cocoa mass, cocoa, fat-reduced cocoa (or any combination) and sucrose, with or without the addition of extracted cocoa butter and meeting the requirements in the table below.

Milk chocolate any product obtained from cocoa nib, cocoa mass, cocoa, fat-reduced cocoa (or any combination) and sucrose, and from milk or milk solids, with or without the addition of extracted cocoa butter and meeting the requirements in the table below.

Reserved descriptions

	Minimum total dry cocoa solids (%)	*Minimum non-fat dry cocoa solids* (%)	*Minimum cocoa butter* (%)
Chocolate (1)	35	14	18
Quality chocolate (1)	43	14	26
Plain chocolate (1)	30	12	18
Chocolate vermicelli (2)	32	14	12
Chocolate flakes (2)	32	14	12
Gianduja nut chocolate (2,3)	32	8	18
Couverture chocolate (1)	35	2.5	31
Dark couverture chocolate	35	16	31

	Minimum total dry cocoa solids (%)	*Minimum dry non-fat cocoa solids* (%)	*Minimum milk solids* (%)	*Minimum milk fat* (%)	*Maximum sucrose* (%) (4)	*Minimum total fat* (%)
Milk chocolate (1) (a)	25	2.5	14	3.5	55	25
or (b)	20	2.5	20	5	55	25
Quality milk chocolate (1)	30	2.5	18	4.5	50	25
Milk chocolate vermicelli (2)	20	2.5	12	3	66	12
Milk chocolate flakes (2)	20	2.5	12	3	66	12
Gianduja nut milk chocolate (2,5)	25	2.5	10	3.5	55	25
Couverture milk chocolate (1)	25	2.5	14	3.5	55	31
White chocolate (1)		(6)	14	3.5	55	
Cream chocolate (1)	25	2.5	(7)	7	55	25
Skimmed milk chocolate (1)	25	2.5	(8)	(9)	55	25

Notes: All figures calculated excluding additional ingredients

(1) Permitted additional ingredients
  (a) 5–40% any edible substance in clearly visible and discrete pieces (except flour, starch or non-milk fat)
  (b) max 30% any edible substance not in clearly visible and discrete pieces (except flour, starch, sucrose, dextrose, fructose, lactose, maltose or non-milk fat)
  (c) max 5% vegetable fat (not derived from cocoa beans)
  (d) max 10% partial coating or decoration (except for couverture and couverture milk chocolate)
  (e) max 40% combinations of (a)–(d)
  (f) max 30% combinations of (b)–(d)

(2) May also contain any flavouring substance which does not impart the flavour of chocolate or milk fat

(3) Contains 20–40% finely ground hazelnuts and may also contain
  (a) whole or broken nuts up to a total nut content of 60%
  (b) milk or dry matter produced by partial or complete dehydration of whole milk or partially or fully skimmed milk to product with max 5% dry milk solids including max 1.25% butterfat

(4) Sucrose may be replaced by dextrose, fructose, lactose and/or maltose up to, in each case, 5% of product weight; if only dextrose is used it may be up to 20% of product weight

(5) Contains 15–40% finely ground hazelnuts and may also contain whole or broken nuts up to a total nut content of 60%

(6) Cocoa butter min 20%

(7) Dry non–fat milk solids 3–14%

(8) Dry non–fat milk solids min 14%

(9) Less than 3.5% milk fat

General points

1) All chocolate products may contain the following emulsifiers to the maximum figure stated:
Lecithins and ammonium phosphatides (total 0.5% phosphatides), except for vermicelli, flakes or milk chocolate satisfying composition (b) in the table this figure is 1.0%, polyglycerol esters of polycondensed fatty acids of castor oil (0.5%), sorbitan tristearate (1.0%), any combination complying with the stated figures (1.5%).

2) The use of any of the above descriptions (or derivative or similar expression) may not be used unless the product conforms to the above standards except:
a) 'choc ice' or 'choc bar' may be used for an ice-cream with a coating resembling a chocolate product and containing min 2.5% dry non-fat cocoa solids, and
b) 'choc roll' may be used for a swiss roll with such a coating, but, in both cases, the words must be accompanied by an appropriate designation to avoid confusion.

3) Labelling: there are detailed regulations governing statements to accompany the reserved description. The Regulations should be consulted for full details. The presence of the following must not be indicated (except in an ingredients list) unless:
a) for milk the product is milk chocolate, couverture milk chocolate, white chocolate, cream chocolate or skimmed milk chocolate,
b) for spirits the amount of spirits is min 1% of the chocolate product,
c) for coffee the amount of coffee solids (dry matter) is min 1% of the chocolate product,

4.1

d) for other edible substance not in discrete visible pieces min 5% of the chocolate product.

4) Reserved descriptions and labelling requirements are also applied to 'filled chocolate', 'X-filled Y' (or similar), 'a chocolate' and 'chocolates' (see Regulations).

5) The Regulations do not apply to products specially prepared for diabetics or to which a slimming claim is applied and which has thus been specially made by the addition of any ingredient other than an edible substance (as defined in the Regulations).

Cocoa products

Regulation: Cocoa and Chocolate Products Regulations 1976 (1976/541)
Amendments: Emulsifiers and Stabilizers in Food Regulations 1980 (1980/1833)
Miscellaneous Additives in Food Regulations 1980 (1980/1834)
Food Labelling Regulations 1980 (1980/1849)
Cocoa and Chocolate Products (Amendment) Regulations 1982 (1982/17)
Food Labelling Regulations 1984 (1984/1305)

Definitions

Cocoa product any product listed in General Point 5) below and any product whose reserved description is given below but does not include any product specially prepared for diabetics or to which a slimming claim is lawfully applied and which has been specially prepared in connection with that claim by the addition of any ingredient other than an edible substance (as defined in the Regulations).

Reserved descriptions

	Maximum water (%)	*Minimum cocoa butter on dry matter* (%)
Cocoa	9	20
Cocoa powder	9	20
Fat reduced cocoa	9	8
Fat reduced cocoa powder	9	8

	Minimum cocoa when mixed with sucrose (%)
Sweetened cocoa	32
Sweetened cocoa powder	32
Drinking chocolate	25

	Minimum fat reduced cocoa when mixed with sucrose (%)
Sweetened fat reduced cocoa	32
Sweetened fat reduced cocoa powder	32
Fat reduced drinking chocolate	25

Note: Sucrose may be replaced by dextrose, fructose, lactose and/or maltose up to, in each case, 5% of product weight; if only dextrose is used it may be up to 20% of product weight

General points

1) Cocoa products in the tables above may contain, as emulsifiers, lecithins and/or ammonium phosphatides up to a maximum 1.0% phosphatides or 5.0% phosphatides for products in the form of an instant preparation.
2) Products in the first table above may contain any permitted base up to a maximum of 5.0% (calculated as potassium carbonate on the weight of the dry defatted matter) and when used may also contain any of the following acids up to a total quantity of 0.5%: citric acid, tartaric acid, or orthophosphoric acid. The resulting product must have an ash content of maximum 14% (dry defatted matter).
3) All products may contain any flavouring substance which does not impart the flavour of chocolate or milk fat.
4) Labelling: there are detailed regulations governing statements to accompany the reserved description. The Regulations should be consulted for full details.
5) The Regulations also contain definitions and standards for the following cocoa products:
   cocoa bean, cocoa nib, cocoa dust, cocoa fines, cocoa mass, cocoa press cake, fat-reduced cocoa press cake, expeller cocoa press cake, cocoa butter, press cocoa butter, expeller cocoa butter, refined cocoa butter, cocoa fat.
6) The Regulations do not apply to products specially prepared for diabetics or to which a slimming claim is applied and which has thus been specially made by the addition of any ingredient other than an edible substance (as defined in the Regulations).

Coffee products

Regulation: Coffee and Coffee Products Regulations 1978 (1978/1420)
Amendments: Food Labelling Regulations 1980 (1980/1849)
Coffee and Coffee Products (Amendment) Regulations 1982 (1982/254)
Coffee and Coffee Products (Amendment) Regulations 1987 (1987/1986)

Definitions

Coffee the dried seed of the coffee plant (whether or not roasted and/or ground).

Coffee extract the product in any concentration which contains the soluble and aromatic constituents of coffee, and is obtained by extraction from roasted coffee using only water as the medium of extraction (excluding any process of hydrolysis involving the addition of an acid or base) and which may contain insoluble oils derived from coffee, traces of other insoluble substances derived from coffee and insoluble substances not derived from coffee or from the water used for extraction.

4.1 *Reserved descriptions*

Coffee and chicory mixture a mixture of only roasted coffee and chicory.

French coffee - coffee and chicory mixture 51% minimum coffee with no matter other than roasted coffee and chicory.

Coffee with fig flavouring (Viennese coffee) 85% minimum coffee with no matter other than roasted coffee and fig.

	Dry matter (%)	*When present, added sugar* (%)
Dried coffee extract (dried extract of coffee, soluble coffee, instant coffee)	min 95 (2)	
Coffee extract paste	70 - 85 (2)	
Liquid coffee extract	15 - 55 (2)	max 12
Dried chicory extract (soluble chicory, instant chicory)	min 95 (3)	
Chicory extract paste	70 - 85 (3)	
Liquid chicory extract	25 - 55 (3)	max 35
Dried coffee and chicory extract (1)	min 95 (4)	
Coffee and chicory paste (1)	70 - 85 (4)	
Liquid coffee and chicory extract (1)	15 - 55 (4)	max 25
Chicory and coffee essence	(6)	(7)
Dried coffee and fig extract (1)	min 95 (5)	
Coffee and fig paste (1)	70 - 85 (5)	
Liquid coffee and fig extract (1)	15 - 55 (5)	max 25

Notes:
(1) Name of ingredient of which higher proportion used in manufacture to appear first
(2) Coffee-based dry matter content
(3) Chicory-based dry matter content
(4) Coffee and chicory-based dry matter content
(5) Coffee and fig-based dry matter content
(6) 20% min chicory-based dry matter and 5% min coffee-based dry matter
(7) May contain added sugar

Additional Labelling Provisions

Products should, for retail sale, be labelled with:

a) a reserved description;
b) the word 'decaffeinated' if it has been subject to a decaffeination process and in which the residual anhydrous caffeine content does not exceed (based on coffee-based dry matter): 0.10% for coffee, coffee and chicory mixtures, coffee with fig flavouring; 0.30% for coffee extracts;
c) in the case of products above with added sugar, - 'roasted with sugar' if the raw material has been roasted with sugar, - 'with sugar', 'preserved with sugar' or 'with added sugar' if sugar added after

roasting, and in both cases the word sugar may be replaced by the reserved description of the sugar used;

d) in the case of coffee/chicory extract paste and liquid coffee/chicory extract (or mixtures with these), a declaration of the minimum % coffee/chicory based dry matter;

e) in the case of liquid coffee extract with minimum 25% coffee-based dry matter or liquid chicory extract with minimum 45% chicory-based dry matter, the word 'concentrated' may be used.

Permitted ingredients

1) Permitted anti-caking agent
   May be added to dried coffee extract and to dried chicory extract when intended for vending machines. Product to be labelled 'for use in vending machines only'
   Subject to the Miscellaneous Additives in Food Regulations.
2) Decaffeination agent
   May be added to decaffeinated coffee which satisfies Notes (1) or (2) in the table above as long as permitted by Food Safety Act 1990.
3) Added sugar products
   Permitted only where indicated in above table.
4) Permitted preservative
   May be added to chicory and coffee essence.
   Subject to the Preservatives in Food Regulations.

General points

1) All raw materials should be sound, wholesome and in marketable condition.
2) The word 'coffee' may be used to describe a beverage prepared from the following: dried coffee extract, coffee extract paste or liquid coffee extract, and 'dandelion coffee' may be used to describe a product consisting of or made from roasted dandelion root.

Cream

A Product standards

Regulation: Cream Regulations 1970 (1970/752)
Amendments: Emulsifiers and Stabilizers in Food Regulations 1975 (1975/1486)
Food Labelling Regulations 1980 (1980/1849)

Definitions

Cream that part of milk rich in fat which has been separated by skimming or otherwise.

Clotted cream cream which has been produced and separated by the scalding, cooling and skimming of milk or cream.

Specified descriptions

	Minimum fat content (%)
Clotted cream	55
Double cream	48
Whipping cream	35
Whipped cream	35
Sterilised cream	23
Single cream	18
Cream	18
Sterilised half cream	12
Half cream	12

Note: (1) Figures calculated excluding any added sugar

Permitted ingredients

1) Except where listed in 2) to 7), cream shall contain no flavouring or other added ingredient (whether or not that ingredient is a constituent of milk).
2) Clotted cream may contain nisin.
3) Whipped cream or cream in an aerosol may contain
   a) sodium alginate, or a mixture of sodium bicarbonate, tetrasodium pyrophosphate and alginic acid,
   b) sodium carboxymethylcellulose,
   c) carageenan,
   d) gelatine,

   such that the maximum % of the total of all of these is 0.3%.
4) Whipped cream or cream in an aerosol may contain
   a) not more than 13% sugar,
   b) nitrous oxide.
5) Cream in an aerosol may contain not more than 0.5% glyceryl monostearate.
6) Sterilized cream or UHT cream may contain
   a) calcium chloride,
   b) sodium or potassium salts of carbonic acid, citric acid or orthophosphoric acid,

   such that the maximum % of the total of all of these ingredients is 0.2%.
7) Cream sold to a manufacturer or caterer
   a) if for use in flour confectionery may contain up to 13% sugar,
   b) if whipping cream may contain up to 13% sugar,
   c) if whipping cream may contain any of the additives listed in 3) above with the same maximum %.

General points

1) The description of the cream, except for clotted cream, shall include the appropriate method of treatment (see next section): pasteurised

(includes cream made from pasteurized milk), ultra heat treated (or UHT), or untreated.

2) If the cream is obtained from milk from any animal other than a cow, the name of the animal must be included.
3) The word 'cream', or any derivative thereof, may only be used for cream or products containing cream unless it is indicated explicitly (or there is a clear indication) that the product is not, or does not contain, cream. However, except for certain specified dairy products, the word 'creamed' may be used.
4) Whipped cream, or cream in an aerosol container, containing sugar shall be labelled with a declaration of the content and type of sugar.

B Processing standards

Regulation: Milk and Dairies (Heat Treatment of Cream) Regulations 1983 (1983/1509)

Amendment: Milk and Dairies (Heat Treatment of Cream) (Amendment) Regulations 1986 (1986/721)

The following standards apply to all cream except:

a) when imported under the Importation of Milk Regulations, or
b) produced in the UK, untreated and obtained from untreated milk, or
c) when the cream is for use in the preparation of food other than cream, or
d) when the cream has been heat treated in Scotland or Northern Ireland and satisfies the equivalent Regulations in force in those countries.

	Minimum heat treatment		*Specified tests*
	Temperature (°C)	*Time*	
Pasteurisation (1)			
a)	63	30 minutes	Coliform test (2) and/or phosphatase test
or b)	72	15 seconds	
Sterilisation (3)	108	45 minutes	Colony count
Ultra High Temperature (UHT) (3,4)	140	2 seconds	Colony count

Notes:

(1) Or similar process designed to have equivalent effect on the elimination of vegetative pathogenic organisms. Cream to be cooled to a maximum of 10°C and must not rise above 10°C

(2) Only to be used not later than the day following heat treatment and before departure from premises of treatment

(3) Or similar process designed to have equivalent effect in rendering cream free from viable micro-organisms and their spores

(4) Direct application of steam is permitted only if the equivalent amount of water is removed by evaporative cooling. Only certain specified additives may be used to treat the water used for generating the steam (see Regulations)

General points

1) Only milk or cream produced in the UK shall be subjected to the above treatments to produce heat treated cream, except when the cream is imported under the Importation of Milk Regulations.
2) For these Regulations, 'cream' is defined as that part of cows' milk rich in fat which has been separated by skimming or otherwise and includes cream with permitted additives and reconstituted cream (i.e. a substance which resembles cream and contains no ingredient not derived from milk except water or ingredients permitted in cream).

Fish

Regulations: Preserved Sardines (Marketing Standards) Regulations 1990 (1990/1084)
EEC Council Regulation 2136/89

Only products meeting certain specified requirements may be marketed as preserved sardines and using specified trade descriptions. Included are the following points (see Council Regulation 2136/89 for full details):

1) Only fish of the species '*Sardinia pilchardus* Walbaum' may be used (with an exception concerning products using homogenised sardine flesh).
2) They must be pre-packaged with an appropriate covering medium. The following are listed and shall be indicated in the trade description: olive oil (not to be mixed with other oils); other refined vegetable oils, including olive-residue oil used singly or in mixtures; tomato sauce; natural juice (liquid exuding from the fish during cooking), saline solution or water; marinade, with or without wine. Other covering media may be used on condition that it is clearly distinguished from those in the above list.
3) The pack should be sterilised by appropriate treatment.
4) Preserved sardines may be marketed in the following presentations:
   a) sardines;
   b) sardines without bones;
   c) sardines without skin or bones;
   d) sardine fillets;
   e) sardine trunks.

   Other presentations may be used on condition that it is clearly distinguished from those in the above list.
5) The ratio of the weight of the sardines (for the presentations a) to e) in 4)) in the container after sterilisation and the net weight depends upon covering media and shall be not less than: olive oil; other refined vegetable oils; natural juice, saline solution or water; marinade: 70%
   tomato sauce: 65%
   other media: 50%
   For other presentations, the ratio must be not less than 35%.

4.1

Fish cakes

Regulations: Food Standards (Fish Cake) Order 1950 (1950/589)

Fish cakes fish content: min 35%

Flour

Regulation: Bread and Flour Regulations 1984 (1984/1304)
Amendment: Potassium Bromate (Prohibition as a Flour Improver) Regulations 1990 (1990/399)

Definitions

Flour the product derived from, or separated during, the milling or grinding of cleaned cereal, whether or not the cereal has been malted or subjected to any other process, and includes meal, but does not include other cereal products, such as separated cereal bran, separated cereal germ, semolina or grits.

Malt flour flour derived from malted cereal.

Cereal fruit of any cultivated grass of the family *Gramineae*.

Reserved descriptions

Description	*Requirement*
1) Where all the flour is derived from wheat the name shall be (1):	
'Wholemeal' or 'wholemeal flour'	Consists of the whole product obtained from the milling or grinding of cleaned wheat.
'Brown flour'	Has a crude fibre content derived from wheat of min 0.6% (dry matter) but does not comprise wholemeal.
'Flour'	Any other case.
2) Where the flour is derived from cereals with or without wheat the name shall be (1):	
'Flour'	Must be preceded by the names of all the cereals. May be qualified by 'wholemeal' if it is derived from the whole product of the cereals.
3) Miscellaneous additional descriptions:	
'Self-raising'	Minimum available carbon dioxide of 0.4%.

Note: (1) No account shall be taken of any barley malt flour used in small quantities for technological purposes.

4.1 The following ingredients may be used without their presence being indicated in the name of the flour:

a) prepared wheat gluten, barley malt flour or wheat malt flour (all in small quantities for technological purposes):
b) any substance added to satisfy the requirements given below under 'Composition of wheat flour'.

The name 'wheatmeal' is not to be used to describe any flour.

Composition of wheat flour
(Note: the requirements of this section can only be enforced by sampling according to a specified procedure at a mill or dock.)

1) All flour, except wholemeal, self-raising flour (with a calcium content of min 0.2%), and wheat malt flour, shall contain:
   calcium carbonate   between 235 and 390 mg/100 g of flour
2) All flour shall contain (per 100 g of flour):
   iron   min 1.65 mg
   thiamin (vitamin B_1)   min 0.24 mg
   nicotinic acid or nicotinamide   min 1.60 mg
   For wholemeal, the substances should be naturally present and not added.
3) These standards do not apply to flour which is authorized for stockpiling or experimental purposes, for use in the manufacture of communion wafers, matzos, gluten, starch or a concentrated preparation used in facilitating the addition to flour of the above substances, or for use for the purposes of diagnosis, treatment or research.

Permitted additional ingredients
See table of 'Permitted additional ingredients of bread and flour' given under 'Bread'.

Fruit juices and nectars

Regulation: Fruit Juices and Fruit Nectars Regulations 1977 (1977/927)
Amendments: Lead in Food Regulations 1979 (1979/1254)
Food Labelling Regulations 1980 (1980/1849)
Fruit Juices and Fruit Nectars (Amendment) Regulations 1982 (1982/1311)
Fruit Juices and Fruit Nectars (England, Wales and Scotland)(Amendment) Regulations 1991 (1991/1284)

Definitions
Fruit juice   the food consisting of fermentable but unfermented juice which is either obtained from

a) fruit by mechanical processes and has the characteristic colour, aroma and flavour of the fruit from which it is obtained, or

b) concentrated fruit juice by the addition of water and has the same organoleptic and analytical characteristics of fruit juice obtained from fruit of the same kind by mechanical processes, or
c) fruit (other than apricots, citrus fruits, grapes, peaches, pears or pineapples) by diffusion processes and is intended for use in the preparation of concentrated fruit juice.

or is fruit purée where the nature of the fruit from which the juice is to be obtained is such that it is impossible to extract the juice without the pulp.

Fruit purée the fermentable but unfermented product obtained by sieving the entire edible part of the whole or peeled fruit.

Fruit nectar the food consisting of the fermentable but unfermented product obtained by the addition of water and sugar to fruit juice, concentrated fruit juice, fruit purée or concentrated fruit purée with the following limits:

either a) added sugar max 20% (dry matter basis)
or b) added honey max 20%
and satisfies the following table:

Fruit from which the product is obtained	*Minimum quantity of acid expressed as tartaric acid and in grammes per litre of the finished product*	*Minimum quantity of juice or purée or of juice and purée expressed as a percentage of the weight of the finished product*
1. Apricots	3 (1)	40
Bilberries	4	40
Blackberries	6	40
Blackcurrants	8	25
Cherries (other than sour cherries)	6 (1)	40
Cranberries	9	30
Elderberries	7	50
Gooseberries	9	30
Lemons	–	25
Limes	–	25
Mulberries	6	40
Passion fruit (*Passiflora edulis*)	8	25
Plums	6	30
Quetsches	6	30
Quinces	7	50
Quito Naranjillos (*Solanum quitoense*)	5	25
Raspberries	7	40
Redcurrants	8	25
Rose hips (fruits of the species *Rosa*)	8	40
Rowanberries	8	30
Sallowthorn berries	9	25
Sloes	8	30
Sour cherries	8	35
Strawberries	5 (1)	40
Whitecurrants	8	25
Any other fruit with acid juice unpalatable in the natural state	–	25

4.1

(continued)

Fruit from which the product is obtained	*Minimum quantity of acid expressed as tartaric acid and in grammes per litre of the finished product*	*Minimum quantity of juice or purée or of juice and purée expressed as a percentage of the weight of the finished product*
2. Azeroles (Neopolitan medlars)	–	25
Bananas	–	25
Bullock's heart (Custard apple) (*Annona reticulata*)	–	25
Cashew fruits	–	25
Guavas	–	25
Lychees	–	25
Mangoes	–	35
Papayas	–	25
Pomegranates	–	25
Soursop (*Annona muricata*)	–	25
Spanish plums (*Spondia purpurea*)	–	25
Sugar apples	–	25
Umbu (*Spondias tuberosa aroda*)	–	30
Any other low acid, pulpy or highly flavoured fruit with juice unpalatable in the natural state	–	25
3. Apples	3 (1)	50
Peaches	3 (1)	45
Pears	3 (1)	50
Pineapples	4	50
Citrus fruits other than lemons and limes	5	50
Any other fruit with juice palatable in the natural state	–	50

Note: (1) Does not apply when product obtained exclusively from fruit purée or concentrated fruit purée, or a mixture

Permitted additional ingredients

When for sale for consumption, only the following additional ingredients are permitted in fruit juice, concentrated or dried fruit juice or fruit nectar (or concentrated fruit juice or fruit juice intended for the preparation of these).

1) Fruit juice, concentrated or dried fruit juice and fruit nectar may contain L-Ascorbic acid subject to Antioxidants in Food Regulations.
2) Concentrated fruit juice, fruit juice derived from concentrated fruit juice and dried fruit juice may contain volatile components of the same fruit, which need not be included in the ingredients list.
3) Pineapple juice and concentrated pineapple juice may contain the permitted antifoaming agent dimethylpolysiloxane up to 10 mg/l after dilution.

4) Fruit juice or fruit nectar may contain carbon dioxide, subject to Miscellaneous Additives in Food Regulations provided that if the level of carbon dioxide exceeds 2 g/l it must be labelled 'carbonated'.
5) Fruit juice and concentrated or dried fruit juice may contain, after dilution or reconstitution if appropriate, sugar (types specified in the Regulations) as follows:
grapes/pears not permitted
apples up to 40 g/l
bergamots, blackcurrants, lemons, limes, redcurrants or white currants up to 200 g/l
other fruits up to 100 g/l
For concentrated orange juice not prepackaged and not for sale to the ultimate consumer, added sugar is permitted up to 15 g/l (after dilution).
6) Fruit juice and concentrated fruit juice may contain sulphur dioxide as follows:
apples, grapefruits, oranges or pineapples up to 50 mg/kg
grapes up to 10 mg/kg
lemons or limes up to 350 mg/kg
If the sulphur dioxide does not exceed 10 mg/l it need not be included in the ingredients list.
7) Fruit juice, concentrated fruit juice and fruit nectar may contain added acid as indicated in the following table, except that no fruit juice or concentrated fruit juice may contain both added sugar and added permitted acid (if more than one is used, the total used must not exceed 100% based on the individual maximum levels):

	Permitted acid	*Maximum g/l (after dilution)*
1. Apple nectar (other than 2.)	lactic	5
2. Apple nectar (from apple purée and/or concentrated apple purée)	citric (1)	5
3. Grape juice	citric	3
4. Peach nectar obtained from peach purée and/or concentrated peach purée	citric (1) or	5
	DL-malic or	3
	L-malic	3
5. Pear nectar obtained from pear purée and/or concentrated pear purée	citric (1) or	5
	lactic or	5
	DL-malic or	3
	L-malic	3
6. Pear nectars (other than 5)	lactic	5
7. Nectars (mixed from 2, 4 and 5)	citric (1)	5
8. Pineapple juice and concentrated pineapple juice	citric	3
9. Pineapple juice	DL-malic or	3
	L-malic	3
10. Apple juice	citric	3

Note: (1) Citric acid may be replaced by an equivalent amount of lemon juice

Specific labelling requirements

1) Product to be labelled 'juice', 'concentrated juice', 'dried juice' or 'nectar' as appropriate and preceded by the name (or names in weight descending order) of the fruit(s) used (but not including any lemon juice added as acid to nectar).
2) The word 'dried' may be replaced by 'powdered' and may be accompanied or replaced by 'freeze-dried' (or other word descriptive of the process).
3) Where sugar has been added (in accordance with 5) above) and exceeds 15 g/l, the product shall be labelled 'sweetened' and there should be a declaration of the maximum added sugar (which must not exceed the actual sugar content by more than 15%).
4) Where fruit juice or fruit nectar is made from concentrated fruit juice (or purée), product to be labelled as 'made with concentrated .. juice (purée)' (name of fruit to be added).
5) Fruit nectar shall be marked with the minimum fruit content.
6) Concentrated or dried fruit juice shall be marked with the quantity of water required for reconstitution.

General points

1) Most of the above standards do not apply to any concentrated fruit juice specially prepared for infants and children and labelled as such (see Regulations).
2) Concentrated fruit juice must have been reduced in volume by at least 50%.
3) For citrus fruits, the juice must only be derived from the endocarp (although for lime juice the minimum possible of juice from the outer parts of the fruit is permitted).
4) The preparation of concentrated or dried fruit juice must not involve the application of direct heat.

Honey

Regulation: Honey Regulations 1976 (1976/1832)
Amendment: Food Labelling Regulations 1980 (1980/1849)

Definitions

Honey   the fluid, viscous or crystallized food which is produced by honeybees from the nectar of blossoms, or from secretions of, or found on, living parts of plants other than blossoms, which honeybees collect, transform, combine with substances of their own and store and leave to mature in honeycombs.

Blossom honey   honey produced wholly or mainly from the nectar of blossoms.

Honeydew honey honey, the colour of which is light brown, greenish brown, black or any intermediate colour, produced wholly or mainly from secretions of or found on living parts of plants other than blossoms.
Pressed honey honey obtained by pressing broodless honeycombs with or without the application of moderate heat.

	Minimum apparent reducing sugar content (%) (1)	*Maximum moisture content* (%) (2)	*Maximum apparent sucrose content* (%)	*Maximum water insoluble solids* (%)	*Maximum ash content* (%)
Honeydew honey	60	21	10	0.1	1
Blended honeydew honey and blossom honey	60	21	10	0.1	1
Heather honey	65	23	5	0.1	0.6
Clover honey	65	23	5	0.1	0.6
Acacia honey	65	21	10	0.1	0.6
Lavender honey	65	21	10	0.1	0.6
Banksia menziesii honey	65	21	10	0.1	0.6
Pressed honey	65	21	5	0.5	0.6
Honey	65	21	5	0.1	0.6

Notes:
(1) Calculated as invert sugar
(2) Moisture content may be above specified standard but not more than 25% if such moisture content is the result of natural conditions of production

Bakers' or industrial honey
Honey with one or more of the following conditions:
1) fails above moisture restrictions,
2) has a foreign taste or odour,
3) has begun to ferment or effervesce,
4) has been heated to such an extent that natural enzymes are destroyed or made inactive,
5) is citrus honey (or any other honey with a naturally low enzyme content) with a diastase activity of less than 3,
6) is honey not included in 5) with a diastase activity of less than 4,
7) has a hydroxymethylfurfural content of more than 80 mg/kg.

General points
1) No person shall add to honey (intended for sale) any substance other than honey.
2) Honey (sold, consigned or delivered) shall be free, as far as practicable, from mould, insects, insect debris, brood or any other organic foreign substance. Honey used in the preparation of another food should also be free of inorganic foreign substances.

4.1

3) No honey shall have an acidity of more than 40 mEq acid/kg. No person may sell honey with an artificially changed acidity.
4) Reference to origin:
   a) if a type of blossom or plant is indicated, the honey must be wholly or mainly from that source,
   b) if a name of a country, etc. is indicated, the honey must originate wholly from that place.

Ice-cream

A Product standards

Regulation: Ice-Cream Regulations 1967 (1967/1866)
Amendments: Food Labelling Regulations 1980 (1980/1849)
Sweeteners in Food Regulations 1983 (1983/1211)
Milk and Milk Products (Protection of Designations) Regulations 1990 (1990/607)

Definitions

Ice-cream the frozen product intended for sale for human consumption which is obtained by subjecting an emulsion of fat, milk solids and sugar, with or without the addition of other substances, to heat treatment and either to subsequent freezing or to evaporation, addition of water and subsequent freezing, whether or not fruit, fruit pulp, fruit purée, fruit juice, sugar, flavouring or colouring materials, nuts, chocolate or other similar substances have been added before or after freezing, and includes any ice-cream present as an ingredient of any composite article of food, but does not include any sherbet, sorbet, water ice or ice lolly described as 'sherbet', 'sorbet', 'water ice' or 'ice lolly', as the case may be.

Parev ice includes Kosher ice and means the substance intended for sale for human consumption which resembles ice-cream and which
a) is usually known as Parev ice or Kosher ice, and
b) contains no milk or milk derivatives, and includes any Parev ice present as an ingredient of any composite article of food.

	Minimum fat (%)	*Minimum milk solids other than fat* (%)	*Minimum fat and milk solids other than fat* (%)
Ice-cream	5	7.5	
Dairy ice-cream (dairy cream ice, cream ice)	5 (1)	7.5	
Milk ice (including milk ice with fruit (2))	2.5 (1)	7	
Ice-cream with fruit (2)	5	7.5	
or	7.5	2	12.5 (3)

(continued)

	Minimum fat (%)	Minimum milk solids other than fat (%)	Minimum fat and milk solids other than fat (%)
Dairy ice-cream (dairy cream ice, cream ice) with fruit (2)	5 (1)	7.5	
or	7.5 (1)	2	12.5 (3)
Parev ice (4)	10		

Notes:
(1) All fat to be milk fat (except any present by reason of the use as an ingredient, of any egg, flavouring substance or emulsifier or stabiliser)
(2) Fruit includes fruit pulp, fruit purée or fruit juice
(3) % of the whole product (including fruit, etc.)
(4) Must contain no milk fat or other derivative of milk

Labelling

When a product is described as 'ice-cream' and does not comply with note 1) in the above table, it shall be labelled, in immediate proximity to the description, with the words 'contains non-milk fat' (or 'contains vegetable fat' if all fat is vegetable fat).

General Point

No ice-cream of any kind nor Parev ice may contain acesulfame potassium, aspartame, saccharin, sodium saccharin, calcium saccharin or thaumatin.

B Processing standards

Regulation: Ice-Cream (Heat Treatment, etc) Regulations 1959 (1959/734)
Amendment: Ice-Cream (Heat Treatment, etc) (Amendment) Regulations 1963 (1963/1083)

Definitions

Ice-cream includes any similar commodity.

Complete cold mix a product which is capable of manufacture into a mixture with the addition of water only, is sent out by the manufacturer in airtight containers, and has been made by evaporating a liquid mixture which has already been subjected to heat treatment not less effective than that described in these regulations and to which, after such treatment, no substance other than sugar has been added.

Mixture a product which is capable of manufacture into ice-cream by freezing only.

4.1 *Requirements*

1) Where a complete cold mix is used which is reconstituted with wholesome drinking water (and to which nothing is added other than sugar, colouring or flavouring materials, fruit, nuts, chocolate or other similar substances), the reconstituted mixture shall be converted to ice-cream within one hour of reconstitution.
2) In any other case (unless the mixture is to be used to make water ice or similar frozen confection with a pH of 4.5 or less) the following must be observed:

   a) The mixture should be kept for no longer than one hour at any temperature over 45°F before being pasteurised or sterilised.

   b) One of the following heat treatments is used:

      pasteurisation
      min 150°F for min 30 minutes
      min 160°F for min 10 minutes
      min 175°F for min 15 seconds,

      sterilisation
      min 300°F for min 2 seconds.

   c) After pasteurisation or sterilisation the mix should be reduced to a maximum of 45°F within 1.5 hours, and should be maintained at such a temperature until freezing begins unless:
   either i) it is subject to sterilisation and immediately placed in sterile containers under sterile conditions and the containers remain unopened but, when the containers are opened, the temperature shall be reduced to a maximum of 45°F until freezing begins,
   or ii) added to a mixture having a pH of 4.5 or less for the preparation of water ice (or similar confection) and the combined mixture is frozen within one hour.
3) Once frozen, ice-cream shall be held at a maximum of 28°F prior to sale.

Jam (and similar products)

Regulation: Jam and Similar Products Regulations 1981 (1981/1063)
Amendments: Food Labelling (Amendment) Regulations 1982 (1982/1700)
Sweeteners in Food Regulations 1983 (1983/1211)
Sweeteners in Food (Amendment) Regulations 1988 (1988/2112)
Jam and Similar Products (Amendment) Regulations 1990 (1990/2085)

Note: In these Regulations, fruit includes carrots, ginger, rhubarb and sweet potatoes.

Reserved Descriptions

Jam/extra jam/marmalade a mixture, brought to a suitable gelled consistency, of sweetening agents and fruit (see Note (1) in table below), and complying with the following tables.

Jelly/extra jelly/UK standard jelly an appropriately gelled mixture of sweetening agents and fruit (see Note (1) in table below), and complying with the following tables.

Sweetened chestnut purée a mixture, brought to a suitable gelled consistency, of sweetening agents and puréed chestnuts, and complying with the following tables.

Minimum quantity of fruit (1) used for 1 kg of product:

	Extra jam or extra jelly (g) (2)	*Jam or jelly or UK standard jelly* (g)	*Marmalade* (g)	*Sweetened chestnut purée* (g)
Passion fruit	80	60		
Cashew apples	230	160		
Ginger	250	150		
Blackcurrants, rosehips, quinces	350	250		
Citrus fruit			200 (3)	
Puréed chestnuts				380
Other fruit	450	350		

Notes:

(1) Defined as follows:
for extra jam fruit pulp (but see also note 2)
for jam fruit pulp and fruit purée
for jelly and extra jelly fruit juice and aqueous extract of fruit (but see also note 2)
for UK standard jelly fruit juice or aqueous extract of fruit derived from the quantity stated in the Table of fruit, fruit pulp and/or fruit purée
for marmalade fruit pulp, fruit purée, fruit juice, fruit peel or aqueous extract of fruit, in every case, obtained from citrus fruit

(2) Extra jam and extra jelly, if made from a mixture of fruit, must not include the following: apples, pears, clingstone plums, melons, grapes, pumpkins, cucumbers, tomatoes.

(3) Minimum of 75 g of endocarp

'X' Curd, or 'Y' Flavour Curd

(Where 'X' is a named fruit, 'mixed fruit' or a specified number of fruits; and 'Y' is a named fruit or 'mixed fruit'.)

X curd an emulsion of edible fat or oil (or both), sugar, whole egg or egg yolk (or both), and any combination of fruit, fruit pulp, fruit purée, fruit juice, aqueous extract of fruit or essential oils of fruit, with or without other ingredients, and meeting the following standards.

Y flavour curd an emulsion of edible fat or oil (or both), sugar, whole egg or egg yolk (or both), and flavouring material with or without other ingredients, and meeting the following standards.

4.1

a) fat or oil   min 40 g/kg finished product,
b) egg yolk solids (derived from whole egg and egg yolk)   min 6.5 g/kg finished product,
c) for 'X' curd sufficient fruit (as listed above) or essential oil of fruit to characterise the product,
d) for 'Y' flavour curd sufficient flavouring material to characterise the product.

Lemon cheese
A food conforming to the requirements above appropriate for lemon curd.

Mincemeat
A mixture of sweetening agents, vine fruits, citrus peel, suet or equivalent fat and vinegar or acetic acid, with or without other ingredients, such that the following are found in each kg of finished product:

1) vine fruits and citrus peel   min 300 g,
2) vine fruits   min 200 g,
3) suet (or equivalent fat)   min 25 g,
4) acetic acid   min 5 g.

Permitted ingredients
The Regulations contain a list of permitted ingredients (additional to those contained in the definitions given above), a list of the products in which they may be used and, in some cases, restrictions on the usage (see Regulations). The following are included:

1) reduced sugar products may contain the following specified preservatives in the specified quantities,
   E200, E201, E202, E203   total max 750 mg/kg
   E210, E211, E212, E213   total max 500 mg/kg
   E214, E215   total max 500 mg/kg
   E216, E217   total max 500 mg/kg
   E218, E219   total max 500 mg/kg
2) reduced sugar products and diabetic products (labelled as such) may contain sweeteners as permitted in the Sweeteners in Food Regulations. Other products must use sweetening agents specified in the Regulations.

Soluble solids content (at 20°C):

	Soluble solids (%)
Extra jam, jam (1)	min 60 (2)
Extra jelly, jelly (1)	min 60 (2)
Marmalade (1)	min 60 (2)
Sweetened chestnut purée (1)	min 60 (2)

(*continued*)

	Soluble solids (%)
Reduced sugar jam, reduced sugar jelly, reduced sugar marmalade	30-55 (3)
UK standard jelly (1)	min 60 (2)
'X' curd	min 65
'Y' flavour curd	min 65
Mincemeat	min 65

Notes:

(1) Not applicable to 'diabetic' products labelled as such

(2) If the quantity is greater than a single serving, and the soluble solid is less than 63%, the pack must be marked 'keep in a cool place once opened'

(3) If the quantity is greater than a single serving, the pack must either be marked 'keep in a cool place once opened' or contain sufficient preservative to have a preserving effect on the food

General points

1) Labelling. Full details are given in the Regulations, but the following points should be noted:

a) 'Conserve' and 'preserve' may only be used for foods which are either 'jam' or 'extra jam'.

b) The word 'extra' may be dropped from 'extra jam' and 'extra jelly'.

c) Marmalade: with no insoluble matter (except a small quantity of finely sliced peel) may be called 'jelly marmalade'; containing peel shall state the style of cut of the peel, and not containing peel shall state that it does not contain peel.

d) The name of the food shall, if a single type of fruit is used, include an indication of that fruit, if two types of fruit are used, include an indication of both fruits in descending order of weight, if more than two, either include an indication of all the fruits, or state 'mixed fruit', or state the number of fruits used.

e) All products must be marked with the following statements (except that products made specially for diabetics do not require the sugar statement):

'prepared with X g of fruit per 100 g'

'total sugar content: Y g per 100 g'

with the appropriate figures substituted for X and Y.

2) Authorized treatments and additives. Full details are given in the Regulations, but the following points should be noted:

a) fruit sources (other than fruit juice) may only be used if treated by being heated, chilled, frozen, freeze-dried or concentrated (in the case of fruit juice, the juice must comply with the Fruit Juice Regulations), although apricots may be used in jam if dried otherwise than by freeze-drying,

chestnuts used for sweetened chestnut purée may be soaked for a short time in an aqueous solution of sulphur dioxide,

ginger may have been dried or preserved in syrup, and citrus peel may have been preserved in brine
b) certain specified sources of sulphur dioxide may be used on fruit sources used in the preparation of jam (except in the case of fruit juice), jelly, marmalade, reduced sugar jelly, reduced sugar marmalade, UK standard jelly, fruit curd, fruit flavour curd and mincemeat.

3) Residual sulphur dioxide content permitted:
extra jam, extra jelly, sweetened chestnut purée 10 mg/kg
jelly 50 mg/kg
other products 100 mg/kg.
Where the level exceeds 30 mg/kg, the presence of sulphur dioxide shall be indicated in the list of ingredients.
4) The term 'jelly' may be used for other products where its use would not be confused with products conforming to the specified standards.

Margarine

Regulation: Margarine Regulations 1967 (1967/1867)
Amendments: Food Labelling Regulations 1980 (1980/1849)
Milk and Milk Products (Protection of Designations) Regulations 1990 (1990/607)

Definition
Margarine the food usually known as margarine, being a plasticised emulsion of edible oils and fats with water or skimmed milk, with or without addition of vitamins A and D, sodium chloride, sugars and other minor ingredients and permitted additives (defined as permitted colours, antioxidants, emulsifiers, stabilisers, preservatives or solvents).

Margarine standards
a) maximum moisture 16%
b) minimum total fat 80%
c) maximum fat derived from milk 10% of fat content
d) for retail sale
vitamin A 760–940 IU per oz
vitamin D 80–100 IU per oz
(From 1.1.1995, these will be metricated to read:
vitamin A 800–1000 micrograms per 100 grams margarine
vitamin D 7.05–8.82 micrograms per 100 grams margarine)

General points
1) The above standards do not apply to margarine supplied to a manufacturer or caterer for their business use.
2) There are specific restrictions on the labelling and advertising of margarine so as to limit the associations of margarine with milk or other dairy interests (see Regulations).

Meat

A Meat treatment

Regulation: Meat (Treatment) Regulations 1964 (1964/19)

Definitions

Meat the flesh or other part of any animal (but not including birds or fish).

Processed includes curing by smoking and any treatment or process resulting in a substantial change in the natural state of the meat but does not include boning, paring, grinding, cutting, cleaning or trimming; and 'unprocessed' shall be construed accordingly.

Requirements

No raw or unprocessed meat may contain:

any added ascorbic acid, erythorbic acid, nicotinic acid, nicotinamide or any salt or other derivative of these.

B Use of bovine offal

Regulations: Bovine Offal (Prohibition) Regulations 1989 (1989/2061)
Bovine Offal (Prohibition) (Amendment) Regulations 1992 (1992/306)

Note: These Regulations were introduced specifically to prevent any risk of Bovine Spongiform Encephalopathy (BSE) infected offal being incorporated into food. More general requirements relating to the use of other offal are contained in the Regulations covering meat products and described in that section.

Definition

Specified bovine offal the brain, spinal cord, spleen, thymus, tonsils and intestines of a bovine animal which has been slaughtered in the United Kingdom and no longer comprises a whole dead animal.

Requirements

No person shall sell for human consumption or use in the preparation of food for sale for human consumption any specified bovine offal or any material derived wholly or partly from it.

General points

1) The restrictions do not apply to specified bovine offal from animals not more than six months old when slaughtered.
2) The Regulations contain detailed requirements relating to the movement of specified bovine offal and its sterilising and staining.
3) Under another Order, the Bovine Spongiform Encephalopathy Order 1991 (1991/2246), it is prohibited to export specified bovine offal

4.1 from Great Britain to another EC Member State (but note that the definition of specified bovine offal, in this case, includes offal when part of a whole dead animal).

Meat products and spreadable fish products

Regulation: Meat Products and Spreadable Fish Products Regulations 1984 (1984/1566)

Amendment: Meat Products and Spreadable Fish Products (Amendment) Regulations 1986 (1986/987)

Definitions

Meat means the flesh, including fat, and the skin, rind, gristle and sinew in amounts naturally associated with the flesh used, of any animal or bird which is normally used for human consumption and includes the offals listed in part a) of the definition of offals given below but does not include any other part of the carcase.

Lean meat meat free, when raw, of visible fat.

Meat product any food which consists of meat or has meat as an ingredient except:

raw meat with no added ingredient except proteolytic enzymes;

uncooked chickens, hens, cocks, turkeys, ducks, geese and guinea fowl (or their cuts or offals) with no added ingredient except additives permitted by the additive regulations, flavourings, smoke and smoke solutions (subject to Preservatives in Food Regulations), water, self-basting preparations or seasonings;

haggis, black pudding, white pudding, brawn, collard head;

sandwiches, filled rolls and similar bread products which are ready for consumption unless sold using the words 'burger', 'economy burger' or 'hamburger';

products named 'broth', 'gravy', or 'soup';

stock cubes (and similar flavouring agents);

products commonly known as 'potted head', 'potted meat' and 'potted hough';

products containing only animal or bird fat but no other meat.

Fish the edible portion of any fish including edible molluscs and crustacea.

Spreadable fish product any product containing fish in which 'paste', 'pâté' or 'spread' is used in the name or any other readily spreadable product containing fish (except if they only contain fish oil and no other fish constituent).

Offals (as used in the Food Labelling Regulations) any of the following parts of the carcase:

a) for mammalian species: diaphragm, head meat (muscle meat and associated fatty tissue only), heart, kidney, liver, pancreas, tail meat, thymus, tongue;

for avian species: gizzard, heart, liver, neck;

b) for mammalian species: brains, feet, large intestine, small intestine, lungs, oesophagus, rectum, spinal cord, spleen, stomach, testicles, udder.

Cured meat a food consisting of meat and curing salt and may include water and any of the following ingredients used in small quantities in accordance with good manufacturing practice but no other ingredient: honey, maple syrup, molasses, any food used solely as a garnish or decorative coating, additives permitted by the additive regulations, flavourings, smoke and smoke solutions (subject to the Preservatives in Food Regulations) and salt, herbs or spices used as seasoning;
sucrose, invert sugar, glucose, dextrose, lactose, maltose and glucose syrup (all for sweetening purposes only);
hydrolyzed proteins and yeast extract (both for flavouring purposes only).

Curing salt sodium chloride, potassium chloride, sodium nitrate, potassium nitrate, sodium nitrite, or potassium nitrate whether alone or in any combination except that if only sodium chloride and potassium chloride are used (either alone or mixed) they must be used in sufficient quantity to have a significant preserving effect.

Reserved descriptions

	Definition of 'X'	*Minimum meat content* (as % of food)	*Minimum lean meat content* (as % of required meat content)	*Minimum 'X' content* (as % of food)
Burger (1) a) qualified by 'X'	named meat or cured meat	80	65	80
b) others		80	65	
Economy burger (1) a) qualified by 'X'	named meat or cured meat	60	65	60
b) others		60	65	
Hamburger (1,2)		80	65	
Chopped 'X'	'meat', 'cured meat' or a named meat or cured meat	90	65	
Corned 'X' (3)	named meat unless qualified by the name of another food	120	96	
Luncheon meat, luncheon 'X'	named meat or cured meat	80	65	

4.1 (*continued*)

	Definition of 'X'	*Minimum meat content* (as % of food)	*Minimum lean meat content* (as % of required meat content)	*Minimum 'X' content* (as % of food)
Meat pie, meat pudding, pie or pudding qualified by 'X', Melton Mowbray pie, game pie	named meat or cured meat unless qualified by the name of another food			
a) cooked				
weight ⩾ 200g		25	50	
⩾ 100g, < 200g		21	50	
< 100g		19	50	
b) uncooked				
weight ⩾ 200g		21	50	
⩾ 100g, < 200g		18	50	
< 100g		16	50	
Scottish pie or Scotch pie				
a) cooked		20	50	
b) uncooked		17	50	
Pie or pudding qualified by 'X', pastie or pasty, bridie or sausage roll	'meat' or a named meat or cured meat and also the name of another food			
a) cooked		12.5(4)	50	
b) uncooked		10.5(4)	50	
Sausage, chipolata, link or sausage meat				
a) qualified by 'X'				
(1)	'pork' and no other meat	65	50	80(5)
(2)	'beef' and no other meat	50	50	50(5)
(3)	'liver' and/or 'tongue'	50	50	30(5)
(4)	named meat or cured meat	50	50	80(5)
b) unqualified		50	50	
Paste or pâté (unless preceded by words which include the name of a food other than meat or fish and do not include a named meat, fish, cured meat or fish or 'meat' or 'fish')				
a) if preceded by 'X'	named meat, fish or cured meat			(6)
and if				
b) a meat product				
(1) pâté		70	50	
(2) others		70	65	

(*continued*)

	Definition of 'X'	*Minimum meat content* (as % of food)	*Minimum lean meat content* (as % of required meat content)	*Minimum 'X' content* (as % of food)
c) a spreadable fish product		70(7)		
d) combined meat and spreadable fish product				
(1) pâté		70(8)	50	
(2) others		70(8)	65	70
Spread, with the same condition as for paste, except that the name must be preceded by 'X' and if a meat product	named meat, fish or cured meat or fish or a mixture of them	70	65	

Notes:

(1) Whether or not the description forms part of another word except that for 'burger' excluding names using 'economy burger' or 'hamburger'. Where the name refers to a compound product (e.g. including a roll) the % only applies to the meat component of the product.
(2) Meat must be beef and/or pork and the name of the food must be qualified by the type of meat used.
(3) The food shall only contain corned meat of the named type.
(4) If the name used is pie or pudding qualified by 'meat' or a named meat or cured meat and preceded by 'vegetable' or the name of a type of vegetable, the minimum meat content is 10% (cooked) or 8% (uncooked).
(5) As % of meat content.
(6) Sufficient so that the food is characterized by 'X'.
(7) Fish content.
(8) Sum of fish and meat content.

Specific labelling requirements

1) Every meat product (except those to which 2) and 3) apply but not those requiring an indication of other ingredients under 3 a)) or spreadable fish product must be labelled with a declaration 'minimum X% meat' or 'minimum X% fish' with the correct value being inserted for X. Where a product includes a liquid medium not normally consumed the declaration must indicate that the liquid weight is not included in the calculation. If X is less than 10% the declaration may be 'less than 10% meat' or 'less than 10% fish'. If X is more than 100% the declaration shall be 'not less than 100% meat' or 'not less than 100% fish'. The words meat or fish may be replaced by the name of the meat or fish used (see also 4), 5) and 7)).
2) For corned meat products if only corned meat is used the declaration shall be '100% corned X' where the type of meat is inserted for X. Where the product name is qualified by the name of another food or where 'corned X' is used in the name of a food the declaration should read 'minimum Y% corned X' with the correct value being inserted for Y (see also 4)).

4.1

3) For any product having the appearance (while disregarding the presence of any seasoning, flavouring, garnishing or gelatinous substance) of a cut, joint, slice, portion or carcase of raw meat, cooked meat or cured meat the following shall apply (except in the case of products using the reserved descriptions listed above or food appearing to be shaped minced raw meat):
a) The name used shall include an indication of any ingredient other than water and other than for cooked meat: additives permitted by the additive regulations, flavourings, smoke and smoke solutions (subject to the Preservatives in Food Regulations), salt and herbs or spices used as seasoning; for cured meat: any ingredient listed in the definition of cured meat given above and used according to the conditions specified.
b) If under a) for raw or cooked meat containing added water or uncooked cured meat containing more than 10% added water the name includes an indication of other ingredients, then it shall be labelled with the declaration 'with added water'.
c) If under a) the name does not include an indication of other ingredients but it does contain added water (or for uncooked cured meats, contains more than 10% added water) it should be labelled with a declaration 'with not more than X% added water' where in the case of:
raw or cooked meat, 'X' is the value of the maximum added water
uncooked cured meat 'X' is the value expressed as a multiple of 5 by which the maximum added water exceeds 10%
cooked cured meat, 'X' is the value expressed as a multiple of 5 of the maximum added water.
Declarations under b) and c) shall appear either in the name of the food or in immediate proximity to it.
4) Declarations under 1) and 2) shall, if the product is labelled with an ingredients list, appear in immediate proximity to that list. Where only one type of meat or cured meat, fish or cured fish is present they may appear in immediate proximity to the relevant ingredient in the ingredients' list and (except for cured meat) the word 'meat' or 'fish' or the name of the meat or fish may be omitted from the declaration.
5) Products requiring a declaration under 1) must have a lean meat content of at least 65% of the declared minimum meat content except the following products which must have at least 50%: meat pie or part of a meat pie (includes meat pudding or sausage roll), a sausage (including chipolata, frankfurter, link, salami and any similar products and includes sausage meat) or a meat product of which sausage is an ingredient, or pâté.
6) Products requiring a declaration under 2) must have a lean meat content of at least 96% of the meat content of the product.

7) Where a meat product has a declaration under 1) or 2) and has animal or bird fat which, because of 5) or 6) cannot be taken into account in that declaration then, subject to 8), that fat must be separately identified in any ingredients list.
8) If the declared meat content is below that actually present and thus the fat cannot be taken into account for the declaration then the fat can be disregarded for the purposes of 7) if the lean meat contents specified in 5) are met.

General points

1) Meat content   the meat content is the sum of meat (calculated as raw meat) used in the preparation of the product and, if its presence is indicated in the name of the food, any naturally associated solid bone expressed as a % of the total weight of the product as sold. Where the product is dehydrated, or contains dehydrated ingredients, and is reconstituted before consumption, the calculation shall use the reconstituted weights. For sausages, any edible skin enclosing the sausage shall not be included in either the weight of the meat used or the product weight (where sausage includes chipolata, frankfurter, link, salami and any similar product and sausage meat). For products which include a liquid medium not normally consumed the weight of liquid shall not be included in the weight of the product.
2) Fish content   the fish content is the total weight of fish (calculated as raw fish) used in the preparation of the product expressed as a % of the total weight of the product as sold.
3) Corned meat content   the corned meat content shall be taken to be five-sixths of the meat content of the product.
4) Added water content   the added water content is the total weight of added water in the product expressed as a % of the total weight of the product as sold. The added water is only that water which is added in excess of that which would naturally be present in the meat used in the product when raw.
5) Use of offals   only those offals listed in a) in the definition of offals given above may be used in the preparation of uncooked meat products unless used solely as a sausage skin (which includes chipolata, frankfurter, link, salami and any similar product and sausage meat). (See also separate section on Offals.)
6) The Regulations do not apply to foods marked or labelled as being intended exclusively for consumption by babies or young children.

Milk

A Fresh liquid milk

Regulations: Milk and Dairies (Channel Islands and South Devon Milk) Regulations 1956 (1956/919)

4.1 EEC Council Regulation 1411/71
Drinking Milk Regulations 1976 (1976/1883)
Milk and Dairies (Milk Bottle Caps) (Colour) Regulations 1976 (1976/2186)
Amendments: EEC Council Regulations 1556/74, 556/76, 222/88, 2138/92
Milk and Dairies (Standardisation and Importation) Regulations 1992 (1992/3143)

Definitions
Milk the milk-yield of one or more cows.
Drinking milk the following products for delivery to the consumer: raw milk, whole milk, semi-skimmed milk and skimmed milk.
Raw milk milk which has not been heated or subjected to treatment having the same effect.
Whole milk milk which has been sujected to at least one heat treatment or an authorised treatment of equivalent effect by a milk processor, and with respect to fat content, meets the requirements of the table below.
Semi-skimmed milk/skimmed milk milk which has been subjected to at least one heat treatment or an authorised treatment of equivalent effect by a milk processor, and meets the requirements of the table below.

	Fat content (%)
Channel Islands, Jersey, Guernsey and South Devon milk	min 4.0
Whole milk	
non-standardised	min 3.5 (1)
standardised	min 3.5
Semi-skimmed milk	1.5–1.8
Skimmed milk	max 0.3

Note: (1) Fat content must not have been altered since the milking stage either by the addition or separation of milk fats or by mixture with milk, the natural fat content of which has been altered

Requirement
No person shall sell drinking milk except:
1) raw milk,
2) non-standardised whole milk,
3) standardised whole milk,
4) semi-skimmed milk,
5) skimmed milk.

General points
1) No person shall make any alteration to the composition of drinking milk. Except that standardised whole milk, skimmed milk or semi-skimmed milk may be obtained by adding or separating milk or cream, or by adding skimmed or semi-skimmed milk. Milk containing

additional ingredients is permitted but is subject to the Food Labelling Regulations.

2) If milk is packaged in a bottle with an aluminium foil cap, the cap should be of the following colour (any lettering to be in black or silver except that where silver is indicated in the table, any lettering must be in black):

Milk type	*Cap colour*
1 Pasteurised Channel Islands, Jersey, Guernsey, South Devon (may be homogenised)	Gold
2 Pasteurised homogenised	Red
3 Pasteurised Kosher (including any defined by 1) or 2))	Blue/Silver stripes
4 Pasteurised Kedassia (including any defined by 1) or 2)	Purple/Silver stripes
5 Pasteurised (except 1) to 4))	Silver
6 Sterilised	Blue
7 UHT	Pink
8 Untreated Channel Islands, Jersey, Guernsey, South Devon	Green with Gold stripe
9 Untreated	Green

B Liquid milk, processing standards

Regulations: Milk (Special Designation) Regulations 1989 (1989/2383)
Milk and Dairies (Semi-skimmed and Skimmed Milk)(Heat Treatment and Labelling) Regulations 1988 (1988/2206)
Amendments: Milk and Dairies (Semi-skimmed and Skimmed Milk)(Heat Treatment and Labelling)(Amendment) Regulations 1989 (1989/2382)
Milk and Dairies (Semi-skimmed and Skimmed Milk)(Heat Treatment and Labelling)(Amendment) Regulations 1990 (1990/2491)
Milk (Special Designation)(Amendment) Regulations 1990 (1990/2492)
Milk (Special Designation)(Amendment) Regulations 1992 (1992/1208)
Milk and Dairies (Standardization and Importation) Regulations 1992 (1992/3143)

The Special Designation Regulations require that use of the terms 'untreated', 'pasteurised', 'sterilised' and 'Ultra Heat Treated' (U.H.T.) for milk are only permitted when a licence has been granted by the local authority. In this case, 'milk' means cow's milk but does not include cream, or separated, skimmed, dried, condensed or evaporated milk, or butter milk. Detailed requirements, including heat treatment, for the granting of the licences are given in the Regulations. These include major restrictions on the distribution of 'untreated' milk (e.g. retail sale is not permitted).

The Semi-skimmed and Skimmed Milk Regulations specify the equivalent standards to be applied to semi-skimmed and skimmed milk. Untreated semi-skimmed and skimmed milk is not permitted.

4.1 The following standards are applied to all milk covered by the two sets of Regulations (except when imported under the Importation of Milk Regulations):

	Heat treatment	
	Temperature (°C)	*Time*
Pasteurised (1)		
(a)	62.8–65.6	min 30 minutes
or (b)	min 71.7	min 15 seconds
Sterilised	min 100	not specified
Ultra Heat Treated (UHT) (2)	min 135	min 1 second

Notes:
(1) Alternative time/temperature combinations may be approved by the licensing authority. Product to be immediately cooled to a maximum of 10°C
(2) For whole milk, under specified conditions, direct application of steam is permitted. Only certain specified additives may be used to treat the water used for generating the steam (see Regulations)

	Specified tests	
	Test (1)	*Limit/result*
Untreated milk	Coliform	less than 100 per ml
	Plate count	max 20,000 per ml
Milk for heat treatment		
(a) acceptance for treatment	Plate count	max 100,000 per ml (2)
(b) awaiting treatment more than 36 hours	Plate count	max 200,000 per ml
Pasteurised		
(a) after treatment	Coliform	less than 1 per ml
	Plate count	max 30,000 per ml
(b) after 120 hrs at 6°C	Plate count	max 100,000 per ml
(c) from treatment to delivery	Phosphatase	negative
Sterilised		
(a) after 15 days at 30°C	Plate count	max 10 per 0.1 ml
(b) from treatment to delivery	Turbidity	negative
UHT		
after 15 days at 30°C	Plate count	max 10 per 0.1 ml

Notes:
(1) Test methods are fully described in the Regulations
(2) Geometric average over preceding two months with a minimum of two samples taken each month of producers raw milk

Labelling

Details are specified for the labelling of milk. The general labelling requirement includes the following information:

a) the name of the milk, i.e. 'milk' or 'whole milk' qualified by 'untreated', 'pasteurised', 'ultra heat treated' (or 'U.H.T.'), 'semi-skimmed' or 'skimmed' as appropriate;
b) the appropriate durability indication, i.e. either the 'best before' date or, if highly perishable from a microbiological point of view and in consequence likely after a short period to constitute an immediate danger to human health, the 'use by' date;
c) for 'untreated' milk, the name and address of the licensed producer and details of the distributor, and, for other milks, the name and address of the producer, packer or seller;
d) the place of origin or provenance if necessary to avoid misleading (to a material degree) the purchaser;
e) for 'untreated' milk, the words 'This milk has not been heat treated and may therefore contain organisms harmful to health'.

General points

1) If UHT milk is produced by the direct treatment by steam, the milk fat and milk solids content must be the same after treatment as before.
2) Milk produced in Scotland or Northern Ireland, when produced under the equivalent Regulations in force in the country of production for the specified designations (pasteurised, sterilised or UHT), may be sold in England and Wales.

C Condensed and dried milk

Regulation: Condensed Milk and Dried Milk Regulations 1977 (1977/928)
Amendments: Food Labelling Regulations 1980 (1980/1849)
Condensed Milk and Dried Milk (Amendment) Regulations 1982 (1982/1066)
Condensed Milk and Dried Milk (Amendment) Regulations 1986 (1986/2299)
Condensed Milk and Dried Milk (Amendment) Regulations 1989 (1989/1959)

Definitions

Condensed milk milk, partly skimmed milk or skimmed milk (or any combination) whether with or without the addition of cream, dried milk or sucrose which has been concentrated by the partial removal of water but does not include dried milk.

Dried milk milk, partly skimmed milk or skimmed milk (or any combination) whether with or without the addition of cream, which has been concentrated to the form of a powder, granule or solid by the removal of water.

4.1

	Milk fat (%)	*Minimum total milk solids* (%) (1)	*Maximum moisture* (%)
Unsweetened condensed high-fat milk (2)	min 15	26.5	
Evaporated milk (2)	9–15	31	
Unsweetened condensed milk (2)	7.5–15	25	
Unsweetened condensed partly skimmed milk (2)			
(a) retail sale	4–4.5	24	
(b) other	1.0–7.5	20	
Unsweetened condensed skimmed milk (2)	max 1.0	20	
Sweetened condensed milk (3)			
(a) retail sale	min 9	31	
(b) other	min 8	28	
Sweetened condensed partly skimmed milk (3)			
(a) retail sale	4–4.5	28	
(b) other	1.0–8	24	
Sweetened condensed skimmed milk (3)	max 1.0	24	
Dried high-fat milk or high-fat milk powder	42–65		5
Dried whole milk or whole milk powder	26–42		5
Dried partly skimmed milk or partly skimmed milk powder	1.5–26		5
Dried skimmed milk or skimmed milk powder	max 1.5		5

Notes:

(1) For all products, up to 0.3% of milk solids not fat can consist of lactate; for condensed products, up to 25% of total milk solids can be derived from dried milk
(2) Condensed milk which has been sterilised
(3) Condensed milk with added sucrose

Permitted ingredients

1) Any instant dried milk product containing not less than 1.5% milk fat may contain up to 0.5% lecithins (E322). Product to be labelled 'instant'.
2) Any dried milk products for use in vending machines may contain up to 1.5% anti-caking agents. For non retail sale, product to be labelled 'for use in vending machines only'.
3) Sweetened condensed milk may contain up to 0.02% added lactose.
4) Condensed and dried milk may contain added vitamins.
5) Dried milk products may contain up to a total of 0.05% of the following antioxidants: L-ascorbic acid, sodium L-ascorbate or ascorbyl palmitate.
6) Certain specified condensed and dried milk products may contain specified miscellaneous additives in specified quantities (see Regulations).

General points

1) Any milk source used or any final product must be subject to pasteurisation so that a specified phosphatase test is satisfied.
2) The following declarations are required for retail sale:
   a) for condensed milk (min 1.0% milk fat) and dried milk (min 1.5% milk fat) actual or minimum milk fat content
   b) for condensed milk actual or minimum milk solids not fat
   c) for condensed milk instructions for dilution or use
   d) for dried milk (min 1.5% milk fat) fat content after dilution and instructions for dilution
   e) for unsweetened condensed UHT products 'UHT' or 'ultra heat treated'
   f) for condensed milk (max 1.0% milk fat) and dried milk (max 1.5% milk fat) the statement 'not to be used for babies except under medical advice'
3) Condensed or dried milk specially prepared for infant feeding and labelled as such is exempt from the above controls on additional ingredients and labelling.

D Filled milks

Regulation: Skimmed Milk with Non-Milk Fat Regulations 1960 (1960/2331)
Amendments: Skimmed Milk with Non-Milk Fat (Amendment) Regulations 1976 (1976/103)
Food Labelling Regulations 1980 (1980/1849)
Skimmed Milk with Non-milk Fat (Amendment) Regulations 1981 (1981/1174)
Milk and Milk Products (Protection of Designations) Regulations 1990 (1990/607)
Food Safety (Amendment)(Metrication) Regulations 1992 (1992/2597)

The Regulations specify labelling standards for the following products:
skimmed milk with non-milk fat,
condensed skimmed milk with non-milk fat,
dried skimmed milk with non-milk fat.

In particular, the statement 'Unfit For Babies' or 'Not To Be Used For Babies' is required except for certain specified approved products. If the quantity or proportion and the appropriate designation of each fat or oil (other than milk fat) is given, the statement may be 'Should not be used for babies except under medical advice' or 'Medical advice should be obtained before using this product for baby feeding'.

The Regulations do not apply to foods (not being baby foods) sold under a description of designation which clearly indicates that they are not intended or suitable for use as, or as a substitute for, milk, condensed full cream milk or dried full cream milk.

4.1 Milk-based drinks

Regulation: Milk-based Drinks (Hygiene and Heat Treatment) Regulations 1983 (1983/1508)

Amendment: Milk-based Drinks (Hygiene and Heat Treatment) (Amendment) Regulations 1986 (1986/720)

Definition

Milk-based drink (or Milk drink) a liquid drink (other than a fermented drink) being a mixture comprising minimum 85% milk and other permitted ingredients (see below). The milk shall be cows' milk (whether or not separated) but not cream separated from the milk, dried milk, condensed milk, evaporated milk or butter milk.

Permitted ingredients

1) Any substance suitable for use as food and commonly used as food, which is wholly a natural product whether or not it has been subjected to a process or treatment.
2) Flavouring.
3) Any permitted solvent, colouring matter, emulsifier, stabiliser, miscellaneous additive and sweetener (as defined in the appropriate Regulations).
4) Starch (modified or not).
5) Salt.
6) Vitamin or mineral preparations.
7) Water fit for human consumption.

Processing standards

1) Only milk that has been produced in the UK (unless imported under the provisions of the Importation of Milk Regulations) may be used.
2) The milk and other ingredients must be mixed no longer than 4 hours prior to heat treatment (or pre-heating prior to sterilization).
3) No milk-based drink shall be kept for more than 1 hour at a temperature above 10°C prior to heat treatment (unless pre-heated prior to sterilisation).
4) Heat treatments are specified (see table on next page).

General points

1) No person may sell a food, other than a milk-based drink, which is labelled with the words 'milk-based drink' or 'milk drink'.
2) Milk-based drinks produced in Scotland or Northern Ireland, when produced under the equivalent Regulations in force in the country of production for the specified treatment (pasteurised, sterilised or UHT), may be sold in England and Wales.
3) The Regulations specify additional hygiene conditions which must be met.

	Minimum heat treatment		Specified tests
	Temperature (°C)	Time	
Pasteurisation (1)			
(a)	63	30 minutes	Coliform test (2)
or (b)	72	15 seconds	and/or phosphatase test
Sterilisation (3)	108	45 minutes	Colony count
Ultra High Temperature (UHT)(3,4)	140	2 seconds	Colony count

Notes:

(1) Or similar process designed to have equivalent effect on the elimination of vegetative pathogenic organisms. Drink to be cooled as soon as practicable and retained at a maximum 10°C

(2) Only to be used not later than the day following heat treatment and before departure from the premises of treatment. Must be used if the milk-based drink has a colour which interferes with the phosphatase test

(3) Or similar process designed to have equivalent effect in rendering the milk-based drink free from viable micro-organisms and their spores. Drink to be cooled as soon as practicable after sterilisation

(4) Direct application of steam is permitted. Only certain specified additives may be used to treat the water used for generating the steam (see Regulations)

Natural mineral waters

Regulation: The Natural Mineral Waters Regulations 1985 (1985/71)

Definitions

Natural mineral water water which originates in a ground water body or deposit and is extracted for human consumption from the ground through a spring, well, bore or other exit, and which is recognized in accordance with the Regulations.

Effervescent natural mineral water a natural mineral water which spontaneously and visibly gives off carbon dioxide under ambient conditions of temperature and pressure.

Carbonated natural mineral water an effervescent natural mineral water whose carbon dioxide content derives at least in part from an origin other than the ground water body or deposit from which the water comes.

Naturally carbonated natural mineral water an effervescent natural mineral water whose carbon dioxide content is the same after decanting (if it is decanted) and bottling as it was at source, and includes a natural mineral water to which carbon dioxide from the same ground body or deposit as the water has been added if the amount added does not exceed the amount previously released during decanting or bottling.

4.1 *General points*

1) To be classed as a natural mineral water, the water must originate in a ground water body or deposit and be extracted for human consumption from the ground through a spring, well, bore or other exit and be officially recognised. Official recognition can be obtained by demonstrating that the list of conditions specified in the Regulations are satisfied and by providing relevant details of the source. These include: hydrogeological description of the source, physical and chemical characteristics of the water, microbiological analyses, levels of toxic substances, freedom from pollution and stability of the source. The names of all natural mineral waters which have been officially recognised will be published in the *Official Journal of the European Communities*.
2) Certain general requirements apply to the exploitation of a source of natural mineral water. These Regulations specify that equipment must be installed so as to avoid any possibility of contamination and so as to preserve the properties ascribed to it which the water possesses at the source. In particular the water must be transported from the source in the containers in which it will be sold to the consumer (unless prior to 17/7/1980 it was being transported in tanks to a bottling plant in the UK away from the source).
3) Authorised treatments   no treatment is permitted whether for disinfection or for any other purposes, except:
   a) filtration or decanting, preceded if necessary by oxygenation, provided that it does not alter the composition in respect of the its stable constituents and it is not intended to change its total viable count;
   b) the total or partial elimination of carbon dioxide by exclusively physical methods;
   c) the addition of carbon dioxide.
4) Microbiological requirements   the following microbiological criteria must be satisfied:
   a) at source – total viable colony count to conform to normal values indicating the source protected from contamination;
   b) after bottling (within 12 hours) – the maximum total viable colony count to be   100 per ml at 20–22°C in 72 hours, and 20 per ml at 37°C in 24 hours; thereafter no more than that which results from the normal increase;
   c) at source and thereafter – water to be free from:
   parasites and pathogenic micro-organisms
   Escherichia coli and other coliforms and faecal streptococci (in any 250 ml sample)
   sporulated sulphite-reducing anaerobes (in any 50 ml sample)
   Pseudomonas aeruginosa (in any 250 ml sample).

5) Toxic substances the following maximum are specified and the water must not contain amounts of any other substance which makes it unwholesome: Mercury 1 µg/l; Cadmium 5 µg/l; Antimony, Selenium, Lead 10 µg/l; Arsenic, Cyanide, Chromium, Nickel, 50 µg/l.
6) Organoleptic defects no natural mineral water may be sold which has an organoleptic defect.
7) Bottles the water must be sold in bottles which:
   a) are the ones used at the time of bottling by the exploiter,
   b) are fitted with closures which avoid the possibility of adulteration or contamination, and
   c) are still fitted with the intact original closures.

Specific labelling requirements

1) Every natural mineral water shall be labelled with:
   a) if non-effervescent, 'natural mineral water';
   b) if effervescent, 'naturally carbonated natural mineral water', 'natural mineral water fortified with gas from the spring' or 'carbonated natural mineral water' as appropriate (see definitions above);
   c) 'fully de-carbonated' or 'partially de-carbonated' as appropriate if the water has been treated to remove carbon dioxide;
   d) the name of the place where the source is exploited and the name of the spring, well or borehole;
   e) either the statement 'composition in accordance with the results of the officially recognized analysis of ...' (giving the date of the analysis), or a statement of the analytical composition of the water including details of its characteristic constituents.
2) A commercial designation (name under which water is sold including brand name, trade mark or fancy name) may be used but:
   a) the name of a locality, hamlet or other place may only be used if it is where the source is exploited and its use does not mislead;
   b) only one commercial designation may be used per source (except the brand name, trade mark or fancy name may differ);
   c) the name of the source must be at least one and a half times the height and width of the largest letters used for any other part of the commercial designation.
3) No bottled drinking water may be labelled in a way likely to be confused with a natural mineral water.
4) No labelling must suggest a characteristic which the water does not possess. The following indications may only be used if they meet the conditions specified and in particular no other indication relating to the prevention, treatment or cure of human disease shall be used:

4.1

Indication	*Constituent*	*Requirement*
'Low mineral content'	inorganic constituents	not above 500 mg dry residue/l
'Very low mineral content'	inorganic constituents	not above 50 mg dry residue/l
'Rich in mineral salts'	inorganic constituents	above 1,500 mg dry residue/l
'Contains bicarbonate'	bicarbonate	above 600 mg/l
'Contains sulphate'	sulphate	above 200 mg/l
'Contains chloride'	chloride	above 200 mg/l
'Contains calcium'	calcium	above 150 mg/l
'Contains magnesium'	magnesium	above 50 mg/l
'Contains fluoride'	fluoride	above 1 mg/l
'Contains iron'	bivalent iron	above 1 mg/l
'Acidic'	free carbon dioxide	above 250 mg/l
'Contains sodium'	sodium	above 200 mg/l
'Suitable for a low sodium diet'	sodium	not above 20 mg/l

Olive oil

Regulations: Olive Oil (Marketing Standards) Regulations 1987 (1987/1783)
Tetrachloroethylene in Olive Oil Regulations 1989 (1989/910)
Amendment: Olive Oil (Marketing Standards)(Amendment) Regulations 1992 (1992/2590)

Note: The Regulations provide for procedures to enforce marketing standards applied by EC Council Regulation Nos 136/66 and Commission Regulation 1860/88 as amended by Nos 1915/87 and 356/92. The standards have been supplemented by very detailed controls on characteristics and methods of analysis contained in Commission Regulation 2568/91.

The use of the following definitions (and associated standards) is compulsory in the marketing of olive oil and olive-pomace oil within the UK, in intra-Community trade and in trade with third countries.

Definitions

(Note: All the following definitions are supplemented by the statement 'and the other characteristics which comply with those laid down for this category'. Reference should be made to Commission Regulation 2568/91 for the more detailed characteristics.)

Virgin olive oils   oils derived solely from olives using mechanical or other physical means under conditions, and particularly thermal conditions, that do not lead to deterioration of the oil, and which have undergone no treatment other than washing, decantation, centrifugation and filtration, but excluding oils obtained by means of solvents or of re-esterification and mixtures with other oils.

Refined olive oil   olive oil obtained by refining virgin olive oils.

Olive oil   olive oil obtained by blending refined olive oil and virgin olive oil other than lampante oil.

Crude olive-residue oil oil obtained by treating olive residue with solvents, but excluding oil obtained by re-esterification and mixtures with other types of oils.
Refined olive-residue oil oil obtained by refining crude olive-residue oil.
Olive-residue oil oil obtained by blending refined olive-residue oil and virgin olive oil other than lampante oil.

The following standards are included with the definitions:

	Organoleptic grading (1)	*Free acid content* (expressed as oleic acid) g/100g
Virgin olive oils:		
extra virgin olive oil	min 6.5	max 1
virgin olive oil (2)	min 5.5	max 2
ordinary virgin olive oil	min 3.5	max 3.3
lampante virgin olive oil (3)	less than 3.5	more than 3.3
Refined olive oil		max 0.5
Olive oil		max 1.5
Refined olive-residue oil		max 0.5
Olive-residue oil		max 1.5

Notes:
(1) As measured according to the procedure specified in Commission Regulation 2568/91.
(2) The expression 'fine' may be used at the production and wholesale stage.
(3) Only one of the specified levels needs to be met for the oil to be in this category.

General points

1) Only extra virgin olive oil, virgin olive oil, olive oil and olive-residue oil may be sold by retail.
2) No olive oil or olive-residue oil with a tetrachloroethylene content of more than 0.1 mg/kg can be sold by retail.

Poultry

(See also Meat products and spreadable fish products)

A Raw poultry

Regulation: Poultry Meat (Hygiene) Regulations 1976 (1976/1209)
Amendments: Poultry Meat (Hygiene) (Amendment) Regulations 1979 (1979/693)
Poultry Meat (Hygiene) (Amendment) Regulations 1981 (1981/1168)

Note: These Regulations primarily concern hygiene and fuller details are given in Section 4.6 (page 159). However, the following point is included and is more relevant to this section.

4.1 No person shall sell as fresh poultry meat, poultry meat that has been:

a) treated with hydrogen peroxide or other bleaching substance or with any natural or artificial colouring matter,
b) treated with antibiotics, preservatives or tenderisers.

B Frozen poultry

Regulations: Poultry Meat (Water Content) Regulations 1984 (1984/1145)
EEC Council/Commission Regulations 2967/76, 2785/80
Amendments: EEC Council/Commission Regulations 1691/77, 641/79, 2632/80, 2835/80, 3204/83.

Frozen and deep-frozen chickens, hens and cocks may be marketed only if the water content absorbed during preparation does not exceed the technically unavoidable minimum determined by specified methods.

Products treated with polyphosphates are exempt provided they are clearly described with their treatment.

Product may be described as 'dry chilled poultry' if no water is added during chilling.

	Maximum extraneous water (%)
Slaughterhouse check (prior to freezing)	5
Rapid detection check (thawing loss) (1)	
standard freezing	5.2 (2)
dry chill poultry	2 (2)
Standard procedure (analytical) (3)	
standard freezing	(4)
dry chilled poultry	(4)

Notes:
(1) Based on a sample of 20 carcases. Not to be used if polyphosphates have been used to increase water retention.
(2) If these figures are exceeded, then the standard procedure should be followed.
(3) Based on a sample of 7 carcases.
(4) Result obtained by comparing two figures obtained by calculation (See amended Annex III of Council Regulation 2967/76)

Soft drinks

Regulation: Soft Drinks Regulations 1964 (1964/760)
Amendments: Soft Drinks (Amendment) Regulations 1969 (1969/1818)
Soft Drinks (Amendment) Regulations 1970 (1970/1579)
Labelling of Food (Amendment) Regulations 1972 (1972/1510)
Soft Drinks (Amendment) Regulations 1976 (1976/295)
Fruit Juices and Fruit Nectars Regulations 1977 (1977/927)
Food Labelling Regulations 1980 (1980/1849)
Sweeteners in Food Regulations 1983 (1983/1211)
Food Safety (Amendment)(Metrication) Regulations 1992 (1992/2597)

Definitions

Soft drink any liquid intended for sale as drink for human consumption, either without or after dilution, and includes –
any fruit drink, and any other fruit juice squash, crush or cordial; soda water, Indian or quinine tonic water, and any sweetened artificially carbonated water whether flavoured or unflavoured; ginger beer and any herbal or botanical beverage but does not include –
water (except as aforesaid); water from natural springs, either in its natural state or with added mineral substances; fruit juice, concentrated fruit juice, dried fruit juice or fruit nectar (as defined in the relevant Regulations); milk or any preparation of milk; tea, coffee, dandelion coffee, cocoa or chocolate; any egg product; and cereal product, except
(a) flavoured barley water and liquid products used in the preparation of barley water, and
(b) cereal products containing alcohol, which are not intoxicating liquor as defined in the Licensing Act 1953;
meat, yeast or vegetable extracts, soup or soup mixtures, or any similar product; tomato juice, vegetable juice or any preparation of any such juice or juices; intoxicating liquor as defined in the Licensing Act 1953; any other unsweetened drink except soda water;
and for the purposes of this definition a product shall not be deemed not to be a soft drink by reason only of the fact that it is capable of being used as a medicine.

Comminuted citrus drink a soft drink produced by a process involving the comminution of the entire citrus fruit.

Crush a soft drink containing fruit juice, not being a comminuted citrus drink, intended for consumption without dilution and includes any cordial intended for consumption without dilution.

Squash a soft drink containing fruit juice, not being a comminuted citrus drink, intended for consumption after dilution and includes any cordial intended for consumption after dilution.

The following compositional standards are specified (provision has been made for the metrication of the standards as from 1.1.1995):

	For consumption without dilution			*For consumption with dilution*		
	Minimum fruit content (%)	*Minimum added sugar* (1) (lb/10 gal)	*Maximum saccharin* (1) (grains/ 10 gal)	*Minimum fruit content* (%)	*Minimum added sugar* (1) (lb/10 gal)	*Maximum saccharin* (1) (grains/ 10 gal)
Citrus juice and barley water (2)	3 (3)	4.5	56	15 (3)	22.5	280
Lime crush, lime juice and soda (2)	3 (4)	4.5	56			

4.1 *(continued)*

	For consumption without dilution			*For consumption with dilution*		
	Minimum fruit content (%)	*Minimum added sugar* (1) (lb/10 gal)	*Maximum saccharin* (1) (grains/ 10 gal)	*Minimum fruit content* (%)	*Minimum added sugar* (1) (lb/10 gal)	*Maximum saccharin* (1) (grains/ 10 gal)
Other citrus crushes (2)	5 (3)	4.5	56			
Citrus squashes (2)				25 (3)	22.5	280
Other soft drinks (2) (mixed citrus and non citrus)	5 (5)	4.5	56	25 (5)	22.5	280
Comminuted citrus fruit and barley drinks (2)	1.5 (6)	4.5	56	7 (6)	22.5	280
Other comminuted citrus drinks (with other fruits) (2)	2 (6)	4.5	56	10 (6)	22.5	280
Soft drinks with fermented apple or pear juice	5 (7)	4.5	56			
Any other fruit juice soft drink (2)	5 (5)	4.5	56			
Indian or quinine tonic water (8)		4.5	56			
Dry ginger ale		3	56			
Brewed ginger beer (10)		2	80			
Non citrus fruit squashes (2)				10 (9)	22.5	280
Other soft drinks		4.5	56		22.5	280

Notes:

(1) Not applicable to low calorie soft drinks or to diabetic drinks labelled as such
(2) For 'Semi-sweet' soft drinks the following figures apply
fruit content: as specified above
added sugar (lb/10 gal):
2.25–3 for consumption without dilution
11.25–15 for consumption with dilution
maximum saccharin (grams/10 gal):
28 for consumption within dilution
140 for consumption with dilution
(3) Citrus fruit juice by volume
(4) Lime juice by volume
(5) Fruit juice by volume
(6) Potable citrus fruit content (lb/10 gal)
(7) Fermented apple or pear juice by volume
(8) To contain not less than 0.5 grain quinine per pint
(9) Non-citrus fruit juice by volume
(10) Includes herbal and botanical beverages

Permitted acids

Only the following acids can be added to soft drinks:

1) all drinks: ascorbic acid, citric acid, lactic acid, malic acid, nicotinic acid, tartaric acid, and any acid permitted in soft drinks by the preservatives and colouring matter regulations (subject to any restrictions);
2) all drinks except fruit squash, fruit crush and comminuted citrus drinks: acetic acid, phosphoric acid.

General points

1) Low calorie soft drinks:
   for consumption after dilution max 7.5 cal/fluid oz
   for consumption without dilution max 1.5 cal/fluid oz.
   (From 1.1.95, these will be metricated to read:
   for consumption after dilution max 264 kcals/l and 1105 kJ/l
   for consumption without dilution max 53 kcals/l and 221 kJ/l)
2) Soda water:
   minimum 5 grains sodium bicarbonate per pint.
3) Sweeteners: any sugar or permitted sweetener may be used, but if saccharin is used the maximum quantity is given in the above table.
4) Diabetic drinks: no added sugar permitted but no maximum quantity of saccharin specified.

Labelling

1) Citrus squash shall be labelled with the word 'squash' preceded by the name(s) of the fruit(s) used, except:
   a) clear squash made from lime juice shall be called 'lime juice cordial'.
   b) other clear citrus squashes may be termed 'cordial'.
   c) squash prepared from citrus fruit and barley water (and no other juice) shall be called 'barley water' (preceded by the name of the fruit(s)).
2) Citrus crush shall be labelled with the word 'crush' preceded by the name(s) of the fruit(s) used, except:
   a) clear citrus crushes may be termed 'cordial'.
   b) crush prepared from citrus fruit and barley water (and no other juice) shall be called 'barley crush' (preceded by the name of the fruit(s)).
3) Comminuted citrus drink shall be labelled with the word 'drink' preceded by the name(s) of the fruit(s) used, except:
   drink prepared from comminuted citrus fruit and barley water (and no other juice) shall be called 'barley drink' (preceded by the name of the fruit(s)).
4) Drinks for consumption after dilution must have appropriate dilution instructions and must require at least 4 parts water to 1 part drink.

5) Soft drinks are permitted below the specified fruit standards if they are termed 'fruit-ade' when the name of a fruit is substituted or the word flavour is used immediately after the name of the fruit(s).
6) Semi-sweet soft drinks must be labelled 'semi-sweet'.
7) Diabetic and low calorie soft drinks shall be labelled with the name of the drink preceded by 'diabetic' or 'low calorie' (as appropriate).
8) Soft drinks from vending machines must display the correct name and, if containing saccharin, an appropriate statement (e.g. 'saccharin and sugar added' or 'sweetened with sugar and saccharin' - see Regulations).

Sugar products

Regulation: Specified Sugar Products Regulations 1976 (1976/509)
Amendments: Miscellaneous Additives in Food Regulations 1980 (1980/1834)
Food Labelling Regulations 1980 (1980/1849)
Specified Sugar Products (Amendment) Regulations 1982 (1982/255)

Definitions

Candy sugar crystalline sugar with crystals having any dimension greater than 1 cm.

Loaf sugar a piece of agglomerated crystalline sugar, usually conically shaped, weighing not less than 250 g.

Reserved descriptions

(Descriptions to be applied only to the products stated and conforming to the standards below.)

Dextrose anhydrous purified and crystallised D-glucose (except icing dextrose) containing no water of crystallisation.

Dextrose monohydrate purified and crystallised D-glucose (except icing dextrose) containing one molecule of water of crystallisation.

Glucose syrup purified and concentrated aqueous solution of nutritive saccharides obtained from starch.

Dried glucose syrup glucose syrup which has been partially dried.

Extra white sugar/white sugar/sugar purified and crystallised sucrose (except icing sugar, candy sugar or loaf sugar).

Semi-white sugar purified and crystallised sucrose (except candy sugar or loaf sugar).

Sugar solution an aqueous solution of sucrose.

Invert sugar solution an aqueous solution of sucrose which has been partially inverted by hydrolysis.

Invert sugar syrup an aqueous solution, whether or not crystallised, of sucrose which has been partially inverted by hydrolysis.

White soft sugar/soft sugar fine-grain purified moist sucrose.

Lactose the carbohydrate normally obtained from whey; it may be anhydrous or contain one molecule of water of crystallisation or be a mixture of both forms.

Icing dextrose/powdered dextrose   fine particles of dextrose monohydrate or anhydrous (or mixture).

Icing sugar/powdered sugar   fine particles of white sugar or extra white sugar (or mixtures).

	Minimum dry matter (%)	*Minimum D-glucose content* (% of dry matter)	*Maximum sulphated ash* (% of dry matter)
Dextrose anhydrous	98	99.5	0.25
Dextrose monohydrate	90	99.5	0.25
Dried glucose syrup	93	20(1)	1.0
Glucose syrup	70	20(1)	1.0

	Minimum dry matter (%)	*Invert sugar content* (% of dry matter)	*Invert sugar fructose: dextrose ratio*	*Maximum conductivity ash content* (% of dry matter)
Sugar solution (2,5)	62	max 3	1.0 ± 0.2	0.1
Invert sugar solution (5)	62	3–50	1.0 ± 0.1	0.4
Invert sugar syrup (5)	62	min 50	1.0 ± 0.1	0.4

	Minimum sucrose and invert sugar content (as sucrose) (%)	*Invert sugar content* (%)	*Maximum ash content* (%)	*Maximum loss on drying* (%)
White soft sugar (2)	97	0.3–12	0.2 (3)	3
Soft sugar	88	0.3–12	3.5 (4)	4.5

	Minimum polarization (°)	*Maximum invert sugar* (%)	*Maximum loss on drying* (%)
Extra white sugar (2)	99.7	0.04	0.1
White sugar, sugar (2)	99.7	0.04	0.1
Semi-white sugar	99.5	0.1	0.1

Notes:

(1) Minimum dextrose equivalent expressed as D-glucose (% of dry matter)
(2) Extra standards are specified for colour standards (see Regulations)
(3) Conductivity ash contents
(4) Sulphated ash content
(5) May only be qualified by the word ‘white’ if certain colour standards are satisfied (see Regulations)

4.1

Permitted additional ingredients

1) Icing sugar or icing dextrose may contain:
   a) max 5% starch (except modified starch), or
   b) max 1.5% anti-caking agents, subject to the Miscellaneous Additives in Food Regulations and product to be marked, as appropriate, 'contains starch' or 'contains X' where X is the name of the anti-caking agent.
2) Glucose syrup or dried glucose syrup may contain max 15 mg/kg antifoaming agent (or emulsifier acting as antifoaming agent), subject to the Miscellaneous Additives or Emulsifiers and Stabilisers in Food Regulations. Product to be marked 'contains X' where X is the name of the additive.
3) If a sugar product is intended for use as an ingredient of another food it may contain colour subject to the Colouring Matter in Food Regulations. Product to be marked 'contains permitted colour' or 'contains colour' or 'contains X' where X is the name of the colour.
4) Sulphur dioxide (or the alternative forms specified in the Preservative Regulations) as in the following table:

	Maximum sulphur dioxide (mg/kg)
Dextrose anhydrous, dextrose monohydrate, extra white sugar, semi-white sugar, white sugar	15
Invert sugar solution, invert sugar syrup, sugar solution	15 (1)
Icing dextrose, icing sugar	20
Soft sugar, white soft sugar	40
Glucose syrup (for manufacturing purposes) (2)	400
Glucose syrup (for other purposes)	20
Dried glucose syrup (for manufacturing purposes) (2)	150
Dried glucose syrup (for other purposes)	20

Notes:
(1) On dry matter
(2) To be marked 'not for retail sale'

Labelling requirements

1) Extra white sugar may be called 'sugar' or 'white sugar'.
2) Dextrose monohydrate or dextrose anhydrous may be called 'dextrose'.
3) Any invert sugar syrup containing a significant proportion of crystals must be qualified by the word 'crystallised'.
4) For sugar solution, invert sugar solution or syrup, a declaration of the dry matter and of the invert sugar content must be given.

4.2 Additives

Antioxidants

Regulation: Antioxidants in Food Regulations 1978 (1978/105)
Amendments: Antioxidants in Food (Amendment) Regulations 1980 (1980/1831)
Sweeteners in Food Regulations 1983 (1983/1211)
Bread and Flour Regulations 1984 (1984/1304)
Antioxidants in Food (Amendment) Regulations 1991 (1991/2540)
Food Additives Labelling Regulations 1992 (1992/1978)

Definition
Any substance which is capable of delaying, retarding or preventing the development in food of rancidity or other flavour deterioration due to oxidation, does not include any substance permitted in other additive Regulations (except a permitted diluent combined with an antioxidant) or any esters of L-ascorbic acid with straight chain C14 and C18 fatty acids used or for use to dilute or dissolve colouring matter.

Permitted antioxidants

(1)	*Name (and synonyms)*
E300	L-Ascorbic acid
E301	Sodium L-ascorbate
E302	Calcium L-ascorbate
E304	6-*o*-Palmitoyl-L-ascorbic acid (ascorbyl palmitate)
E306	Extracts of natural origin rich in tocopherols
E307	Synthetic alpha-tocopherol
E308	Synthetic gamma-tocopherol
E309	Synthetic delta-tocopherol
E310	Propyl gallate (propyl 3,4,5-trihydroxybenzoate) (2)
E311	Octyl gallate (octyl 3,4,5-trihydroxybenzoate) (2)
E312	Dodecyl gallate (dodecyl 3,4,5-trihydroxybenzoate) (2)
E320	Butylated hydroxyanisole (BHA) (2)
E321	Butylated hydroxytoluene (BHT) (2,6-di-*tert*-butyl-*p*-cresol) (2)
–	Ethoxyquin (2)

Notes:
(1) Serial number permitted for use on labels
(2) Only permitted in certain foods (see below)

Permitted diluents
Drinking water, demineralized water, distilled water, edible oils and fats.

Antioxidants permitted only in certain foods:

	Permitted antioxidant	*Maximum* (mg/kg)
Any of the following dairy products for use in the preparation of food: Butter, butter fat, dried cream, dried cheese, dried whey, dried whey derivatives.	(1) (2) (3)	100 (4) 200 (4) 300 (4,5)

4.2 (*continued*)

	Permitted antioxidant	*Maximum (mg/kg)*
Anhydrous edible oils and fats and vitamin oils and concentrates other than preparations of Vit. A or Vit. A esters containing more than 30 000 μg retinol equivalents per gram	(1) (2) (3)	100 200 300 (5)
Any permitted emulsifier or stabiliser containing combined fatty acids whether or not those fatty acids have been polymerised.	(1) (2) (3)	100 200 300 (5)
Essential oils and isolates from the concentrates of essential oils.	(1) (2) (3)	1000 1000 1000
Potato powder, potato flakes and potato granules.	(2)	25
Walnuts (shelled)	BHA BHT Any mixture of BHA and BHT	70 70 140 (6)
Apples and pears	Ethoxyquin	3
Preparations of Vit. A and Vit. A esters containing more than 30 000 μg retinol equivalents per gram	(2)	33.3 (7)
Preparations of Vit. A and Vit. A esters for use as ingredients in the preparation of food described directly or indirectly as intended for babies or young children.	(2)	0.35 (7)
Chewing gum base	BHT	1000
Chewing gum manufactured from chewing gum base containing BHT.	BHT	200
Chewing gum manufactured from chewing gum base containing BHA and/or BHT and imported from another EC Member State	(2)	(8)

Notes:

(1) Propyl gallate, octyl gallate or dodecyl gallate or any mixture of them
(2) BHA or BHT or any mixture of them
(3) Any mixture of any of (1) or (2)
(4) Calculated on the milk fat content
(5) Of which not more than 100 shall be from (1) and not more than 200 shall be from (2)
(6) Of which not more than 70 shall be BHA and not more than 70 shall be BHT
(7) mg/kg of preparation for every 1000 μg retinol equivalents per gram
(8) Must meet legal requirements of country of origin

General points

1) The following are not permitted in foods intended for babies or young children (except as specifically permitted for babies and young children in the above table): BHA, BHT, propyl gallate, octyl gallate, dodecyl gallate or ethoxyquin.
2) Diphenylamine may be used on or in apples and pears up to a maximum of 10 mg/kg where it is present solely following use as a scald inhibitor.

3) Any food (except butter, butter fat, cream, dried cream, milk, condensed milk, evaporated milk, dried milk, cheese, dried cheese, dried whey or dried whey derivative) containing as an ingredient one of the dairy products listed in the first item of the above table (or containing milk fat derived from any of the dairy products listed in the first item of the above table) may contain the antioxidant in proportion to its use.
4) Any food containing as an ingredient any food listed in the above table (except dairy products listed in the first item of the above table) may contain the antioxidant in proportion to its use.

Colours

Regulation: Colouring Matter in Food Regulations 1973 (1973/1340)
Amendments: Preservatives in Food Regulations 1974 (1974/1119)
Colouring Matter in Food (Amendment) Regulations 1975 (1975/1488)
Colouring Matter in Food (Amendment) Regulations 1976 (1976/2086)
Colouring Matter in Food (Amendment) Regulations 1978 (1978/1787)
Lead in Food Regulations 1979 (1979/1254)
Colouring Matter in Food (Amendment) Regulations 1987 (1987/1987)
Food Additives Labelling Regulations 1992 (1992/1978)

Note: There is no definition in the Regulations for 'colouring matter'.

Permitted colouring matter

(1)	*Name*
E100	Curcumin
E101	Riboflavin or Lactoflavin
101a	Riboflavin-5′-phosphate
E102	Tartrazine
E104	Quinoline Yellow
E110	Sunset Yellow FCF or Orange Yellow S
E120	Cochineal or Carminic acid
E122	Carmoisine or Azorubine
E123	Amaranth
E124	Ponceau 4R or Cochineal Red A
E127	Erythrosine BS
128	Red 2G
E131	Patent Blue V
E132	Indigo Carmine or Indigotine
133	Brilliant Blue FCF
E140	Chlorophyll
E141	Copper complexes of chlorophyll and chlorophyllins
E142	Green S or Acid Brilliant Green BS or Lissamine Green
154	Brown FK
155	Chocolate Brown HT
E150	Caramel
E151	Black PN or Brilliant Black BN
E153	Carbon black or Vegetable carbon
E160	Carotenoids:

4.2 *(continued)*

(1)	*Name*
E160(a)	alpha-, beta-, gamma-carotene
E160(b)	annatto, bixin, norbixin
E160(c)	capsanthin or capsorubin
E160(d)	lycopene
E160(e)	beta-apo-8′-carotenal
E160(f)	ethyl ester of beta-apo-8′-carotenoic acid
E161(a)	Flavoxanthin
E161(b)	Lutein
E161(c)	Crytoxanthin
E161(d)	Rubixanthin
E161(e)	Violaxanthin
E161(f)	Rhodoxanthin
E161(g)	Canthaxanthin
E162	Beetroot Red or Betanin
E163	Anthocyanins
–	The following natural substances having a secondary colouring effect: paprika, turmeric, saffron, sandalwood or their pure colouring principle
E171	Titanium dioxide
E172	Iron oxides and hydroxides
E173	Aluminium (2)
E174	Silver (2)
E175	Gold (2)
E180	Pigment Rubine or Lithol Rubine BK (2)
–	Methyl violet (2)
–	The synthetic equivalent identical with the pure colouring principle of any natural colouring matter described in this table.

Notes:
(1) Serial number permitted for use on labels
(2) Permitted only for certain foods (see below)

Permitted diluents
Sodium carbonate, sodium hydrogen carbonate, sodium chloride, sodium sulphate, glucose, lactose, sucrose, dextrins, starches, sorbitol, edible fats and oils, beeswax, water, citric acid, tartaric acid, lactic acid, gelatin, pectins, ammonium or sodium or potassium alginates, esters of l-ascorbic acid with straight chain C14, C16 and C18 fatty acids (only for E160 and E161), acetic acid, sodium hydroxide, ammonium hydroxide (ammonia solution), and any permitted solvent.

Colouring matter permitted only in certain foods:

Food	*Colours*	*Restrictions*
Dragees	Aluminium, gold, silver	For external colouring only
Sugar coated flour confectionery	Aluminium, gold, silver	For decoration only
Hard cheeses	Pigment Rubine or Lithol Rubine BK	On the rind only
Raw or unprocessed meat	Methyl violet	For marking only

General points

1) No food shall have in it or on it any colouring matter other than a permitted colouring matter.
2) The following raw or unprocessed foods shall have no added colouring matter (except for marking purposes): meat, game, poultry, fish, fruit or vegetable (except the husk of any nut may have any permitted colouring).
3) The following foods shall have no added colouring: food specially prepared for babies or young children (except use of the vitamin sources Riboflavin (E101), Riboflavin-5′-phosphate and beta-Carotene (E160(a)) is permitted), tea (leaf or essence), coffee, coffee product, condensed milk, dried milk.

Emulsifiers and stabilisers

Regulation: Emulsifiers and Stabilisers in Food Regulations 1989 (1989/876)
Amendments: Emulsifiers and Stabilisers in Food (Amendment) Regulations 1992 (1992/165)
Food Additives Labelling Regulations 1992 (1992/1978)

Definition

Any substance which is capable:

a) in the case of an emulsifier, of aiding the formation of, and
b) in the case of a stabiliser, of maintaining the uniform dispersion of two or more immiscible substances.

It does not include any natural food substance, or any substance permitted in other additive Regulations, or caseins or caseinates, or proteins, protein concentrates and protein hydrolysates, or starches (whether modified or not), or normal straight chain fatty acids derived from food fats.

Permitted emulsifiers and stabilisers

(1)	*Name (and synonyms)*
E322	Lecithins
E400	Alginic acid
E401	Sodium alginate

4.2 (*continued*)

(1)	*Name (and synonyms)*
E402	Potassium alginate
E403	Ammonium alginate
E404	Calcium alginate
E405	Propane-1,2-diol alginate (propylene glycol alginate)
E406	Agar
E407	Carrageenan
E410	Locust bean gum (carob gum)
E412	Guar gum
E413	Tragacanth
E414	Acacia (gum arabic)
E415	Xanthan gum
416	Karaya gum (sterculia gum)
432	Polyoxyethylene (20) sorbitan monolaurate (polysorbate 20)
433	Polyoxyethylene (20) sorbitan mono-oleate (polysorbate 80)
434	Polyoxyethylene (20) sorbitan monopalmitate (polysorbate 40)
435	Polyoxyethylene (20) sorbitan monostearate (polysorbate 60)
436	Polyoxyethylene (20) sorbitan tristearate (polysorbate 65)
E440	Pectin
E440	Amidated pectin
442	Ammonium phosphatides
E460	Microcrystalline cellulose
E461	Methylcellulose
E463	Hydroxypropylcellulose
E464	Hydroxypropylmethylcellulose
E465	Ethylmethylcellulose (methyethylcellulose)
E466	Carboxymethylcellulose (sodium carboxymethycellulose)
E470	Sodium, potassium and calcium salts of fatty acids (2)
E471	Mono- and di-glycerides of fatty acids
E472(a)	Acetic acid esters of mono- and di-glycerides of fatty acids (acetylated mono- and di-glycerides)
E472(b)	Lactic acid esters of mono- and di-glycerides of fatty acids (lactylated mono- and di-glycerides; lactoglycerides)
E472(c)	Citric acid esters of mono- and di-glycerides of fatty acids (citroglycerides)
E472(d)	Tartaric acid esters of mono- and di-glycerides of fatty acids
E472(e)	Mono- and diacetyltartaric acid esters of mono- and di-glycerides of fatty acids (mono- and diacetyltartaric acid esters of mono- and di-glycerides)
E472(f)	Mixed acetic and tartaric acid esters of mono- and di-glycerides of fatty acids
E473	Sucrose esters of fatty acids
E474	Sucroglycerides
E475	Polyglycerol esters of fatty acids
476	Polyglycerol esters of polycondensed fatty acids of castor oil (polyglycerol polyricinoleate)
E477	Propane-1,2-diol esters of fatty acids (propylene glycol esters of fatty acids)
E481	Sodium stearoyl -2-lactylate
E482	Calcium stearoyl -2-lactylate
E483	Stearyl tartrate

(continued)

(1)	*Name (and synonyms)*
491	Sorbitan monostearate
492	Sorbitan tristearate
493	Sorbitan monolaurate
494	Sorbitan mono-oleate
495	Sorbitan monopalmitate
–	Extract of Quillaia (2)
–	Polyglycerol esters of dimerised fatty acids of soya bean oil (2)
–	Oxidatively polymerised soya bean oil (2)
–	Pectin extract

Notes:
(1) Serial number permitted for use on labels
(2) Only permitted in certain foods (see below)

Emulsifiers and stabilisers permitted only in certain foods (or foods using certain foods as ingredients):

Emulsifier/stabiliser	*Food or ingredient*	*Maximum quantity in food* (mg/kg)
Extract of Quillaia	Soft drinks	200 (1)
Sodium, potassium and calcium salts of fatty acids:		
(a) all such salts	Dutch type rusks	15 000 (2,3)
	E471, E472(b), E473, E474, E475, E477	60 000 (2)
(b) sodium octanoate	Malted barley	(4)
Oxidatively polymerised soya bean oil and polyglycerol esters of dimerised fatty acids of soya bean oil	Tin greasing emulsions	(4)

Notes:
(1) Of the dry matter content of the extract
(2) Calculated as sodium oleate
(3) On the weight of the flour
(4) In accordance with good manufacturing practice

Foods in which the use of emulsifiers and stabilisers is limited:

Bread (see details under Bread).

Soft cheese, whey cheese, processed cheese and cheese spread (see details under Cheese).

Cocoa products and chocolate products (see details under Cocoa and Chocolate).

General points

1) No food may contain more than 150,000 milligrams of guar gum (E412) and/or locust bean gum (E410) per kilogram.

4.2

2) If a tin-greasing emulsion has been used, a food may contain:
   oxidatively polymerised soya bean oil
   max 50 mg/kg
   polyglycerol esters of dimerised fatty acids of soya bean oil
   max 20 mg/kg.
3) If a tin-greasing emulsion has been used in the preparation of bread, it may contain a max 50 mg/kg of any permitted emulsifier or stabiliser (not mentioned in 2)) by reason of its use.
4) No flour may contain any emulsifier or stabiliser.

Flavourings

Regulation: Flavourings in Food Regulations 1992 (1992/1971)

Definitions

Flavouring as a noun, material used or intended for use in or on food to impart odour, taste or both (and as an adjective, flavouring shall be construed accordingly)

Relevant flavouring flavouring which does not consist entirely of excepted material and the components of which include at least one of he following:

i) a flavouring substance,
ii) a flavouring preparation,
iii) a process flavouring,
iv) a smoke flavouring.

Flavouring substance a chemical substance with flavouring properties the chemical structure of which has been established by methods normally used among scientists and which is:

i) obtained by physical (including distillation and solvent extraction), enzymatic or microbiological processes from appropriate material of vegetable or animal origin (termed 'natural flavouring substances' for labelling for business sales);
ii) either obtained by chemical synthesis or isolated by chemical processes and which is chemically identical to a substance naturally present in appropriate material of vegetable or animal origin (termed 'flavouring substances identical to natural substances' for labelling for business sales); or
iii) obtained by chemical synthesis but not included under (ii) (termed 'artificial flavouring substances' for labelling for business sales).

Flavouring preparation a product (other than a flavouring substance), whether concentrated or not, with flavouring properties which is obtained by physical processes (including distillation and solvent extraction) or by enzymatic or microbiological processes from appropriate material of vegetable or animal origin.

Process flavouring a product which is obtained according to good manufacturing practices by heating to a temperature not exceeding 180°C for a continuous period not exceeding 15 minutes a mixture of ingredients (whether or not with flavouring properties) of which at least one contains nitrogen (amino) and another is a reducing sugar.

Smoke flavouring means an extract from smoke of a type normally used in food smoking processes.

Permitted flavouring relevant flavouring which:

i) has in it or on it no specified substance which has been added as such;
ii) contains no element or substance in a toxicologically dangerous quantity, and
iii) contains less that the following: 3 mg/kg arsenic, 10 mg/kg lead, 1 mg/kg cadmium, and 1 mg/kg mercury.

Excepted material any edible substance (including herbs and spices) or product, intended for human consumption as such, with or without reconstitution, and, any substance which has exclusively a sweet, sour or salt taste.

Specified substance those substances given in the table below.

Appropriate material of vegetable or animal origin material of vegetable or animal origin which is either raw or has been subjected to a process (including drying, torrefaction and fermentation) normally used in preparing food for human consumption and to no process other than one normally so used.

Specified substances

The following substances are specified and

a) must not be added to permitted flavourings (see definition above);
b) no food sold which has in it or on it any relevant flavouring shall contain any specified substance other than a specified substance which is present in the food naturally or as a result of the inclusion of the relevant flavouring where that relevant flavouring is prepared from natural raw materials;
c) no food sold which has in it or on it any relevant flavouring shall contain a proportion greater than that specified in the table except where the proportion of the specified substance in the food is not greater than it would have been had the food not had the relevant flavouring in it or on it.

Specified substance	*Standard permitted proportion*	*Permitted proportion in the case of particular descriptions of food*
Agaric acid	20 mg/kg	(a) Alcoholic drinks: 100 mg/kg (b) Food (other than drinks) containing mushrooms: 100 mg/kg
Aloin	0.1 mg/kg	Alcoholic drinks: 50 mg/kg

4.2

(continued)

Specified substance	*Standard permitted proportion*	*Permitted proportion in the case of particular descriptions of food*
Beta asarone	0.1 mg/kg	(a) Alcoholic drinks: 1 mg/kg (b) Seasonings used in snack foods: 1 mg/kg
Berberine	0.1 mg/kg	Alcoholic drinks: 10 mg/kg
Coumarin	2 mg/kg	(a) Chewing gum: 50 mg/kg (b) Alcoholic drinks: 10 mg/kg (c) Caramel confectionery: 10 mg/kg
Hydrocyanic acid	1 mg/kg	(a) Nougat, marzipan, a nougat or marzipan substitute or a similar product: 50 mg/kg (b) Tinned stone fruit: 5 mg/kg (c) Alcoholic drinks: 1 mg/kg for each percentage of alcohol by volume therein
Hypericine	0.1 mg/kg	(a) Alcoholic drinks: 10 mg/kg (b) Confectionery: 1 mg/kg
Pulegone	25 mg/kg	(a) Mint confectionery: 350 mg/kg (b) Mint or peppermint flavoured drinks: 250 mg/kg (c) Other drinks: 100 mg/kg
Quassine	5 mg/kg	(a) Alcoholic drinks: 50 mg/kg (b) Confectionery in pastille form: 10 mg/kg
Safrole, isosafrole or any combination of safrole and isosafrole	1 mg/kg	(a) Food containing mace, nutmeg or both: 15 mg/kg (b) Alcoholic drinks containing more than 25% of alcohol by volume: 5 mg/kg (c) Other alcoholic drinks: 2 mg/kg
Santonin	0.1 mg/kg	Alcoholic drinks containing more than 25% of alcohol by volume: 1 mg/kg
Thuyone (alpha), thuyone (beta) or any combination of thuyone (alpha) and thuyone (beta)	0.5 mg/kg	(a) Bitters: 35 mg/kg (b) Food (other than drinks) containing preparations based on sage: 25 mg/kg (c) Alcoholic drinks containing more than 25% of alcohol by volume: 10 mg/kg (d) Other alcoholic drinks: 5 mg/kg

General points

1) Any relevant flavourings added to food must be permitted flavourings.
2) Any relevant flavouring added to food must not increase the proportion of 3,4-benzopyrene by more than 0.03 μg per kilogram of food above that which would otherwise occur in the food.
3) The Regulations contain detailed labelling provision (see Regulations). These are more demanding for business sales which include a requirement to specify, in weight descending order, the components of

relevant flavourings using the following classification (see definitions above): 'natural flavouring substances', 'flavouring substances identical to natural substances', 'artificial flavouring substances', 'flavouring preparations', 'process flavourings' and 'smoke flavourings' and for each other substance, its name or 'E' number.

4) Relevant flavouring may not be described as 'natural' in any business sale unless it is either in compliance with 3), or that relevant flavouring is a permitted flavouring the flavouring components of which are exclusively comprised of
   a) flavouring substances which come within the category of 'natural flavouring substances',
   b) flavouring preparations, or
   c) both.
5) In a business sale of relevant flavouring, the word 'natural' may not be used to qualify any substance used in its preparation unless that relevant flavouring is a permitted flavouring the flavouring component of which has been isolated solely, or almost solely, from that substance by physical processes, enzymatic or microbiological processes or processes normally used in preparing food for human consumption.

Mineral hydrocarbons

Regulation: Mineral Hydrocarbons in Food Regulations 1966 (1966/1073)

Definition

Any hydrocarbon product, whether liquid, semi-liquid or solid, derived from any substance of mineral origin and includes liquid paraffin, white oil, petroleum jelly, hard paraffin and micro-crystalline wax.

Permitted mineral hydrocarbons

(1)	*Name*
905	Mineral hydrocarbons (liquid, semi-liquid or solid)
907	Micro-crystalline wax

Note: (1) Serial number permitted for use on labels

Food permitted to contain mineral hydrocarbons (meeting specifications given in the Regulations):

1) Dried fruit (i.e. prunes, currants, sultanas and raisins)   max use 0.5%
2) Citrus fruit   max use 0.1%
3) Sugar confectionery, by reason of its use as a polishing or glazing agent   max use 0.2%

4.2

4) Chewing compound max use 60% solid mineral hydrocarbon (with a separate special specification)
5) Rind of whole pressed cheese no limit
6) Eggs, provided that any hydrocarbon is present for preservation purposes (by dipping or spraying) and the eggs are marked 'SEALED' no limit
7) Foods containing any of the foods specified in 1), 2) or 3) which themselves contain mineral hydrocarbons up to the limit specified, may contain mineral hydrocarbons as a result.
8) Foods which, during their preparation, are in contact with a surface on which a mineral hydrocarbon has been used as a lubricant or greasing agent max 0.2%

No other food may use any mineral hydrocarbon in its preparation.

Miscellaneous additives

Regulation: Miscellaneous Additives in Food Regulations 1980 (1980/1834)
Amendments: Food Labelling Regulations 1980 (1980/1849)
Miscellaneous Additives in Food (Amendment) Regulations 1982 (1982/14)
Sweeteners in Food Regulations 1983 (1983/1211)
Bread and Flour Regulations 1984 (1984/1304)
Potassium Bromate (Prohibition as a Flour Improver) Regulations 1990 (1990/399)
Food Additives Labelling Regulations 1992 (1992/1978)

Definition

Any acid, anti-caking agent, anti-foaming agent, base, buffer, bulking aid, firming agent, flavour modifier, flour bleaching agent, flour improver, glazing agent, humectant, liquid freezant, packaging gas, propellant, release agent or sequestrant (all having separate definitions in the Regulations). It does not include any substance permitted in other additive Regulations, or starches (modified or not), or caseinates, or proteins, protein concentrates and protein hydrolysates, or sodium chloride, or normal straight chain fatty acids derived from food fats, or any natural food substance.

Permitted miscellaneous additives

(1)	*Name (and synonyms)*
E260	Acetic acid
262	Sodium acetate, anhydrous
262	Sodium acetate
E262	Sodium hydrogen diacetate (sodium diacetate)
E261	Potassium acetate
E263	Calcium acetate
355	Adipic acid
–	2-Aminoethanol (2) (monoethanolamine)
927	Azodicarbonamide (2)

(*continued*)

Permitted miscellaneous additives

(1)	*Name (and synonyms)*
901	Beeswax, white
901	Beeswax, yellow
–	Benzoyl peroxide (2)
–	Calcium phytate (calcium *meso*inositolhexaphosphate)
E290	Carbon dioxide
503	Ammonium carbonate
503	Ammonium hydrogen carbonate (ammonium bicarbonate)
500	Sodium carbonate
500	Sodium hydrogen carbonate (ammonium bicarbonate)
500	Sodium sesquicarbonate
504	Magnesium carbonate, heavy
504	Magnesium carbonate, light
501	Potassium carbonate
501	Potassium hydrogen carbonate (potassium bicarbonate)
E170	Calcium carbonate
903	Carnauba wax (2)
E460(ii)	alpha-cellulose (powdered cellulose)
925	Chlorine (2)
926	Chlorine dioxide (2)
E330	Citric acid
380	*tri*Ammonium citrate (ammonium citrate)
E331	Sodium dihydrogen citrate
E331	*tri*Sodium citrate, *di*Sodium citrate
E332	Potassium dihydrogen citrate
E332	*tri*Potassium citrate
E333	Calcium citrate (*mono-*,*di-*,*tri-*)
381	Ammonium ferric citrate (ferric ammonium citrate)
381	Ammonium ferric citrate, green (green ferric ammonium citrate)
920	L-Cysteine hydrochloride (2)
–	Dichlorodifluoromethane (2)
900	Dimethylpolysiloxane (dimethyl silicone)
–	*di*Sodium dihydrogen ethylenediamine-NNN′N′-tetra-acetate (2) (disodium edetate)
385	Calcium disodium ethylenediamine-NNN′N′-tetra-acetate (2) (sodium calciumedetate)
535	Sodium ferrocyanide (sodium hexacyanoferrate (II))
536	Potassium ferrocyanide (potassium hexacyanoferrate (II))
297	Fumaric acid
575	D-Glucono-1,5-lactone (glucono delta-lactone)
576	Sodium gluconate
577	Potassium gluconate
578	Calcium gluconate
620	L-Glutamic acid (2)
621	Sodium hydrogen L-glutamate (*mono*Sodium glutamate, sodium glutamate, glutamic acid sodium salt)
622	Potassium hydrogen L-glutamate (2)
623	Calcium dihydrogen di-L-glutamate (2)
–	Glycine
370	1,4-Heptonolactone (heptonolactone)
–	Sodium heptonate
–	Calcium heptonate

4.2 *(continued)*

Permitted miscellaneous additives

(1)	*Name (and synonyms)*
507	Hydrochloric acid
510	Ammonium chloride
508	Potassium chloride
509	Calcium chloride, anhydrous
509	Calcium chloride
–	Hydrogen
527	Ammonium hydroxide
524	Sodium hydroxide
528	Magnesium hydroxide
530	Magnesium oxide, heavy
530	Magnesium oxide, light
525	Potassium hydroxide
526	Calcium hydroxide
529	Calcium oxide
E270	Lactic acid
E325	Sodium lactate
E326	Potassium lactate
E327	Calcium lactate
296	DL-Malic acid
296	L-Malic acid
350	Sodium hydrogen malate
350	Sodium malate
351	Potassium malate
352	Calcium malate
352	Calcium hydrogen malate
353	Metatartaric acid (2)
375	Nicotinic acid
–	Nitrogen
–	Nitrous oxide
–	Octadecylammonium acetate (2) (octadecylamine acetate)
–	Oxygen
–	Oxystearin
E338	Orthophosphoric acid
–	Ammonium dihydrogen orthophosphate (ammonium phosphate, monobasic)
–	*di*Ammonium hydrogen orthophosphate (ammonium phosphate, dibasic)
E339	Sodium dihydrogen orthophosphate
E339	*di*Sodium hydrogen orthophosphate
E339	*tri*Sodium orthophosphate
E340(a)	Potassium dihydrogen orthophosphate
E340(b)	*di*Potassium hydrogen orthophosphate
E340(c)	*tri*Potassium orthophosphate
E341(a)	Calcium tetrahydrogen diorthophosphate
E341(b)	Calcium hydrogen orthophosphate
E341(c)	*tri*Calcium diorthophosphate
541	Sodium aluminium phosphate, acidic
541	Sodium aluminium phosphate, basic
E450(a)	*di*Sodium dihydrogen diphosphate
E450(a)	*tri*Sodium diphosphate
E450(a)	*tetra*Sodium diphosphate
E450(a)	*tetra*Potassium diphosphate

(*continued*)

Permitted miscellaneous additives

(1)	*Name (and synonyms)*
540	*di*Calcium diphosphate (dicalcium pyrophosphate, calcium pyrophosphate)
E450(b)	*penta*Sodium triphosphate
E450(b)	*penta*Potassium triphosphate
E450(c)	Sodium polyphosphates
E450(c)	Potassium polyphosphates
544	Calcium polyphosphates
545	Ammonium polyphosphates
542	Edible bone phosphate
627	Guanosine 5′-(disodium phosphate) (sodium 5′-guanylate)
631	Inosine 5′-(disodium phosphate) (sodium 5′-inosinate)
–	Polydextrose
635	Sodium 5′-ribonucleotide
636	Maltol (3)
637	Ethyl maltol (3)
904	Shellac
551	Silicon dioxide (silica, chemically prepared)
558	Bentonite
559	Kaolin, heavy
559	Kaolin, light
554	Aluminium sodium silicate (sodium aluminium silicate, sodium aluminosilicate, sodium silicoaluminate)
556	Aluminium calcium silicate (calcium aluminium silicate, calcium aluminosilicate, calcium silicoaluminate)
552	Calcium silicate
553a	Magnesium silicate, synthetic
553a	Magnesium trisilicate
553b	Talc
–	Spermaceti
–	Sperm oil
572	Magnesium stearate
–	Calcium stearate
–	Butyl stearate
363	Succinic acid
513	Sulphuric acid
–	Ammonium sulphate
514	Sodium sulphate
518	Magnesium sulphate
515	Potassium sulphate
–	Aluminium potassium sulphate (2) (potassium aluminium sulphate, potash alum)
516	Calcium sulphate
–	Tannic acid (tannin)
E334	L-(+)-Tartaric acid
–	DL-Tartaric acid
E335	*mono*Sodium L-(+)-tartrate
–	*mono*Sodium DL-tartrate
E335	*di*Sodium L-(+)-tartrate
–	*di*Sodium DL-tartrate
E336	*mono*Potassium L-(+)-tartrate

4.2 *(continued)*

Permitted miscellaneous additives

(1)	*Name (and synonyms)*
–	*mono*Potassium DL-tartrate
E336	*di*Potassium L-(+)-tartrate
–	*di*Potassium DL-tartrate
E337	Potassium sodium L-(+)-tartrate
–	Potassium sodium DL-tartrate

Notes:
(1) Serial number permitted for use on labels
(2) Only permitted in certain foods (see below)
(3) These additives are not legally 'Miscellaneous additives' being usually used as flavours. They are however sometimes used as flavour enhancers and are therefore included here with the other flavour enhancers

Miscellaneous additives permitted only in certain foods (or foods using certain foods as ingredients):

Food or ingredient	*Additive*	*Maximum quantity in food* (mg/kg)
Ammonium chloride	Octadecylammonium acetate	500
Brandy	*di*Sodium dihydrogen ethylenediamine NNN'N' -tetra-acetate	25 (1)
Bread	Azodicarbonamide, benzoyl peroxide, chlorine dioxide, L-cysteine hydrochloride	(2)
Canned fish	(3)	(4)
Canned shellfish	(3)	(4)
Chocolate confectionery	Carnauba wax	200
Chocolate products	Carnauba wax	200
Dietetic foods	L-glutamic acid, potassium hydrogen L-glutamate or calcium dihydrogen di-L-glutamate (5)	
Flour	Azodicarbonamide, benzoyl peroxide, chlorine, chlorine dioxide, L-cysteine hydrochloride	(2)
Frozen food	Dichlorodifluoromethane	100 (6)
Glacé cherries	(3)	(4)
	Aluminium potassium sulphate	10 000 (7)
Peeled fruit	2-Aminoethanol	100
Peeled vegetables	2-Aminoethanol	100
Sugar confectionery	Carnauba wax	200
Wine	Metatartaric acid	100 (1)

Notes:
(1) Milligrams/litre
(2) See details under Bread
(3) Calcium disodium ethylenediamine NNN'N'-tetra-acetate
(4) In accordance with good manufacturing practice
(5) These additives are not 'permitted miscellaneous additives' but dietetic foods may contain these additional additives
(6) Determined when the food is fully thawed at and to 20°C
(7) On a dry matter basis

General point

Food specially prepared for babies and young children may not contain:

2-aminoethanol
alpha-cellulose
sodium hydrogen L-glutamate
guanosine 5′-(disodium phosphate)
inosine 5′-(disodium phosphate)
polydextrose
sodium 5′-ribonucleotide.

Preservatives

Regulation: Preservatives in Food Regulations 1989 (1989/533)
Amendments: Preservatives in Food (Amendment) Regulations 1989 (1989/2287)
Food Additives Labelling Regulations 1992 (1992/1978)

Definition

Any substance which is capable of inhibiting, retarding or arresting the growth of micro-organisms or any deterioration of food due to micro-organisms or of masking the evidence of any such deterioration. It does not include any substance permitted in other additive Regulations, or vinegar, or any soluble carbohydrate sweetening matter, or potable spirits or wines, or herbs, spices, hop extract or flavouring agents when used for flavouring purposes, or common salt, or any substance added to food during curing by smoking (i.e. treating with smoke or smoke solutions derived from wood or ligneous vegetable matter in the natural state, and excludes smoke or smoke solutions derived from wood or ligneous vegetable matter which has been impregnated, coloured, gummed, painted or otherwise treated in a similar manner).

Permitted preservatives

		Alternative form in which the permitted preservative may be used	
(1)	*Name (and synonym)*	*(1)*	*Name (and synonym)*
E200	Sorbic acid	E201	Sodium sorbate
		E202	Potassium sorbate
		E203	Calcium sorbate
E210	Benzoic acid	E211	Sodium benzoate
		E212	Potassium benzoate
		E213	Calcium benzoate
E214	Ethyl 4-hydroxybenzoate (ethyl *para*-hydroxybenzoate)	E215	Ethyl 4-hydroxybenzoate, sodium salt (sodium ethyl *para*-hydroxybenzoate)
E216	Propyl 4-hydroxybenzoate (propyl *para*-hydroxybenzoate)	E217	Propyl 4-hydroxybenzoate, sodium salt (sodium propyl *para*-hydroxybenzoate)

4.2 (*continued*)

		Alternative form in which the permitted preservative may be used	
E218	Methyl 4-hydroxybenzoate (methyl *para*-hydroxybenzoate)	E219	Methyl 4-hydroxybenzoate, sodium salt (sodium methyl *para*-hydroxybenzoate)
E220	Sulphur dioxide	E221	Sodium sulphite
		E222	Sodium hydrogen sulphite (acid sodium sulphite)
		E223	Sodium metabisulphite
		E224	Potassium metabisulphite
		E226	Calcium sulphite
		E227	Calcium hydrogen sulphite (calcium bisulphite)
E228	Potassium bisulphite		
E230	Biphenyl		
E231	2-Hydroxybiphenyl (orthophenylphenol)	E232	Sodium biphenyl-2-yl oxide (sodium orthophenylphenate)
E233	2-(Thiazol-4-yl) benzimidazole (thiabendazole)		
E239	Hexamine (hexamethylenetetramine)		
E250	Sodium nitrite	E249	Potassium nitrite
E251	Sodium nitrate	E252	Potassium nitrate
E280	Propionic acid	E281	Sodium propionate
		E282	Calcium propionate
		E283	Potassium propionate
234	Nisin		

Note: (1) Serial number permitted for use on labels

Foods in which the use of preservatives is permitted:

(Note: The Regulations contain numerous definitions which provide a detailed interpretation of some of the foods specified below. These may be checked to confirm whether a particular food is included in a category.)

Specified food	*Permitted preservative*	*Except where otherwise stated: max level* (mg/kg)
Beer (1)	E220 and	70
	E210 or	70
	E218 or	70
	E214 or	70
	E216	70

(*continued*)

Specified food	*Permitted preservative*	*Except where otherwise stated: max level* (mg/kg)
Beetroot, cooked and pre-packed	E210 or E218 or E214 or E216	250 250 250 250
Bread	E280	As prescribed in the Bread Regulations
Cauliflower, canned	E220	100
Cheese	E200	1000
Cheese, other than Cheddar, Cheshire, Granapadano or Provolone type of cheeses or soft cheese	E251 and E250	50 (only 5 may be E250) (2)
Provolone cheese	E239	25 (expressed as formaldehyde)
Chicory and coffee essence	E210 or E218 or E214 or E216	450 450 450 450
Christmas pudding	E280	1000
Cider	E220 or E200	200 200
Coconut, desiccated	E220	50
Colouring matter, except E150 Caramel, if in the form of a solution of a permitted colouring matter	E210 or E218 or E214 or E216 or E200	2000 2000 2000 2000 1000
Colouring matter E150 Caramel	E220	1000
Crabmeat, canned	E220	30
Desserts, fruit based milk and cream	E220 or E200	100 300
Desert sauces, fruit based with a total soluble solids content of less than 75%	E220 or E210 or E218 or E214 or E216 or E200	100 250 250 250 250 1000

4.2 (*continued*)

Specified food	*Permitted preservative*	*Except where otherwise stated: max level* (mg/kg)
The permitted miscellaneous additive, Dimethylpolysiloxane	E220 or	1000
	E210 or	2000
	E218 or	2000
	E214 or	2000
	E216 or	2000
	E200	1000
Enzymes:		
Papain, solid	E220	30 000
Papain, aqueous solutions	E220 or	5000
	E200	1000
Aqueous solutions of enzyme preparations not otherwise specified including immobilized enzyme preparations in aqueous media	E220 or	500
	E210 or	3000
	E218 or	3000
	E214 or	3000
	E216 or	3000
	E200	3000
Fat spreads consisting of an emulsion principally of water in oil with a fat content not exceeding 70%	E200	2000
Figs, dried	E220 or	2000
	E200	500
Fillings and toppings for flour confectionery which consist principally of a sweetened oil and water emulsion with a min sugar solids content of 50%	E200	1000
Finings when sold by retail:		
Wine finings	E220	12 500
Beer finings	E220	50 000
Flavourings	E220 or	350
	E210 or	800
	E218 or	800
	E214 or	800
	E216	800
Flavourings syrups	E220 or	350
	E210 or	800
	E218 or	800
	E214 or	800
	E216	800
Flour confectionery	E280 or	1000
	E200	1000
Foam headings, liquid	E220 or	5000
	E210 or	10 000
	E218 or	10 000
	E214 or	10 000
	E216	10 000

(*continued*)

Specified food	*Permitted preservative*	*Except where otherwise stated: max level* (mg/kg)
Freeze drinks	E220 or	70
	E210 or	160
	E218 or	160
	E214 or	160
	E216 or	160
	E200	300
Fruit based pie fillings	E220 or	350
	E210 or	800
	E218 or	800
	E214 or	800
	E216 or	800
	E200	450
Fruit, dried, other than prunes or figs	E220	2000
Fruit, fresh:		
Bananas	E233	3
Citrus fruit	E230 or	70 (3)
	E231 or	12 (3)
	E233	10
Grapes	E220	15
Fruit, fruit pulp, or fruit purée (including tomatoes, tomato pulp, tomato paste and purée) which in each case is not fresh or canned	E220 or	350
	E210 or	800
	E218 or	800
	E214 or	800
	E216	800
Fruit juices:		
Fruit juice, concentrated fruit juice, fruit nectar or dried fruit juice for sale for consumption (after dilution or reconstitution as required) and fruit juice or concentrated fruit juice for use in the preparation of these products	E220	As prescribed in the Fruit Juice Regulations
Any other fruit juice or concentrated fruit juice	E220 or	350
	E210 or	800
	E218 or	800
	E214 or	800
	E216	800
Fruit or plants (including flowers and seeds), crystallized, glacé or drained (syruped), or candied peel or cut and drained (syruped) peel (1)	E220 and	100
	E210 or	1000
	E218 or	1000
	E214 or	1000
	E216 or	1000
	E200	1000

4.2

(continued)

Specified food	*Permitted preservative*	*Except where otherwise stated: max level* (mg/kg)
Fruit pieces in stabilised syrup for use as ingredients of ice-cream or other edible ices	E200	1000
Fruit spread	E220 and E200	100 1000
Garlic, powdered	E220	2000
Gelatin	E220	1000
Gelatin capsules	E200	3000
Ginger, dry root	E220	150
Glucose drinks containing not less than 235 g of glucose syrup per litre of drink	E220 or E210 or E218 or E214 or E216	350 800 800 800 800
Grape juice products (unfermented intended for sacramental use) (1)	E220 and E210 or E218 or E214 or E216	70 2000 2000 2000 2000
Grape juice, concentrated, intended for home wine making and labelled as such	E220	2000
Hamburgers or similar products	E220	450
Herring, marinated whose pH does not exceed 4.5	E210 or E218 or E214 or E216	1000 1000 1000 1000
Herring, marinated whose pH exceeds 4.5 (1)	E239 and E210 or E218 or E214 or E216	50 1000 1000 1000 1000
Hops, dried, sold by retail	E220	2000
Horseradish, fresh grated, and horseradish sauce	E220 or E210 or E218 or E214 or E216	200 250 250 250 250
Jam and similar products:		
Reduced sugar jam, reduced sugar jelly, and reduced sugar marmalade (1)	E220 and E210 or E218 or E214 or E216 or E200	As prescribed in the Jam Regulations

(*continued*)

Specified food	*Permitted preservative*	*Except where otherwise stated: max level* (mg/kg)
Extra jam, jam, extra jelly, jelly, marmalade, chestnut purée, UK standard jelly, X curd, Y flavour curd, and mincemeat	E220	As prescribed in the Jam Regulations
Mackerel, marinated whose pH does not exceed 4.5	E210 or E218 or E214 or E216	1000 1000 1000 1000
Mackerel, marinated whose pH exceeds 4.5 (1)	E239 and E210 or E218 or E214 or E216	50 1000 1000 1000 1000
Mallow, chocolate covered	E200	1000 (calculated on the weight of the mallow and chocolate together)
Meat, cured (including cured meat products):		
Cured meat (including cured meat products) packed in a sterile pack whether or not it has been removed from the pack	E251 and E250	150 (of which not more than 50 may be E250) (2)
Acidified and/or fermented cured meat products (including salami and similar products) not packed in a sterile pack	E251 and E250	400 (of which not more than 50 may be E250) (2)
Uncooked bacon and ham; cooked bacon and ham that is not and has not been packed in any hermetically sealed container	E251 and E250	500 (of which not more than 200 may be E250) (2)
Any cured meat or meat product not specified above	E251 and E250	250 (of which not more than 150 may be E250) (2)
Mushrooms, frozen	E220	50
Nut pastes, sweetened	E200	1000

4.2 (*continued*)

Specified food	*Permitted preservative*	*Except where otherwise stated: max level* (mg/kg)
Olives, pickled	E220 or	100
	E210 or	250
	E218 or	250
	E214 or	250
	E216 or	250
	E200	500
Peas, garden, canned containing no added colouring matter	E220	100
Pectin, liquid	E220	250
Perry	E220 or	200
	E200	200
Pickles (other than pickled olives)	E220 or	100
	E210 or	250
	E218 or	250
	E214 or	250
	E216 or	250
	E200	1000
Potatoes raw, peeled	E220	50
Prawns, shrimps, scampi other than prawns and shrimps in brine	E220	200 (in edible part)
Prawns and shrimps in brine (1)	E220 and	200 (in edible part)
	E200 or	2000
	E210 and	2000
	E214 or	300
	E216 or	300
	E218	300
Preparations of saccharin, sodium saccharin or calcium saccharin and water only (1)	E210 and	750
	E218 or	250
	E214 or	250
	E216	250
Prunes	E220 or	2000
	E200	1000
Salad cream (including mayonnaise) and salad dressing	E220 or	100
	E210 or	250
	E218 or	250
	E214 or	250
	E216 or	250
	E200	1000
Sambel oelek	E210 and	850
	E200	1000

(*continued*)

Specified food	*Permitted preservative*	*Except where otherwise stated: max level* (mg/kg)
Sauces, other than horseradish sauce	E220 or E210 or E218 or E214 or E216 or E200	100 250 250 250 250 1000
Sausages or sausage meat	E220	450
Snack meals, concentrated (moisture 15–60%)	E200 and E218	1500 175
Soft drinks for consumption after dilution not otherwise specified in this table	E220 or E210 or E218 or E214 or E216 or E200	350 800 800 800 800 1500
Soft drinks for consumption without dilution not otherwise specified in this table	E220 or E210 or E218 or E214 or E216 or E200	70 160 160 160 160 300
Soup concentrates (moisture 25–60%)	E200 and E218	1500 175
Starches, including modified starches	E220	100
Sugars:		
Specified sugar products	E220	As prescribed by the Sugar Regulations
Hydrolysed starches (other than specified sugar products)	E220	400
Other sugars except lactose	E220	70
Tea extract, liquid	E210 or E218 or E214 or E216	450 450 450 450
Vegetables, dehydrated:		
Brussels sprouts	E220	2500
Cabbage	E220	2500
Potato	E220	550
Others	E220	2000

4.2 (*continued*)

Specified food	*Permitted preservative*	*Except where otherwise stated: max level* (mg/kg)
Vinegar:		
Cider or wine vinegar	E220	200
Other	E220	70
Wine (including alcoholic cordials) other than Community controlled wine	E220 and E200	450 (mg/l) 200 (mg/l)
Yogurt, fruit	E220 or E210 or E218 or E214 or E216 or E200	60 120 120 120 120 300

Notes:
(1) See General point (2) below
(2) Expressed in both cases as sodium nitrate
(3) See Regulations for detailed sampling and analysis procedures

General points

1) Any specified food (except those subject to 2) below) in relation to which two or more preservatives are specified as alternatives, may have a mixture of the preservatives, only if, when the quantity of each such preservative present in that food is expressed as a % of the maximum permitted, the sum of the percentages does not exceed 100.
2) Those products indicated by note 1) in the table may have the first permitted preservative in the quantity stated and a mixture of the other preservatives, provided that the mixture conforms to 1) above. In the case of prawns and shrimps in brine two mixtures are involved (E200/E210 and E214/E216/E218) and the rule applies to both mixtures.
3) An ingredient of a specified food may contain a permitted preservative but must conform to special labelling (including 'not for retail sale').
4) Food may contain up to 5 mg/kg formaldehyde derived from any wet strength wrapping containing any resin based on formaldehyde or from any plastic food container or utensil manufactured from any resin of which formaldehyde is a condensing component.
5) The miscellaneous additive dimethylpolysiloxane may contain formaldehyde up to 1000 mg/kg. Products containing the additive may contain formaldehyde in proportion to the additive's use.
6) Cheese, clotted cream and canned food (or food manufactured using these) may contain nisin.

7) Compounded foods containing, as ingredients, foods listed above (except unfermented grape juice product intended for sacramental use), may contain preservative in proportion to ingredient's use or a maximum as follows (whichever is the greater):
for E220 50 mg/kg
for E210, E218, E214, E216 120 mg/kg
For ice-cream or edible ice with fruit pieces in stabilised syrup, for E200 the maximum is 300 mg/kg.
For compounded foods (except cured meat products) which are specified in the table, the figures in the table apply.
8) Food specially prepared for babies or young children may not contain any added E251 (sodium nitrate) or E250 (sodium nitrite).
9) Flour may contain E220 (sulphur dioxide) or E223 (sodium metabisulphite) as prescribed by the Bread and Flour Regulations.
10) Community controlled wine may contain the preservatives E220, E228, E224, E200, E202 or any other preservative authorized by any Community Regulation.
11) The presence of other preservatives (or of permitted preservatives at above the specified level) is allowed if it can be shown that it was as a result of their use as:
an acaricide, fungicide, insecticide or rodenticide for the protection of food whilst in storage;
a sprout inhibitor or depressant otherwise than in a place where food is stored.
12) No other foods may contain preservative.

Solvents

Regulation: Solvents in Food Regulations 1967 (1967/1582)
Amendments: Solvents in Food (Amendment) Regulations 1967 (1967/1939)
Solvents in Food (Amendment) Regulations 1980 (1980/1832)
Sweeteners in Food Regulations 1983 (1983/1211)
Bread and Flour Regulations 1984 (1984/1304)

Definition
Any liquid substance, not being a natural food substance and the primary use of which is not as a flavouring, which is capable of the extraction and dissolution of food, and is generally used to facilitate the incorporation of ingredients in food, but does not include water or any substance permitted under other additive Regulations.

4.2

Permitted solvents	
(1)	*Name*
–	Ethyl alcohol, ethanol
–	Ethyl acetate
–	Diethyl ether, solvent ether
E422	Glycerol
–	Glycerol mono-acetate, monoacetin
–	Glycerol di-acetate, diacetin
–	Glycerol tri-acetate, triacetin
–	Iso-propyl alcohol
–	Propylene glycol

Note: (1) Serial number permitted for use on labels

General point

No person shall sell any food which contains added solvent except permitted solvents listed above.

Sweeteners

Regulation: Sweeteners in Food Regulations 1983 (1983/1211)
Amendment: Sweeteners in Food (Amendment) Regulations 1988 (1988/2112)
Food Additives Labelling Regulations 1992 (1992/1978)

Definition

Any substance, other than a carbohydrate, whose primary organoleptic characteristic is sweetness. It does not include any natural food substance, any substance permitted in other additive Regulations or any starch, whether modified or not.

Permitted sweeteners	
(1)	*Name (and synonyms)*
–	Acesulfame potassium (acesulfame K)
–	Aspartame
–	Hydrogenated glucose syrup (hydrogenated high maltose glucose syrup)
–	Isomalt
–	Lactitol (lactit, lactositol, lactobiosit)

(continued)

Permitted sweeteners

(1)	*Name (and synonyms)*
E421	Mannitol
–	Saccharin
–	Sodium saccharin
–	Calcium saccharin
E420	Sorbitol
E420	Sorbitol syrup
–	Thaumatin
–	Xylitol

Note: (1) Serial number permitted for use on labels

General points

1) No person shall sell any food containing added sweetener except permitted sweeteners listed above.
2) No food specially prepared for babies or young children may contain added sweetener, unless for special dietary requirements.

Tryptophan

Regulation: Tryptophan in Food Regulations 1990 (1990/1728)

Definition

Dextrorotatory tryptophan, laevorotatory tryptophan, or racemic tryptophan, or any salt or peptide prepared from any of these forms.

General points

1) The addition of tryptophan to food intended for sale for human consumption and the sale of food containing tryptophan (where the tryptophan has been added) are prohibited.
2) Exemptions are provided where there is an appropriate medical certificate indicating that a person requires food with added tryptophan.

4.3

4.3 Contaminants

Aflatoxin

Regulation: Aflatoxins in Nuts, Nut Products, Dried Figs and Dried Fig Products Regulations 1992 (1992/3236)

Definitions

Aflatoxins All or any of aflatoxin B_1, aflatoxin B_2, aflatoxin G_1 and aflatoxin G_2.

Total aflatoxins The sum of the concentrations of aflatoxins.

Nuts The following nuts (based on EC combined nomenclature subheadings): Brazil nuts (in shell/shelled), cashew nuts, almonds (bitter/other; in shell/shelled), hazelnuts or filberts (*Corylus spp.*)(in shell/shelled), walnuts (in shell/shelled), chestnuts (*Castanae spp.*), pistachios, pecans, areca (or betel) and cola nuts, other nuts and peanuts (not roasted or otherwise cooked (in shell/shelled)/prepared or preserved in immediate packings below 1kg/greater than 1kg))

Nut product (for import controls below) Any food at least half of which consists (by weight) of nuts or of any substance (except where exclusively edible oil) derived from nuts.

Nut product (for consumer sale controls below) Any food consisting of any quantity of nuts or of any substance (including edible oil) derived from nuts, and, edible oils derived wholly or partly from nuts.

Dried fig product (for import controls below) Any food at least half of which consists (by weight) of dried figs.

Dried fig product (for consumer sale controls below) Any food consisting of any quantity of dried figs.

Import controls

1) Importers of nuts, nut products, dried figs or dried fig products into Great Britain from outside the EC shall inform the authorities of a consignment of one of these by giving them a certificate detailing what constitutes the consignment. It must be no more than 25,000 kg and must be of one type (i.e. nuts, nut products, dried figs or dried fig products).
2) The import must be through an authorised place of entry and according to detailed procedures allowing for inspection and sampling by the authorities. Provision is made for the examination to be deferred to another place.
3) Sampling procedures specify the number of samples and the size of each sample (depends upon product - see Regulations) and require that samples are taken as randomly as possible from throughout the consignment. Preparation of subsamples is detailed. Analysis may be by any method which meets specified performance parameters.
4) The following actions are specified:

a) If total aflatoxins more than 10 micrograms/kg either return to the consignor, or use for purpose other than human consumption or destroy

b) If total aflatoxins more than 4 micrograms/kg but less than 10 micrograms/kg

as a) but, in addition, the importer may undertake to process the consignment to ensure that, when a consumer sale takes place, the level is below 4 micrograms/kg but, in this case, merely blending or mixing with a consignment with a lower level of aflatoxins is not a permitted process.

Consumer sales

1) No person may sell any nut, nut product, dried fig or dried fig product which, when analysed using a method meeting specified performance parameters, has a level of total aflatoxins more than 4 micrograms/kg.
2) If a sale under 1) is found to exceed the limit, it is a defence to show that the nuts or figs concerned came from a lot or batch which had been certified (following the specified sampling and analysis methods) as containing no more than 4 micrograms/kg nuts or dried figs. The laboratory used must be participating in a proficiency testing scheme meeting internationally recognized protocols and must have achieved certain specified results in the scheme.

General point

The Regulations only apply to any nuts, nut products, dried figs or dried fig products which are intended for sale for human consumption.

Arsenic

Regulation: Arsenic in Food Regulations 1959 (1959/831)
Amendments: Arsenic in Food (Amendment) Regulations 1960 (1960/2261)
Bread and Flour Regulations 1963 (1963/1435)
Bread and Flour (Amendment) Regulations 1972 (1972/1391)
Arsenic in Food (Amendment) Regulations 1973 (1973/1052)
Colouring Matter in Foods Regulations 1973 (1973/1340)
Emulsifiers and Stabilizers in Food Regulations 1975 (1975/1486)
Bread and Flour Regulations 1984 (1984/1304)
Flavourings in Food Regulations 1992 (1992/1971)

The permitted level for arsenic in foods is:

a) unspecified foods max 1 ppm,
b) specified foods see table under Trace metals.

General points

1) Where a specified food is used as a component of an unspecified food, in a quantity exceeding 25%, the unspecified food may exceed 1 ppm

having regard to the quantity of the specified food that is used and the maximum arsenic that is permitted in the specified food.

2) For fish, edible seaweed or products containing these, where arsenic exceeds 1 ppm naturally, arsenic may exceed 1 ppm by virtue of its fish or edible seaweed content.
3) The Regulations do not apply to hops or hop concentrates intended for use for commercial brewing, or to foods where limits are specified in other regulations.

Chloroform

Regulation: Chloroform in Food Regulations 1980 (1980/36)

Added chloroform
No-one may sell or import any food which has in it or on it any added chloroform.

Erucic acid

Regulation: Erucic Acid in Food Regulations 1977 (1977/691)
Amendment: Erucic Acid in Food (Amendment) Regulations 1982 (1982/264)

Note: Erucic acid is not strictly a contaminant being a normal constituent of some foods.

Restrictions
Oil or fat (or mixture): Erucic acid content should not exceed 5% of the fatty acid content.
Any food with added oil or fat: Erucic acid content of all the fat and oil in the food should not exceed 5% of the fatty acid content.

Exemptions
The following are exempt from the above standards:

a) any food, except food for infants or young children, containing not more than 5% oil or fat;
b) any oil, fat or food sold to a manufacturer (for manufacturing) or caterer (for catering purposes).

Hormonal Substance and Other Residues in Meat

Regulation: The Animals, Meat and Meat Products (Examination for Residues and Maximum Residue Limits) Regulations 1991 (1991/2843)

Note: These Regulations are supported by related sections of certain other Regulations.

Definitions

Animal any of the following food sources namely animals of the bovine species (including buffalo of species *Bubalus bubalus* and *Bison bison*) swine, goats, solipeds, camelids, rabbits, deer and birds reared for human consumption.

Meat the flesh or other part of an animal suitable for human consumption.

Transmissible substance any substance having a pharmacological action or any conversion product thereof or any other substance which if transmitted to meat would be likely to be dangerous to human health.

Authorised substance a transmissible substance the presence of which in any animal, meat or meat product is permitted by or in implementation of Community law.

Hormonal substance any substance within either of the following categories -

a) stilbenes and thyrostatic substances;

b) substances with oestrogenic, androgenic or gestagenic action.

Maximum residue limit in relation to a concentration of an authorised substance in the tissues or body fluids of an animal or in any meat or meat product, means

a) for the substances listed in the following table, the limits specified in the specified part of the animal, or

b) for hormonal substances, the maximum natural physiological level for that substance.

Substance	*Maximum residue limit*	*Part of the animal*
Chloramphenicol	10 μg/kg	Any edible tissues
Sulphonamides	100 μg/kg	Any edible tissues
Trimethoprim	50 μg/kg	Any edible tissues
Nitrofurans	5 μg/kg	Any edible tissues
Dapsone	25 μg/kg	Any edible tissues
Dimetridazole	10 μg/kg	Any edible tissues
Ronidazole	2 μg/kg	Any edible tissues
Febantel	1,000 μg/kg 10 μg/kg	Liver Any other edible tissues
Fenbendazole	1,000 μg/kg 10 μg/kg	Liver Any other edible tissues
Oxfendazole	1,000 μg/kg 10 μg/kg	Liver Any other edible tissues
Ivermectin	15 μg/kg 20 μg/kg	Liver Any other edible tissues

4.3 (*continued*)

Substance	*Maximum residue limit*	*Part of the animal*
Levamisole	10 μg/kg	Any edible tissues
Carazolol	30 μg/kg 5 μg/kg	Liver, kidney Any other edible tissues
Streptomycin	1,000 μg/kg	Any edible tissues
Azaperone	100 μg/kg 50 μg/kg	Kidney Any other edible tissues
Benzylpenicillin	50 μg/kg	Any edible tissues
Ampicillin	50 μg/kg	Any edible tissues
Amoxycillin	50 μg/kg	Any edible tissues
Oxacillin	300 μg/kg	Any edible tissues
Cloxacillin	300 μg/kg	Any edible tissues
Tetracycline	600 μg/kg 300 μg/kg 100 μg/kg	Kidney Liver Any other edible tissues
Oxytetracycline	600 μg/kg 300 μg/kg 100 μg/kg	Kidney Liver Any other edible tissues
Chlortetracycline	600 μg/kg 300 μg/kg 100 μg/kg	Kidney Liver Any other edible tissues
Clenbuterol	0.5 μg/kg	Any edible tissues

General points

1) It is prohibited to sell any meat (whether or not mixed with other food) or any meat product in which there is:
   a) any prohibited substance - i.e. a hormonal substance (defined above) unless administered by a veterinary surgeon or practitioner for certain specified purposes;
   b) an unlicensed substance - i.e. a substance for which there is no veterinary medicinal product licence;
   c) beta-agonist (unless it can be demonstrated that it was authorised by a veterinary surgeon); or
   d) an authorised substance (defined above) at a concentration exceeding the maximum residue limit (also defined above).
2) The Regulations contain details of inspection, analysis (including indicator residues) and other related requirements.

Lead

Regulation: Lead in Food Regulations 1979 (1979/1254)
Amendments: Lead in Food (Amendment) Regulations 1985 (1985/912)
Flavourings in Food Regulations 1992 (1992/1971)

The permitted level for lead in foods is:

a) Unspecified foods 1.0 mg/kg
b) Specified foods see table under Trace metals.

General points

1) Unspecified compound foods may contain more than 1 mg/kg if
   a) more than 10% of the food is an ingredient for which a higher level is permitted, and
   b) if the components were separate, the specified standards would be met.
2) Additive premixes (marked as not being for retail sale) may be sold above the 1 mg/kg level if the components, if sold separately, would meet the specified standards.
3) The Regulations do not apply to foods where limits are specified in other regulations.

Pesticides

Regulation: Pesticides (Maximum Residue Levels in Food) Regulations 1988 (1988/1378)

The Regulations specify certain maximum residue levels (MRLs) on certain foods (including cereals intended for human consumption).

Cereals

The following types of cereals are included: wheat, rye, barley, oats, maize, paddy rice, other cereals (not including rice).

For the above cereals, the following pesticides have the following MRLs (mg residue/kg food)

Aldrin and dieldrin 0.01
Captafol 0.05
Carbaryl 0.5 (except paddy rice 1)
Carbendazim 0.5 (only specified for wheat, rye, barley and oats)
Carbon disulphide 0.1
Carbon tetrachloride 0.1
Chlordane 0.02
Chlorpyrifosmethyl 10 (no MRL specified for paddy rice)
DDT 0.05
Diazinon 0.05
1,2-dibromoethane 0.05
Dichlorvos 2

4.3 Endosulfan 0.1 (except maize 0.2)
Endrin 0.01
Etrimfos 10 (no MRL specified for paddy rice)
Hexachlorobenzene (HCB) 0.01
Hexachlorocyclohexane (HCH) sum of α and β 0.02 γ 0.1
Heptachlor 0.01
Hydrogen cyanide 15
Hydrogen phosphate 0.1
Inorganic bromide 50
Malathion 8
Mercury compounds 0.02 (no MRL specified for paddy rice)
Methacrifos 10 (no MRL specified for paddy rice)
Methyl bromide 0.1
Phosphamidon 0.05
Pirimiphosmethyl 10 (no MRL specified for paddy rice)
Pyrethrins 3
Trichlorfon 0.1

Products of animal origin

MRLs for these are given in the following table (values are mg residue/kg food but subject to the notes in the table):

Pesticide	*Meat, fat and preparations of meat (1)*	*Milk (2)*	*Dairy produce (>2% fat) (3)*	*Eggs (4)*
Aldrin and dieldrin	0.2	0.006	0.15	0.1
Carbendazim		0.1		0.1
Chlordane	0.05	0.002	0.05	0.02
Chlorfenvinphos	0.2	0.008		
Chlorpyrifosmethyl	0.05	0.01		0.05
DDT	1	0.04	1	0.5
Diazinon	0.7	0.02		
Dichlorvos	0.05	0.05		0.05
Endrin	0.05	0.0008	0.02	0.2
Hexachlorobenzene (HCB)	0.2	0.01	0.25	1
Hexachlorocyclohexane (HCH)				
α	0.2	0.004	0.1	
β	0.1	0.003	0.075	
γ	2 (5) or 1 (6)	0.008	0.2	0.1
Heptachlor	0.2	0.004	0.1	0.05

4.3

Notes:

(1) Levels are measured on fat, except in the case of foods with a fat content of 10% or less by weight. In these cases the residue is related to the total weight of the boned foodstuffs, and the MRL is one tenth of the value given in the table, but must be no less than 0.01 mg/kg

(2) The levels are for fresh raw cow's milk and fresh whole cow's milk expressed on the whole milk

(3) For preserved, concentrated or sweetened cow's milk; for raw milk and whole cream milk of another animal origin; and for butter, cheese or curd whether made from cow's milk or other milk or a combination, the following levels apply:
- fat content $<2\%$, the MRL is 50% that for raw milk and whole cream milk;
- fat content $\geqslant 2\%$, the MRL is expressed in mg/kg of fat and is 25 times that set for raw milk and whole cream milk

(4) Birds' eggs in shell (other than eggs for hatching) and whole egg products and egg yolk products (whether fresh, dried or otherwise prepared)

(5) Sheepmeat only

(6) All meat except sheepmeat

Fruits, vegetables and fungi

For certain categories of fruits, vegetables and fungi MRLs have been specified. Some have a common MRL and these are listed below and apply to all those categories given in the table (subject to the stated exceptions). Others have MRLs which vary. For these, MRLs are given in the table which follows. All values (in the list and table) are mg residue/kg food.

Aminotriazole 0.05
Captafol 0.05
Chlordane 0.02
DDT 0.1 (except oranges, other citrus fruit and bananas 1)
Diazinon 0.5
1,2-dibromoethane 0.01
Dicofol 5 (except tomatoes 1 and cucumbers 2)
Endrin 0.02
Fenitrothion 0.5 (except oranges and other citrus fruit 2 and potatoes 0.05)
2,4,5-T 0.05

Groups to which food belongs	Food	Pesticides															
		Aldrin and Dieldrin	2-Aminobutane	Azinphosmethyl	Bitertanol	Captan	Carbaryl	Carbendazim	Carbophenothion	Chlorfenvinphos	Dichlofluanid	Dichlorvos	Diflubenzuron	Dimethipin	Dimethoate	Dithiocarbamates	Endosulfan
Citrus fruit	Oranges	0.05	5	2		0.1	7	10	2	1	5	0.1	1		2		2
	Other citrus	0.05	5	2		0.1	7	10	2	1	5	0.1	1		2		2
Pomme fruit	Apples	0.05		1	1	3	5	5	1	0.05	5	0.1	1		1	3	2
	Pears	0.05		1	1	3	5	5	1	0.05	5	0.1	1		1	3	2
Stone fruit	Peaches and Nectarines	0.05		4	1	2	10	10	1	0.05	5	0.1			2	3	2
	Plums	0.05		1	1	2	10	2	1	0.05	5	0.1	1		2	1	2
Berries, small fruit and soft fruit	Grapes	0.05		2		3	5	10		0.05	15	0.1			1	5	2
	Strawberries	0.05		1		3	7	5		0.05	10	0.1			1	3	2
	Raspberries	0.05		1		3	10	5		0.05	15	0.1			1	5	2
	Blackcurrants	0.05		1		3	10	5		0.05	15	0.1			2	5	2
Assorted fruit	Bananas	0.05		1	0.5	0.1	5	1		0.05	5	0.1			1	1	2
Root and tuber vegetables	Potatoes	0.05	50	0.2		0.1	0.2	3		0.5	0.1	0.5		0.1(1)	0.05	0.1	0.2
	Carrots	0.05		0.5		0.1	2			0.5	5	0.5			1	0.5	0.2
	Turnips	0.05		0.5		0.1	1			0.5	5	0.5			1		2
	Swedes	0.05		0.5		0.1	2			0.5	5	0.5			1		2
Bulb vegetables	Onions	0.05		0.5		0.1	1	2		0.5	5	0.5			1		1
Fruiting vegetables	Tomatoes	0.05		0.5		3	5	5		0.1	5	0.5	1		1	3	2
	Cucumbers	0.05		0.5		0.1	3	0.5		0.1	5	0.5			2	0.5	2
Brassica vegetables	Cabbage	0.05		0.5		0.1	5			0.1	5	0.5	1		2		2
	Cauliflowers	0.05		0.5		0.1	1		0.5	0.1	5	0.5			2		2
	Brussels sprouts	0.05		1		0.1	1	0.5	0.5	0.1	5	0.5	1		2		2
Legume vegetables	Beans	0.5		0.5		2	5			0.1	5	0.5			2	0.5	2
	Peas	0.5		0.5		2	5			0.1	5	0.5			1		2
Stem vegetables	Celery	0.5		2		0.1	3	2		0.5		0.5			1		2
	Leeks	0.5		0.5		2	1			0.1	5	0.5			1		2
Leaf vegetables	Lettuce	0.05		0.5		2	10	5		0.1	10	1					2
Fungi	Mushrooms	0.05				0.1	1	1		0.05		0.5	0.1		1		

Groups to which food belongs	Food	Pesticides																						
		Ethion	Fluazifop	Flurochloridone	Haloxyfop	Heptachlor	Hexachlorocyclo-hexane (HCH) γ	Imazalil	Inorganic Bromide	Ioxynil	Iprodione	Malathion	Mercury compounds	Mevinphos	Omethoate	Parathion	Parathionmethyl	Phosalone	Pirimiphosmethyl	Quintozene	Tecnazene	Thiabendazole	Triazophos	Vinclozolin
Citrus fruit	Oranges	2				0.01	1	5/0.1(2)	30			2		0.2	1	1	0.2	1	0.5					
	other citrus	2				0.01	1	5/0.1(2)	30			2		0.2	1	1	0.2	1	0.5					
Pomme fruit	Apples	0.5			0.05(1)	0.01(1)	1		20		10	0.5	0.02	0.2	1			2						1
	Pears	0.5			0.05(1)	0.01(1)	1		20		10	0.5	0.02	0.2	1			2						1
Stone fruit	Peaches and Nectarines	0.5				0.01(1)	1		20		10	0.5		0.5	1			2						5
	Plums	0.5				0.01(1)	1		20		10	0.5		0.5	1			1						
Berries, small fruit and soft fruit	Grapes	0.5				0.01(1)	0.5		20		10	0.5		0.1	1			1						5
	Strawberries	0.1				0.01(1)	3		30		10	0.5		0.1	1			1						10
	Raspberries	0.1				0.01(1)	3		20		5	0.5		0.1	1			1						5
	Blackcurrants	0.1				0.01(1)	3		20		5	0.5		0.1	1			1						5
Assorted fruit	Bananas	0.1				0.01(1)	1		20			0.5			0.2			1		1			1	
Root and tuber vegetables	Potatoes		0.1	0.01(1)		0.05	0.05(1)					0.5	0.02	0.1	0.05			0.1(1)		0.2		5	0.05(1)	0.1
	Carrots	0.1		0.01(1)		0.2	0.2					0.5	0.02	0.1	0.2			0.1					0.1	
	Turnips	0.1		0.01(1)		0.05	1					0.5	0.02	0.1	0.2			0.1						
	Swedes	0.1		0.01(1)		0.05	1					0.5	0.02	0.1	2			0.1						
Bulb vegetables	Onions	0.1		0.01(1)		0.05	1			0.1	0.1	3	0.02	0.1	0.1			1					0.05(1)	1
Fruiting vegetables	Tomatoes	0.1				0.02	2		75		5	3	0.02	0.1	1			1		0.1				3
	Cucumbers	0.1				0.05	1		50		5	3	0.02	0.1	0.2			1						1
Brassica vegetables	Cabbage	0.1				0.05	2		100			3	0.02	0.1	0.2			1		0.02			0.1	1
	Cauliflowers	0.1				0.05	2					3	0.02	0.1	0.2			1		0.02				1
	Brussels sprouts	0.1				0.05	2					3	0.02	0.1	0.2			1					0.1	
Legume vegetables	Beans	0.1				0.05	1					3		0.1	0.2			1		0.01				2
	Peas	0.1				0.05	0.1					3		0.1	0.2			1						1
Stem vegetables	Celery	0.1				0.05	1					3	0.02	0.1	0.2			1						5
	Leeks	0.1				0.05	1					3	0.02	0.1	2			1						
Leaf vegetables	Lettuce	0.1				0.05	2					3	0.02	0.5	0.2			1		3	2			5
Fungi	Mushrooms	0.1				0.05	1					3	0.02	0.1	0.2			1						

Notes:
(1) Level at or about limit of determination
(2) 5 mg/kg applies to whole fruit; 0.1 mg/kg applies to fruit without peel

4.3

General points

1) No person may leave or cause to be left in any of the above foods a level of residue exceeding that specified.
2) The substances which are regarded as comprising the specified residues are listed in the Regulations.
3) Levels of residues should be determined (as far as practicable) using procedures recommended in publications of the *Codex Alimentarius*.

Tin

Regulation: Tin in Food Regulations 1992 (1992/496)

No-one may sell or import any food containing a level of tin exceeding 200 mg/kg.

Trace metals

The standards for the trace metals arsenic and lead in specified foods are as given below:

	Statutory limit (ppm, mg/kg)	
	Lead	*Arsenic*
Angelica, glacé	2.0	
Apples	1.0	
Beer	0.2	
Beer: black beer or black beer and rum		0.5
Beverages: alcoholic, not otherwise specified		0.2
Beverages: non-alcoholic ready to drink, not otherwise specified	0.2	0.1
Brandy	0.2	
Chemicals: not otherwise specified	10	2.0
Chemicals: for which arsenic limits are specified in the British Pharmacopoeia or the British Pharmaceutical Codex (excluding synthetic colours)		(1)
Chemicals: for which lead limits are specified in the British Pharmacopoeia or the British Pharmaceutical Codex or the European Pharmacopoeia	(1)	
Chicory: dried and roasted		4.0
Cider	0.2	
Cocktails	1.0	
Cocoa powder	2.0 (2)	
Corned beef	2.0	
Curry powder	10	
Dandelion coffee including soluble dandelion coffee compound	5.0	
Fats: edible	0.5	
Finings and clearing agents		5.0
Fish: not otherwise specified	2.0	
Fish: dried	5.0	
Flavourings	10.0	3.0
Frozen confections (and any other similar commodity)		0.5

(*continued*)

	Statutory limit (ppm, mg/kg)	
	Lead	*Arsenic*
Fruit: dried or dehydrated	2.0	
Fruit juices: concentrated (excluding lime or lemon)	1.0	
Fruit juices: ready to drink (excluding lime or lemon)	0.5	
Fruit juices: undiluted		0.5
Game, game pâté	10	
Gelatine: edible		2.0
Geneva	0.2	
Gin	0.2	
Herbs: dried	10	5.0
Hops concentrates: excluding those for commercial brewing		5.0
Hops: dried, excluding those for commercial brewing		2.0
Hops	10	
Ice-cream		0.5
Ice-cream: or similar frozen confection but excluding water ices	0.5	
Infant food (excluding dried, dehydrated or concentrated infant food)	0.2	
Iron: reduced iron, used in the preparation of flour		10
Lemon/lime juice:		
a) for manufacturing	2.0	
b) for other use	1.0	
Liquorice: dried extract		2.0
Liver	2.0	
Milk: condensed	0.5	
Mustard	10	5.0
Oils: edible	0.5	
Onions: dehydrated	2.0	2.0
Pears	1.0	
Perry	0.2	
Pickles and sauces	2.0	
Protein: hydrolysed	2.0	
Rum	0.2	
Rusks	0.5	
Shellfish	10	
Soft drink concentrates: for use in the manufacture of soft drinks		0.5
Soft drinks: concentrated		0.5
Soft drinks: ready to drink	0.2	
Spices: including ground spices	10	5.0
Sugar:		
a) sulphated ash content max 0.25%	0.5	
b) sulphated ash content 0.25–1.0%	1.0	
c) sulphated ash content over 1.0% (not for further refining)	5.0	
d) sulphated ash content over 1.0% (for further refining)	10	
Tea	5.0	
Tomato juice, Tomato juice cocktails: concentrated	1.0	
Tomato juice, Tomato juice cocktails: ready to drink	0.5	
Tomato paste, purée or powder		
a) total solids 15–25%	2.0	
b) total solids over 25%	3.0	

4.3 (*continued*)

	Statutory limit (ppm, mg/kg)	
	Lead	*Arsenic*
Vegetable juices: concentrated	1.0	
Vegetable juices: ready to drink	0.5	
Vegetables: dehydrated or dried but excluding onion	2.0	
Vodka	0.2	
Water ices: or similar frozen confection	0.2	
Whisky	0.2	
Yeast: brewers' yeast for the manufacture of yeast products		5.0 (3)
Yeast and yeast products: but excluding yeast extract or brewers' yeast for the manufacture of yeast products	5.0 (3)	2.0 (3)
Yeast extract	2.0	

Notes:
(1) As specified in named publications
(2) Calculated on the dry fat free substance
(3) Calculated on dry matter

4.4. Processing and packaging

4.4

Frozen foods

Regulation: Quick-frozen Foodstuffs Regulations 1990 (1990/2615)

Note: These Regulations only apply to a frozen food if it falls within the definition of a 'quick-frozen foodstuff'.

Definition

Quick-frozen foodstuff a product

a) comprising food which has undergone a freezing process known as 'quick-freezing' whereby the zone of maximum crystallisation is crossed as rapidly as possible, depending on the type of product, and
b) which is labelled for the purpose of sale to indicate that it had undergone that process.

Specified processing conditions

1) Quick-frozen foodstuffs must meet the following conditions:
   a) it has been manufactured from raw materials of sound, genuine and merchantable quality and no other raw materials;
   b) no raw material has been used in its manufacture unless, at the time of its use, it would have been lawful for it to be sold for human consumption;
   c) its preparation and quick-freezing have been carried out with sufficient promptness, and by the use of technical equipment appropriate, to minimise any chemical, biochemical and microbiological changes to the food comprised in it;
   d) only authorised cryogenic media may be used in direct contact with any food comprized in it (see 2) below);
   e) the quick-freezing of each food comprised in it has resulted in the temperature of that food after thermal stabilisation being −18°C or colder; and
   f) following the quick-freezing and thermal stabilisation of any food to which e) applies the temperature of that food has been maintained or has, save during the application of any one of the permitted exceptions, been maintained at a level or levels no warmer that −18°C (see 3) below).
2) Authorised cryogenic media are: air, nitrogen and carbon dioxide.
3) The following temperature exceptions are permitted:
   a) brief periods during transport other than local distribution warmer than −18°C but not warmer than −15°C;
   b) during local distribution (delivery to the point of retail sale or to a catering establishment) warmer than −18°C (to an extent consistent with good distribution practice) but not warmer than −12°C (before 10.1.1997; after 10.1.1997, −15°C);

4.4

c) in a retail display cabinet (before 10.1.1997) warmer than −18°C to an extent consistent with good storage practice;
d) in a retail display cabinet (after 9.1.1997) warmer than −18°C to an extent consistent with good storage practice but not warmer than −12°C.

Packaging and labelling
Prepackaging must be suitable to protect the food from microbial and other forms of external contamination and against dehydration, and the food must remain in the packaging until sale.

Irradiation

Regulation: Food (Control of Irradiation) Regulations 1990 (1990/2490)

Definition
Ionising radiation any gamma rays, X rays or corpuscular radiations which are capable of producing ions either directly or indirectly other than -

a) those rays or corpuscular radiations: which are emitted by measuring or inspection devices; which are emitted at an energy level no higher than 10 MeV in the case of X rays and 5 MeV otherwise; and, the dose of energy imparted by which does not exceed 0.5 Gy; and
b) those rays or corpuscular radiations applied in respect of food prepared under medical supervision for patients requiring sterile diets.

Only the following foods can be treated with ionising radiation to the maximum dose indicated:

Food description	*Maximum overall average dose* (kGy) (1)
Fruit (including fungi, tomatoes and rhubarb)	2
Vegetables (excluding fruit, cereals, bulbs, and tubers, and spices and condiments but including pulses)	1
Cereals (2)	1
Bulbs and tubers (meaning potatoes, yams, onions, shallots and garlic)	0.2
Spices and condiments (meaning dried substances normally used for seasoning)	10
Fish and shellfish (including eels, crustaceans and molluscs)	3
Poultry (meaning domestic fowls, geese, ducks, guinea fowls, pigeons, quails and turkeys)	7

Notes:
(1) An additional requirement states that the maximum dose must be the lower of either (a) 3 times the minimum dose, or (b) 1.5 times the level stated in this table
(2) Cereals are defined by reference to an EC Council Regulation

General points

1) No person shall treat food for sale by ionising radiation unless he holds a current irradiation licence, he is permitted by the licence to irradiate the food and the irradiation complies with the conditions of the licence. Full details concerning the issuing of licences are given in the Regulations.
2) No person shall import irradiated food unless it is permitted (see table above), is of recognised appropriate origin and is accompanied by appropriate documentation (see Regulations for full details).
3) No person shall store or transport irradiated food unless accompanied by specified documentation.
4) No person shall sell irradiated food unless either 1) or 2) were observed and 3) was observed.
5) Food for export to the EC may be treated, stored or transported only if it complies with the legislation of the member state concerned.

Materials and articles in contact with food

A General

Regulation: Materials and Articles in Contact with Food Regulations 1987 (1987/1523)

No person shall sell, import or use in connection with food any material which does not satisfy the following standards.

General points

1) Materials and articles for food use shall be manufactured in such a way that under normal or foreseeable conditions of use they do not transfer their constituents to food in quantities which could:
   a) endanger human health,
   b) bring about a deterioration in the organoleptic characteristics of such food or an unacceptable change in its nature, substance or quality.
2) The following particulars are required when any food contact material and article is sold in its finished state:
   a) the description 'for food use', or a specific indication of the use of the material, or the designated symbol for food contact materials (see below) (for retail sale, this provision does not apply if the material or article is by its nature clearly intended to come into contact with food),
   b) any special conditions to be observed in use,
   c) the name and address or trade mark of the producer.

4.4 

Vinyl chloride monomer
Materials manufactured with vinyl chloride polymers or copolymers shall not contain vinyl chloride monomer in a quantity exceeding 1 mg/kg of the material. In addition, they should be manufactured so that they do not transfer vinyl chloride to food in which they are in contact to make it detectable in the food at a level of 0.01 mg/kg.

Regenerated cellulose film

1) Regenerated cellulose film is defined as - a thin sheet material obtained from refined cellulose derived from unrecycled wood or cotton, with or without the addition of suitable substances, either in the mass or on one or both surfaces.
2) Controls are placed on film intended to come into contact with food (or is in contact with food and intended for that purpose) and which
   a) constitutes a finished product in itself, or
   b) is a part of a finished product containing other materials.
   However, excluded is film which
   a) has a coating exceeding 50 mg/dm^2 on the side intended to come into contact with food, and
   b) synthetic casings of film.
3) The following specific provisions relate to regenerated cellulose film:
   a) It must be manufactured from a list of specified substances (see Regulations).
   b) It must be manufactured so that it does not transfer any detectable quantity of adhesive or colourant to food.
   c) If coated, it must not transfer bis(2-hydroxyethyl) ether, ethanediol (or both these substances) in excess of 50 mg/kg food.
   d) In the course of business (involving storage, preparation, packaging, selling or serving food):
   - regenerated cellulose film containing bis(2-hydroxyethyl) ether, ethanediol (or both) shall not be used for food containing water physically free at the surface;
   - no printed surface of regenerated cellulose film shall come into contact with food.

Defences
It shall be a defence for a person to prove that:

1) he took all reasonable precautions and exercised all due diligence,
2) he purchased the material as being lawful under these Regulations with a written warranty to that effect, and he had no reason to believe it otherwise, and it was in the same state as he purchased it. A description in an invoice can be taken to be a written warranty.

B Plastic

Regulation: Plastic Materials and Articles in Contact with Food Regulations 1992 (1992/3145)

Note: Plastic materials are subject to the General controls described above in addition to these more specific controls.

Transfer of constituents
Maximum overall migration limits are specified as follows:

a) In the case of containers (capacity 500 ml – 10 l), articles for filling where the surface cannot be estimated, and caps, gaskets, stoppers or similar sealing devices: 60 mg/kg of food
b) In any other case: 10 mg/dm^2 of plastic surface area.

Monomers
The Regulations specify the permitted monomers and place restrictions on the use of some of them (i.e. quantity in the plastic material or maximum specific migration limits). Certain monomers are only permitted to be used until 31.12.1996 (See Regulations). The following are exempt from this part of the Regulations:

surface coatings obtained from resinous or polymerized products in liquid, powder or dispersion form, including varnishes, lacquers and paints; silicones; epoxy resins; products obtained by means of bacterial fermentation; adhesives and adhesion promoters; printing inks.

Simulants
For the purposes of assessing whether plastic materials transfer constituents to food, the Regulations specify, in some cases, simulants appropriate for various foods (see Regulations). The simulants specified are:

Simulant A: distilled water or water of equivalent quality
Simulant B: 3% acetic acid (w/v) in aqueous solution
Simulant C: 15% ethanol (v/v) in aqueous solution

4.4 Simulant D: rectified olive oil (or, if technically necessary, a mixture of synthetic triglycerides or sunflower oil) (as defined in the Regulations)

Where no simulant is specified but the food is listed, the food should be used; where a food is not listed, the simulant which corresponds most closely in extractive capacity should be used.

4.5 Labelling

General Labelling Requirements

Regulation: Food Labelling Regulations 1984 (1984/1305)
Amendments: Meat Products and Spreadable Fish Products Regulations 1984 (1984/1566)
Natural Mineral Waters Regulations 1985 (1985/71)
Caseins and Caseinates Regulations 1985 (1985/2026)
Condensed Milk and Dried Milk (Amendment) Regulations 1986 (1986/2299)
Coffee and Coffee Products (Amendment) Regulations 1987 (1987/1986)
Sweeteners in Food (Amendment) Regulations 1988 (1988/2112)
Food Labelling (Amendment) Regulations 1989 (1989/768)
Caseins and Caseinates (Amendment) Regulations 1989 (1989/2321)
Milk and Milk Product (Protection of Designations) Regulations 1990 (1990/607)
Food Labelling (Amendment) Regulations 1990 (1990/2488)
Food Labelling (Amendment)(Irradiated Food) Regulations 1990 (1990/2489)
Flavourings in Food Regulations 1992 (1992/1971)
Food Additives Labelling Regulations 1992 (1992/1978)
Food Safety (Amendment)(Metrication) Regulations 1992 (1992/2597)

Notes:

1) The MAFF issued some 'Notes For Guidance' to help in the interpretation of these Regulations. However they have no status in law and the details that follow have made no reference to them.
2) These Regulations are not applicable to cow's milk. Similar requirements have been introduced for milk, semi-skimmed milk and skimmed milk by incorporating the requirements into milk Regulations. The following should be consulted for full details:
   Milk: Milk (Special Designation) Regulations 1986 (1986/723)
   Semi-skimmed/skimmed milk: Milk and Dairies (Semi-skimmed and Skimmed Milk) (Heat Treatment and Labelling) Regulations 1986 (1986/722) (as amended)

Presentation

The presentation of food shall not be such that a purchaser is likely to be misled to a material degree as to the nature, substance or quality of the food.

Food to be delivered to the ultimate consumer or caterer

The following foods are not subject to the Regulations of this section: Specified sugar products, cocoa and chocolate products, honey, condensed and dried milk for delivery to a catering establishment (unless prepared and labelled for infant consumption), hen eggs, wines or grape musts, sparkling wines and aerated sparking wines, additives, drinks bottled before 1/1/1983 having an alcoholic strength greater than 1.2% (vol.).

4.5 The following foods are not subject to the Regulations of this section except the requirement for an ingredients' list:

Coffee and coffee products for delivery to a catering establishment.

(The above foods are all subject to the labelling requirements given in other UK or EC Regulations relating to that food, except that alcoholic drinks bottled before 1/1/1983 are subject to the labelling requirements in force at the time of bottling.)

General labelling requirement

All food to be marked with:

a) the name of the food,
b) a list of ingredients,
c) the appropriate durability indication:
   i) for foods which are highly perishable from a microbiological point of view and in consequence likely after a short period of time to constitute an immediate danger to health, a 'use by' date;
   ii) for other foods, the minimum durability.
d) any special storage conditions or conditions of use,
e) name and address of manufacturer, packer or seller,
f) place of origin if necessary to avoid misleading the purchaser,
g) instructions for use if necessary.

1) Name of food

If a legally prescribed name exists, it shall be used. (For fish, Schedule 1 of the Regulations should be consulted; for melons and potatoes sold as such, the species and variety respectively must be included; for vitamins either the name used in the table on page 141 or one of the following if appropriate – vitamin B_6 pantothenic acid, biotin, vitamin E, vitamin K).

If no legal name exists, a customary name may be used.

If no legal or customary name exists, a name sufficiently precise to inform the purchaser of the true nature and to avoid confusion shall be used (and, if necessary, a description of its use).

Trade marks, brand names, or fancy names shall not be substituted.

The name should include reference to the physical condition and any previous treatment if the purchaser could be misled without such information. In particular the following treatments are specified:

a) Food frozen by contact freezing with dichlorodifluoromethane must be accompanied by the statement 'contact frozen with dichlorodifluoromethane'.
b) Meat and offal which has previously been frozen and thawed must be accompanied by the words 'previously frozen - do not refreeze' or, when not prepacked, there must be a prominent notice stating the fact on the premises.

c) Meat treated (or derived from an animal which has been treated) with proteolytic enzymes must be accompanied by the word 'tenderized'
d) Peas which have been dried, soaked and then canned or frozen must be accompanied by the word 'dried', 'processed' or 'soaked'
e) Food which has been irradiated must be accompanied by the word 'irradiated' or 'treated with ionizing radiation'.

2) List of ingredients
Heading: The list of ingredients should be headed 'ingredients' or a heading which includes the word 'ingredients'.
Order of ingredients: Ingredients to be listed in weight descending order determined at the time of use in preparation of the food, except for the following:

a) Water and volatile ingredients shall be listed in the order of their weight in the finished product. The weight of water is calculated by subtracting the weight of the other ingredients used from the weight of the finished product.
b) If an ingredient is reconstituted from concentrated or dried form during the preparation of the food, it may be positioned according to its weight prior to concentration or dehydration.
c) If a product is to be reconstituted during use, ingredients may be listed in order after reconstitution provided there is a statement 'ingredients of the reconstituted product' or 'ingredients of the ready to use product' or similar.
d) If a product consists of mixed fruit, nuts, vegetables, spices or herbs and no particular one of these ingredients predominates, the ingredients may be listed in any order provided that for foods consisting entirely of such a mixture the heading includes 'in variable proportion' or other words indicating method of listing and for other such foods the relevant ingredients are accompanied by such a statement.

Names of ingredients: the name of an ingredient shall be

a) the name which would be used if the ingredient were sold as a food, including, if appropriate, either 'irradiated' or 'treated with ionizing radiation' (other appropriate indications must be given if a consumer could be misled by its omission); or
b) the generic name given in the following table; or

Generic name	*Ingredients*	*Conditions of use of name*
Caseinates	Any type of caseinate	
Cheese	Any type of cheese	The label of the food must not refer to a specific type of cheese
Citrus peel	Any citrus fruit peel	
Cocoa butter	Press, expeller or refined cocoa butter	

4.5 (*continued*)

Generic name	*Ingredients*	*Conditions of use of name*
Cream	Any cream (except half cream)	
Half cream	Any half cream	
Crumbs or rusks *(as appropriate)*	Any crumbed, baked cereal product	
Dextrose	Anhydrous dextrose or dextrose monohydrate	
Fat	Any refined fat or mixture of refined fats	Must include either a) 'animal' or 'vegetable' or both as appropriate, or b) a specified animal or vegetable origin
Fish	Any fish or shellfish	The label of the food must not refer to a specific species of fish
Other fish	Any fish or shellfish other than one specified on the label of the food	
Flour *(followed by a list of the cereals)*	Any mixture of flour from two or more cereals	
Crystallised fruit	Any crystallised fruit	Crystallised fruit not to exceed 10% of the food
Gum base	Any gum preparation used in chewing gum	
Herbs *or* mixed herbs	Any mixture of two or more herbs	Herbs not to exceed 2% of the food
Honey	Any honey (as defined by Regulations)	
Meat	Any type of meat (as defined by the Meat Product Regulations)	The label of the food must not refer to a specific type of meat
Other meat	Any meat (as defined by the Meat Product Regulations) other than one specified on the label of the food	
Nuts	Any nuts	To be used only if either a) nuts do not exceed 1% of the food, or b) the nuts are mixed with muscatels, raisins, sultanas and/or currants and the pack does not exceed 50 g
Offal	Any offal (as defined on page 56)	Only to be used when an ingredient of cooked food
Oil	Any refined oil or mixture of oils (except olive oil)	Must include either a) 'animal' or 'vegetable' or both as appropriate, or

(continued)

Generic name	*Ingredients*	*Conditions of use of name*
		b) a specified animal or vegetable origin, and hydrogenated oil must include 'hydrogenated' unless only accompanied by 'animal'
Poultry meat	Any type of poultry meat	The label of the food must not refer to a specific poultry meat
Spices *or* mixed spices	Any mixture of two or more spices and/or spice extracts	Spices/spice extracts not to exceed 2% of the food
Starch	Any starch (except chemically modified starch)	
Modified starch	Any chemically modified starch	
Sugar	Any type of sucrose	
Vine fruits	Any muscatels, raisins, sultanas or currants	

c) an additive shall be listed by either the principal function it serves, as given in the following table, followed by its name and/or serial number (subject to the notes in the table) or where the function is not given in the table, its name:

Categories of additives	
Acid (1)	Flavour enhancer
Acidity regulator	Flavouring (2)
Anti-caking agent	Flour improver
Anti-foaming agent	Gelling agent
Antioxidant	Glazing agent
Artificial sweetener	Preservative
Colour	Raising agent
Emulsifier	Stabiliser
Emulsifying salt (3)	Thickener

Notes:
(1) If the name of the additive includes the word 'acid', the category name may be omitted
(2) It shall be sufficient, in the case of an additive which is identified by this category name, to use the category name alone
(3) Only to be used for processed cheese (including cheese spread)

Compound ingredients: the names of the ingredients of a compound ingredient may be given either instead of the compound ingredient or in addition and close to the name of the compound ingredient; except only the name of the compound ingredient need be given if:

4.5 a) the compound ingredient need not bear an ingredients' list if sold separately,
b) the compound ingredient is less than 25% of the finished product,
c) a generic name is used from the table of permitted generic names, but, for b) and c) any additives needing to be named must be listed close to the name of the compound ingredient.

Water: To be declared unless:
a) it is used solely for reconstitution of an ingredient which is concentrated or dehydrated,
b) it is used as, or part of, a medium which is not normally consumed,
c) added water does not exceed 5% of the finished product,
d) it is permitted under EC frozen or deep-frozen poultry Regulations.

Ingredients not needing to be named:
a) constituents which are temporarily separated and re-introduced later (in the same proportions),
b) additives which were in an ingredient and which serve no significant technological function in the finished product,
c) any additive used solely as processing aid,
d) any substance (other than water) used as a solvent or carrier of an additive.

Foods which need not bear a list of ingredients:
a) fresh fruit and vegetables which have not been peeled or cut into pieces,
b) carbonated water (consisting of water and carbon dioxide only, and the name indicates that the water is carbonated),
c) vinegar derived by fermentation (from a single basic product) with no added ingredients,
d) cheese, butter, fermented milk and fermented cream to which only lactic products, enzymes and micro-organism cultures essential to manufacture have been added. In the case of cheese, except fresh curd cheese and processed cheese, salt may be included if required for manufacture,
e) any food consisting of a single component (including flour containing only required nutritional additives),
f) any drink with an alcoholic strength by volume over 1.2%.

For c) and d), if other ingredients are included only those other added ingredients need be listed if the list is headed 'added ingredients' or similar.

3) Special emphasis

Where a food is characterised by the presence of a particular ingredient, and special emphasis is given to it on the label, it must include a declaration of the minimum percentage of the ingredient. Similarly, for the low content of a particular ingredient, the maximum percentage should be given. The % to be calculated on the quantity used and to appear by the name of the food or in the ingredients' list. (Neither reference to an ingredient in the name of the food nor to a flavouring on the label shall of itself constitute special emphasis).

4) Minimum durability/'Use by' date

General requirements:

Minimum durability: to be indicated by 'best before' followed by the date up to and including which the food can reasonably be expected to retain its specific properties if properly stored, and details of the storage conditions necessary for the properties to be retained until that date. Date to be in the form day/month/year except day/month only required if date is within 3 months, or 'best before end' and month/year if date is from 3 to 18 months, or 'best before end' and year if date is more than 18 months. The date may be elsewhere on the packet if reference is made to the position after the 'best before' statement.

'Use by' date: To be indicated by 'use by' followed by the date (expressed in day/month or day/month/year) up to and including which the food, if properly stored, is recommended for use. Details of any storage conditions must also be given. The date may be elsewhere on the packet if reference is made to the position after the 'use by' statement.

Foods exempted from stating minimum durability or 'use by':

a) fresh fruit and vegetables (including potatoes but not including sprouting seeds, legume sprouts and similar products) which have not been peeled or cut into pieces,
b) wine, liqueur wine, sparkling wine, aromatised wine and any similar drink obtained from fruit other than grapes and certain other drinks made from grapes or grape musts (see Regulations),
c) any drink with an alcoholic strength by volume of 10% or more,
d) any soft drink, fruit juice or fruit nectar or alcoholic drink sold in a container of more than 5 l (intended for catering),
e) flour confectionery and bread normally consumed within 24 hours of preparation,
f) vinegar,
g) cooking and table salt,
h) solid sugar and products consisting almost solely of flavoured or coloured sugars,
i) chewing gums and similar products,
j) edible ices in individual portions.

5) Instructions for use

In the case of a concentrate, dry mix or similar food (except custard powder and blancmange powder), which is intended to be made into another food by the addition of any other substance, the instruction shall specify every substance (other than water) required and that part of the instruction shall appear next to the name of the food and may also appear elsewhere.

4.5 *6) Omission of certain particulars*

a) Food which is not prepacked:
(includes food which is prepacked for direct sale and flour confectionery packed in crimp case or transparent packaging unmarked or marked only with price and no other label is attached or details given).

Need not be marked with any of the above requirements except the name of the food, and the following (unless irradiated) do not require the name of the food: flour (which is not exposed for sale), white bread, flour confectionery, carcasses and parts of carcasses not intended for sale in one piece (but see c) below).

b) Fancy confectionery:
Individually wrapped fancy confectionery (i.e. confectionery product in the form of a figure, animal, cigarette, egg or other fancy form) not enclosed in further packaging and intended for sale as single items, need not be marked with any of the above requirements except the name of the food (but see c) below).

c) Additives:
Items in a) or b) which have no list of ingredients and contain additives normally requiring declaration, and which serve as antioxidant, artificial sweetener, colour, flavour enhancer, flavouring or preservative, must be marked with an indication of every category of additive in the food. For edible ices and flour confectionery, a notice displayed in a prominent position stating that products may contain stated categories is sufficient.

d) Items in a) or b) which have no list of ingredients and contain an ingredient which has been irradiated must be marked with a statement of that ingredient accompanied by the word 'irradiated' or 'treated with ionising radiation'.

e) Small packages and certain bottles (unless a), b) or f) apply or if 7) below applies):
If either the largest surface of packaging is less than 10 square centimetres, or, if the container is an indelibly marked glass bottle intended for re-use and having no label, ring or collar, only the name and, if required, the minimum durability or 'use by' need be given. In the case of bottles, the minimum durability/'use by' need not be given until 1.1.97.

f) Food for immediate consumption:
i) If the food is not prepacked and is sold at a catering establishment for immediate consumption, no markings are required unless either the food has been irradiated, when only the name need be marked, or the food is subject to ii) below. If the food is prepacked, sold at a catering establishment as an individual portion and is intended to accompany another food, only the name is required. For prepacked sandwiches, filled rolls (or similar bread products) or prepared meals

sold in a catering establishment for immediate consumption, only the name is required. In all of these cases, where an irradiated ingredient has been used, the food shall be marked with an indication of that ingredient accompanied by 'irradiated' or 'treated with ionising radiation'.

ii) The following foods, when sold other than at a catering establishment for immediate consumption, need not be marked except with the name of the food or the name of the food shall appear on a notice displayed prominently (but see iii) and iv) below): sandwiches, filled rolls (or similar bread products), food which is sold hot and ready for consumption (without any further cooking, heating or other preparation), prepared meals, food from a vending machine which is heated by the purchaser at the establishment where sold (for immediate consumption), any food which is a) not prepacked or which is prepacked for direct sale or which is flour confectionery packed in a crimp case or in wholly transparent packaging and b) is sold at a catering establishment or an establishment (including a vehicle or a fixed or mobile stall) whose business consists mainly of selling food of a kind described in this paragraph.

iii) For food from a vending machine ii) applies also to food sold at a catering establishment for immediate consumption. For prepared meals provided at a hotel the food need not be marked with the name (unless iv) applies).

iv) Where a food has been irradiated, this shall be indicated in the name of the food and where a food contains irradiated ingredients this shall be indicated as in i) above.

7) Additional requirements

Vending machines:

When a name of a food is not visible to a purchaser, it shall be given on a notice on the front of the machine.

Alcoholic drinks:

Every pre-packed alcoholic drink (except Community controlled wine) with its alcoholic strength by volume (being a figure followed by '% vol' which may be preceded by 'alcohol' or 'alc.'). Tolerances are specified in the Regulations. Additional details are given for the indication of alcoholic strength for representative samples of alcoholic drinks (including Community controlled wine) sold otherwise than pre-packed and the information required is then to be given on a menu, wine list or notice.

Any whisky with an alcoholic strength by volume of less than 40% and any brandy, gin, rum or vodka with an alcoholic strength by volume below 37.2% shall be marked 'under strength', except brandy if the strength has fallen below 37.2% only through maturing in cask.

4.5 *8) Manner of marking or labelling*

General:

When sold to the ultimate consumer, the required markings shall be either on the packaging or on a label attached to the packaging or on a label visible through the packaging. If sold otherwise than to the ultimate consumer, as an alternative, the details may be on relevant trade documents (except that the name of the food, its durability indication and the name and address of manufacturer, packer or seller must appear on the external packaging).

For those products which may omit certain details (food not prepacked, fancy confectionery, food for immediate consumption as detailed above):

a) If the food has neither been irradiated nor contains irradiated ingredients, the details which are required shall appear on a label or on a ticket or notice close to the food.
b) If the food has been irradiated or contains irradiated ingredients this shall be indicated on a menu, notice, ticket or label that can be seen when the food is chosen. As an alternative, an indication that an ingredient may have been irradiated is sufficient or, in the case where irradiated dried substances normally used for seasoning are used in a catering establishment, an indication that food contains (or may contain) those irradiated ingredients.

Intelligibility:

Any marking or notice should be easy to understand, clearly legible and, when sold to the ultimate consumer, easily visible. They must not be hidden, obscured or interrupted by written or pictorial matter. For seasonal selection packs containing confectionery or confectionery and chocolate prepacked and labelled according to the Regulations an outer packaging decorated with seasonal designs is permitted.

Field of vision:

The name of the food and, when required, its durability indication and/or alcoholic strength shall be in the same field of vision. Any weight statement shall also be in the same field of vision. These requirements do not apply to foods falling within the 'small packages and certain bottles' section above.

Claims and misleading descriptions

Claims

The following claims in the labelling or advertising of a food are prohibited:

1) A claim that a food has tonic properties (except that the use of the word tonic to describe a soft drink which complies with the requirements of the Soft Drinks Regulations is permitted).

2) A claim that a food which is intended for babies is equivalent or superior to the milk of a healthy mother.

The following claims in the labelling or advertising of a food are only permitted where the conditions specified in the Regulations are met (only summaries of the conditions are given here and the Regulations should be consulted for full details). When considering whether a claim is being made, the following do not constitute claims:

a) a reference in the name of a food to a substance other than vitamins, minerals, polyunsaturated fatty acids or cholesterol;
b) a reference to a substance in an ingredients' list or in a statement of total nutrient content;
c) a statement of the energy value;
d) a reference to protein, polyunsaturated fatty acid or sodium in a statement of the basic nutrient content (being a statement of the energy value and of the protein, carbohydrate and fat content which may be supplemented by further details of that content or by a statement of the sodium or fibre content).

1) Claims relating to particular nutritional uses (i.e. a claim that a food is suitable, or has been specially made, for fulfilling the particular nutritional requirements of either people whose digestive process or metabolism is disturbed, or people who, because of special physiological conditions obtain special benefit from the consumption of certain substances):

   the food must fulfil the claim and the label must indicate the characteristic which justifies the claim; if specially made for the people concerned, the name must indicate the particular characteristic, the prescribed energy statement must be given and the product must be completely enclosed by its packaging.
2) Claims relating to babies or young children (i.e. a claim that a food is suitable, or has been specially made, for fulfilling the particular nutritional requirements of babies or young children):

   the food must fulfil the claim; if specially made the label must state that it is intended for babies or young children, the prescribed energy statement must be given and the product must be completely enclosed by its packaging.
3) Diabetic claims (i.e. a claim that a food is suitable, or has been specially made, for diabetics):

   detailed conditions are imposed on energy content, fat content, readily absorbable carbohydrate content and, subject to certain statements, restrictions are imposed on labelling and advertising.
4) Slimming claims (i.e. a claim that a food is an aid to slimming or weight control or weight reduction or has a reduced or low energy

4.5 value except that the presence of the words 'low calorie' required by the Soft Drinks Regulations does not constitute such a claim):

the food must be capable of contributing to weight control or weight reduction; it must not consist wholly or mainly of vitamins and/or minerals; it must be labelled with the prescribed energy statement and certain other statements may be required; foods claimed to have a reduced energy value must have energy no more than three-quarters of a similar food with no such claim; foods claimed to have a low energy value should usually have a maximum energy of 167 kJ (40 kcal) per 100 g (or 100 ml) and per normal serving.

5) Medicinal claims (i.e. a claim that a food is capable of preventing, treating or curing human disease but excluding claims made under 1) or 2) above):

the food must have a product licence issued under the Medicines Act 1968.

6) Protein claims (i.e. a claim that a food, other than one intended for babies or young children which satisfies the conditions for 2) above, is a source of protein):

a reasonable daily consumption of the food must contribute at least 12 g of protein; foods claimed to be a rich or excellent source of protein must have at least 20% of their energy value provided by protein and in other cases at least 12%; the label must state the protein content (per 100 g or per 100 ml and, where appropriate, per stated serving).

7) Vitamin and mineral claims (i.e. a claim that a food, other than one intended for babies or young children which satisfies the conditions of 2) above, is a source of vitamins or minerals but excluding certain foods consisting solely of vitamins and/or minerals and certain other substances and excluding mineral claims relating to a low or reduced level of minerals):

claims may only be made with respect to minerals or vitamins in the following table and where

a) the claim is not confined to named vitamins or minerals then, if the food is claimed to be a rich or excellent source of vitamins or minerals, it must contain at least one half of the recommended daily amount (RDA) of two or more of the vitamins or minerals listed in the quantity expected to be consumed in one day or, otherwise, at least one-sixth, or where

b) the claim is confined to named vitamins or minerals, the conditions of a) must apply to each named vitamin or mineral

the label must carry a specified statement of the % RDA in a quantified serving of any vitamin or mineral involved in the claim and the number of servings in any pre-packed foods.

Vitamin or mineral	*To be calculated as*	*Recommended daily amount* (RDA)
Vitamin A	μg retinol or retinol equivalent (where 6 μg beta-carotene or 12 μg other biologically active carotenoid equal 1 μg retinol equivalent)	750 μg
Thiamin (vitamin B_1)	mg thiamine	1.2 mg
Riboflavin (vitamin B_2)	mg riboflavine	1.6 mg
Niacin	mg nicotinic acid, mg nicotinamide or mg niacin equivalent (where 60 mg tryptophan equal 1 mg niacin equivalent)	18 mg
Folic acid	μg total folic acid	300 μg
Vitamin B_{12}	μg cobalamines	2 μg
Vitamin C (ascorbic acid)	mg ascorbic acid or mg dehydroascorbic acid	30 mg
Vitamin D	μg ergocalciferol (vitamin D_2) or μg cholecalciferol (vitamin D_3)	2.5 μg
Calcium	mg calcium	500 mg
Iodine	μg iodine	140 μg
Iron	mg iron	12 mg

8) Polyunsaturated fatty acid claims (i.e. a claim relating to polyunsaturated fatty acids in a food): the food must contain at least 35% fat (by weight); at least 45% of the fatty acids must be polyunsaturated and not more than 25% may be saturated; the claim must also state 'low in saturates' or 'low in saturated fatty acids'; the label must carry a statement giving (per 100 g or 100 ml) the amount of fat or oil, the amount of polyunsaturated fatty acids which are *cis, cis*-methylene interrupted and the amount of saturated fatty acid; the claim must not include any suggestion of benefit to health.

9) Cholesterol claims (i.e. a claim relating to the presence or absence of cholesterol):

   the food must have a maximum of 0.005% cholesterol; a claim under 8) above must also be made which must be in equal or larger sized letters than the cholesterol claim; the claim must not include any suggestion of benefit to health.

10) Energy claims (i.e. a claim that a food provides more energy than another food or is a good source of energy):

    the food must fulfil the claim and carry the prescribed energy statement.

11) Claims which depend on another food (i.e. a claim that a food has a particular value or confers a particular benefit):

    the value or benefit must not be derived wholly or partly from another food.

4.5 *Prescribed energy statement*

Where the energy value is 50 kJ (12 kcal) or more per 100 g (or 100 ml) the statement must contain

a) the energy value in kJ and kcal per 100 g (100 ml) and, where appropriate, per quantified serving, and
b) the amount of carbohydrate, protein and fat contained in each 100 g (or 100 ml) and, where appropriate, per quantified serving.

If the energy value is less than stated above, the statement may be either as given above or a statement that the energy value is less than 50 kJ (12 kcal) per 100 g (or 100 ml).

In calculating the energy value the following conversion factors shall be used:

1 g carbohydrate (expressed as monosaccharides) = 16 kJ (3.75 kcal)
1 g protein = 17 kJ (4 kcal)
1 g alcohol = 29 kJ (7 kcal)
1 g fat = 37 kJ (9 kcal)

In any prescribed energy statement, the value of kJ shall predominate and the value in kcal shall not be printed larger than that for kJ.

Misleading descriptions

a) The following words and descriptions may only be used with the foods indicated in the following table if the foods satisfy the conditions stated:

Words and descriptions	*Conditions of use*
'Butter', or any implied butter content	Chocolate confectionery or sugar confectionery (or part so described) must contain min 4% milk fat. Biscuit a) min 50% of fat is milk fat, and b) min 7% of the biscuit is milk fat.
'Cream' or any implied cream content	Chocolate confectionery or sugar confectionery (or part so described) must contain min 4% milk fat.
'Dietary' or 'dietetic'	The food must a) be specially made for people with a particular metabolic or digestive condition and who obtain special benefit from controlled diets, and b) fulfil the nutritional requirements of the particular people.
The name of a designated fish	Names specified in the Regulations may only be used for the species of fish specified.
Food with an implied flavour	May only be used if the flavour is derived wholly or mainly from the food named, except 'chocolate' may be used where the chocolate flavour is derived wholly or mainly from non-fat cocoa solids.

(*continued*)

Words and descriptions	*Conditions of use*
	In other cases, the word 'flavour' should be used preceded by the name of the food giving the implied flavour. (For soft drinks, the Soft Drinks Regulations apply and should be consulted.)
Pictorial indication to imply a flavour	May only be used if the flavour is derived wholly or mainly from the food indicated in the picture. (For soft drinks, the Soft Drinks Regulations apply and should be consulted.)
'Fresh', 'garden' or 'green'	May not be used for canned or frozen peas which have been dried and soaked before being canned or frozen.
'Milk', or any other word or description with implied milk content	Shall not be used as part of the name of a food which contains the milk of an animal other than a cow, unless: a) the milk is in its normal proportions and the animal name is stated; b) the milk has been processed or treated and both the animal name and the process/treatment are stated; c) the word is used in accordance with other Regulations.
'Milk'	Shall not be used as the name of an ingredient where the ingredient is the milk of an animal other than a cow, unless the animal name is stated and its use complies with all other aspects of the Regulations.
'Starch-reduced'	May only be used if less than 50% (wt, dry matter) of the food is anhydrous carbohydrate and the starch content is substantially less than similar foods not so described.
'Vitamin' or similar description implying vitamin	May only be used if food is one of the vitamins in the table on page 141 or is vitamin B_6, pantothenic acid, biotin, vitamin E or vitamin K.
'Alcohol-free'	May only be used for an alcoholic drink from which alcohol has been extracted if the alcoholic strength by volume is max 0.05%, and the drink is marked with the maximum strength (in % mass or % vol preceded by 'not more than') or an indication that it contains no alcohol.
'Dealcoholised'	May only be used for an alcoholic drink from which the alcohol has been extracted if the alcoholic strength by volume is max 0.5%, and the drink is marked with the maximum strength (in % mass or % vol preceded by 'not more than') or an indication that it contains no alcohol.
'Low alcohol' or similar description	May only be used for an alcoholic drink if the alcoholic strength by volume is max 1.2%, and the drink is marked with the maximum strength (in % vol preceded by 'not more than').

4.5 (*continued*)

Words and descriptions	*Conditions of use*
'Non-alcoholic'	May not be used with a name commonly used for an alcoholic drink, except in the composite name 'non-alcoholic wine' when its use is defined in the section below.
'Shandy'	May only be used for a drink if it is a mixture of beer and lemonade, and has an alcoholic strength by volume of min 0.9%.
'Ginger beer shandy' or 'shandygaff'	May only be used for a drink if it is a mixture of beer and ginger beer, and has an alcoholic strength by volume of min 0.9%.
'Cider shandy'	May only be used for a drink if it is a mixture of cider and lemonade, and has an alcoholic strength by volume of min 0.9%.
'Cider and ginger beer shandy' or 'cider shandygaff'	May only be used for a drink if it is a mixture of cider and ginger beer, and has an alcoholic strength by volume of min 0.9%.
'Tonic wine'	May only be used if accompanied by the clear statement: 'the name "tonic wine" does not imply health giving or medicinal properties'. No recommendation as to consumption or dosage shall be given.
'Sweetened liqueur'	May only be used for a drink if it is a flavoured compounded spirit made sweet and viscous only by carbohydrate sweetening matter
'Vintage'	May only be used for a drink if it is a) brandy, or, b) cider or perry made from fruit harvested in a designated vintage year, and the year is indicated on the label, or c) liqueur wine or wine, obtained by the fermentation in its district of origin of the juice of fresh grapes.
'Scotch whisky', 'Irish whiskey', 'blended Scotch whisky' or 'blended Irish whiskey'	May not be used as the name of a spirit distilled after 1/8/1969 unless it conforms to the definitions in the Finance Act 1969.

b) 'Wine' used in a composite name.The use of the word 'wine' is restricted by EC Regulations. However, it may be used in a composite name in the following cases (so long as no confusion is caused):
i) For a drink which is derived wholly or partly from fruit (other than grapes) or other vegetable, plant or carbohydrate material, the word 'wine' shall be preceded by an indication of the fruit, vegetable, plant or carbohydrate material. Where a mixture of such ingredients is used, only those which characterise the drink need by given.
ii) 'Non-alcoholic wine' may only be used for a drink derived from unfermented grape juice intended exclusively for communion or sacramental use (and labelled as such).

Milk and Milk Products

Regulations: Milk and Milk Products (Protection of Designations) Regulations 1990 (1990/607)
EC Council Regulation 1898/87
EC Commission Decision 88/566

Definition

Milk products products derived exclusively from milk, on the understanding that substances necessary for their manufacture may be added provided that those substances are not used for the purpose of replacing, in whole or in part, any milk constituent.

General points

1) Subject to 2) below, the EC Regulation reserves exclusively for milk products:
   a) the following designations - whey, cream, butter, buttermilk, butteroil, caseins, anhydrous milkfat (AMF), cheese, yoghurt, kephir, koumiss;
   b) designations or names actually used for milk products and used in accordance with the 'name' requirements of the Food Labelling Regulations.
2) The designations given in 1) may be used on products, contrary to 1), where the exact nature of the product is clear from traditional usage and/or when the designations are clearly used to describe a characteristic quality of the product. An indicative list has been published (EC Commission Decision 88/566) which includes the following UK products which are considered to meet this exception: coconut milk; 'cream ..' or 'milk' used in the description of a spiritous drink not containing milk or other milk products or milk or milk product imitations (e.g. cream sherry, milk sherry); cream soda; cream filled biscuits (e.g. custard cream, bourbon cream, raspberry cream biscuits, strawberry cream, etc.); cream crackers; salad cream; creamed coconut and other similar fruit, nut and vegetable products where the term 'creamed' describes the characteristic texture of the product; cream of tartar; cream or creamed soups (e.g. cream of tomato soup, cream of celery, cream of chicken, etc.); horseradish cream; ice-cream; jelly cream; table cream; cocoa butter; shea butter; nut butters (e.g. peanut butter); butter beans; butter puffs; fruit cheese (e.g. lemon cheese, damson cheese).

4.5 Lot Marking

Regulation: Food (Lot Marking) Regulations 1992 (1992/1357)

Definition

Sales unit food in the process of being, or which can reasonably be expected to be, sold as an identifiable unit.

Food which is a sales unit and which has been produced, prepared or packaged as part of a batch (being a batch of sales units produced, prepared or packaged under similar conditions) must meet the 'Lot marking rules' unless subject to the exceptions listed below.

Lot marking rules

1) Each prepacked sales unit must be marked on the prepackaging or label, or, if not prepacked, on the outer container or accompanying commercial document.
2) The mark must be preceded by the letter 'L' (except where it is clearly distinguishable from other indications) and it must identify the appropriate batch from which the sales unit comes.
3) The appropriate mark is determined by the producer, preparer or packer of the batch (being a batch of sales units produced, prepared or packaged under similar conditions).
4) The following are exempt from the requirements: agricultural products when sold to a temporary storage, preparation or packaging station or to a producers' organisation or for collection for immediate integration into an operational preparation or processing system; food which is sold to the ultimate consumer and it is not prepacked, is prepacked for direct sale or is packed at the request of the purchaser; sales units which are marked with an indication of minimum durability or 'use by' date (as required by the labelling regulations, or, even if not required by the labelling regulations, in accordance with the labelling regulations);
   sales units in containers where the area of the largest side is less than 10 sq. cm;
   sales units which are prepacked, sold as an individual portion at a catering establishment for immediate consumption, and are intended as an accompaniment to another food;
   individual portions of edible ice supplied in bulk packaging which has a lot mark;
   sales unit marked or labelled before 1.7.1992;
   until 1.7.1997, re-usable glass bottles with no label, ring or collar.

Food Additives

4.5

Regulation: Food Additives Labelling Regulations 1992 (1992/1978)

Definitions

Food additive such food as comprises material (with or without nutritive value) (a) which is within one of the categories in the following table; (b) which is neither normally consumed as a food in itself nor normally used as a characteristic ingredient of food; (c) which is not a processing aid (see definition), an approved plant or plant product protection substance, a permitted flavouring (see Flavouring Regulations) or a substance added to food as a nutrient; and, (d) the intentional addition of which to other food for a technological purpose in the manufacture, processing, preparation, treatment, packaging, transport or storage of that other food results, or may be reasonably expected to result, in that material or its by-products becoming directly or indirectly a component of that other food.

Processing aid substances (a) which are not consumed as food ingredients by themselves; (b) which are intentionally used in the processing of raw materials, foods or their ingredients, to fulfil technological purposes during treatment or processing into finished products; (c) which are capable of resulting in the unintended but technically unavoidable presence of residues of such substances (or their derivatives) in the finished products; and (d) the residues of which (or as the case may be, of the derivatives of which) do not present any risk to human health and do not have any technological effect on the finished products

Supplementary material material the presence of which in or on the food additive may reasonably be expected to facilitate storage, sale, standardisation, dilution or dissolution of the food additive.

The following are the categories of additives specified in the definition of 'food additives':

Categories of food additives	
Colouring matter	Sweeteners
Antioxidants	Raising agents
Preservatives	Anti-foaming agents
Emulsifiers	Glazing agents
Emulsifying salts	Flour bleaching agents
Thickeners	Flour improvers
Gelling Agents	Firming agents
Stabilisers	Humectants
Flavour modifiers	Enzyme preparations
Acids	Sequestrants
Acidity regulators	Bulking agents
Anti-caking agents	Propellant gas
Modified starch	Packaging gas

4.5 *Labelling Requirements*

1) For consumer sales, the name shall be either the legally specified additive name(s) and E number(s), or, where there are no legal names or numbers, a description sufficiently precise to avoid confusion with other products.
2) The following details must be given:
   a) on the container (in the case of both consumer sales and business sales):
   an ingredients' list giving the names and numbers of the additives (in weight descending order);
   the statement 'for use in food' or 'restricted use in food' or a more specific use statement;
   any special storage conditions;
   any special conditions of use;
   b) on the container (in the case of consumer sales or business sales) or in trade documents (in the case of business sales where the container is marked 'intended for manufacture of foodstuffs and not for retail sale'):
   the details of any supplementary material (in weight descending order);
   any necessary instructions for use;
   a batch or lot identifying mark;
   the name and address of the manufacturer, packer or seller (in the EC);
   c) on the container (for consumer sales only):
   an indication of minimum durability;
   d) for business sales only (on the container or in trade documents where the container is marked 'intended for manufacture of foodstuffs and not for retail sale'):
   where an additive has legally restricted use in food, the proportion of the restricted additive in the material sold or information allowing its legal use.

General point

The Regulations do not apply to an additive which has become a part of other food (i.e. when it is added to other food which comprises of or contains material other than food additives except in the case of the addition of supplementary material).

Organic Foods

Regulations: Organic Products Regulations 1992 (1992/2111)
EC Council Regulation 2092/91
Amendment: EC Commission Regulation 1535/92

Definition
Organic products the following products, where such products bear, or are intended to bear indications referring to organic production methods:

a) unprocessed agricultural crop products and unprocessed animal products;
b) products (intended for human consumption) composed essentially of one or more ingredients of plant origin or ingredients of animal origin.

General points

1) The word 'organic' may only be applied to products which have been obtained in accordance with the requirements of the EC Regulation 2092/91 (unless not applied to agricultural products in foodstuffs or clearly has no connection with the method of production).
2) For products in part a) of the above definition, reference to organic production methods may only be used on products where: the reference clearly relates to a method of agricultural production; the product is produced in the EC (or imported from a third country) in accordance with the requirements of the EC Regulation 2092/91; and, it has been inspected in accordance with the requirements of the EC Regulation 2092/91.
3) For products in part b) of the above definition, reference to organic production methods may only be used on products where: (i) all the ingredients of agricultural origin are obtained in accordance with the specified procedures; and
(ii) the product contains only certain substance of non-agricultural origin; the product (or ingredients) have not been subject to irradiation (or other specified substances); and the preparer is subject to inspection.
4) For products in part b) of the above definition prepared partly from ingredients of agricultural origin which are not obtained in accordance with the specified procedures, reference to organic production methods may only be used on products if: at least 50% of the ingredients of agricultural origin meet the requirements; the product meets the requirement of 3)(ii) above; the reference is only in the ingredient list (in the same colour, size and style as other words and clearly refers to the organic ingredients).
5) Where a product is covered by an inspection scheme and meets certain other criteria (see Regulations) the indication 'Organic Farming - EEC Control System' may be used. No claim may be made to suggest that this indication constitutes a guarantee of superior organoleptic, nutritional or salubrious quality.
6) Inspection procedures for producers are being approved, in the UK, by 'Food from Britain'.

4.6

4.6 Hygiene and health

General

Regulation: Food Hygiene (General) Regulations 1970 (1970/1172)
Amendments: Food Hygiene (Amendment) Regulations 1990 (1990/1431)
Food Hygiene (Amendment) Regulations 1991 (1991/1343)
Food Premises (Registration) Regulations 1991 (1991/2825)
Food Safety (Amendment)(Metrication) Regulations 1992 (1992/2597)
Food Safety (Fishery Products) Regulations 1992 (1992/3163)

Note: For the requirements of these Regulations relating to temperature of storage and distribution, see section on 'Temperature Controls' (page 154).

Definitions

Food business any trade or business for the purposes of which any person engages in the handling of food but does not include the handling of food

a) in the course of any agricultural activity (e.g. horticulture, fruit growing, dairy farming, market gardening, breeding and keeping of livestock);
b) at premises covered by other hygiene regulations (docks, carriers, slaughterhouses, market stalls, delivery vehicles, etc.);
c) on any ship where food is handled for the crew or permanent residents.

Food premises any premises in or from which there is carried on any food business.

Open food food which is not in a container of such materials and so closed as to exclude the risk of contamination, but does not include food mentioned in the following table, wrapped as indicated in the table:

Food	*Mode of wrapping*
Butter, margarine, cooking fat	Any total enclosure of greaseproof paper or foil
Meat, except meat which has been cooked or otherwise prepared for sale by any similar process	Any total wrapping of mutton cloth, hessian, jute, paper or film
Fish	Any total enclosure of greaseproof paper or film
Vegetables	Any box, bag, sack, string container or pliable film pack
Flour confectionery and bakery goods	Any total enclosure
Ice-cream	Any total greaseproof enclosure of paper, foil, film, cardboard, carton, cup or similar wrapping
Ice lollies	As for ice-cream (except for cardboard, carton or cup) but including any bag made of such materials to contain the ice lolly which need not be sealed at the end from which the stick protrudes

Hygiene requirements
Note that establishments and factory vessels subject to the Food Safety (Fishery Products) Regulations 1992 are exempt from Regulations 7,8 and 10–26.

The main relevant Regulations are as follows:

Regulation 6 No food business shall be carried on at any insanitary premises or any premises the condition, situation or construction of which is such that food is exposed to the risk of contamination.

Regulation 7 Articles or equipment with which food comes into contact shall be kept clean and, unless non-returnable, constructed so as to

a) enable them to be thoroughly cleaned,
b) prevent absorption,
c) prevent risk of contamination.

Regulation 8 Food shall not be given out for preparation or packing at any domestic premises (other than those of the person carrying on the business and except shrimps and prawns under specified conditions).

Regulation 9 Anyone handling food shall reasonably protect it from risk of contamination and in particular:

a) should not position the food to involve risk,
b) separate food which is unfit for human consumption,
c) food in a forecourt or yard must be at least 18 ins (from 1.1.1995, 45.5 cms) from the ground unless adequately protected from risk,
d) ensure that open food is adequately covered or screened from possible sources of contamination during delivery or sale,
e) keep animal feed in separate rooms or contained to prevent contamination.

Regulation 10 Personal cleanliness: anyone handling food shall

a) keep as clean as may be reasonably practicable all parts of his person and clothing which are liable to contact food,
b) keep any exposed cut or abrasion covered with a suitable waterproof dressing,
c) refrain from spitting,
d) refrain from smoking while handling open food, or in a room in which there is open food.

Regulation 11 Anyone handling open food (except raw vegetables, liquor or soft drinks) shall wear clean and washable overclothing (exempted are waiters in catering businesses, carriers of unskinned rabbits or hares or unplucked game or poultry subject to other reasonable precautions being taken).

Regulation 12 Anyone handling food shall

a) not carry it with any article or animals in a way that could risk contamination,
b) not use a container or wrapping material which is not clean or which is liable to contaminate the food or use printed wrapping material for

food (other than uncooked vegetables or unskinned rabbits or hares or unplucked game or poultry) unless designed exclusively for wrapping or containing food.

Regulation 13 If anyone handling food is aware that he is suffering from (or a carrier of) any of the following, an appropriate medical officer of health must be informed:
typhoid, paratyphoid, other salmonella infections, amoebic or bacillary dysentery, staphylococcal infection likely to cause food poisoning.

Regulations 14–26 Requirements relating to food premises
These Regulations cover:

a) soil drainage systems,
b) cisterns for supplying water to food rooms,
c) sanitary conveniences,
d) water supply,
e) provision of wash-hand basins,
f) first-aid materials,
g) accommodation for clothing,
h) facilities for washing food and equipment,
i) lighting,
j) ventilation,
k) proximity to sleeping place,
l) cleanliness and repair (including protection from the entry of birds, and any risk of infestation by rats, mice, insects or other pests),
m) provision for refuse removal.

Regulation 27 Temperature controls - see page 154.

Regulations 28–30 Administrative provisions.

Regulations 31–32 The application and modification of these Regulations to ships.

Markets, stalls and delivery vehicles

Regulation: Food Hygiene (Markets, Stalls and Delivery Vehicles) Regulations 1966 (1966/791)

Amendments: Food Hygiene (Markets, Stalls and Delivery Vehicles) (Amendment) Regulations 1966 (1966/1487)
Food Hygiene (Amendment) Regulations 1990 (1990/1431)
Food Hygiene (Amendment) Regulations 1991 (1991/1343)
Food Safety (Fishery Products) Regulations 1992 (1992/3163)

Note: For the requirements of these Regulations relating to temperature of storage and distribution, see section on 'Temperature Controls' (page 154).

Definitions

Market to be construed generally and not as limited to a market held by virtue of a grant from the Crown or of prescription or under statutory authority.

Stall includes any stand, marquee, tent, mobile canteen, vehicle (whether movable or not), vending machine, site or pitch from which food is sold (unless a premises or food room covered by the General Regulations above).

Delivery vehicle a vehicle used for the delivery of food in the course of a trade or business (but not a vehicle falling within the definition of stall).

These Regulations control the hygiene standards of:

a) markets,
b) stalls, and
c) delivery vehicles.

They do not apply to establishments and factory vessels subject to the Food Safety (Fishery Products) Regulations 1992 (1992/3163)

The Regulations are similar to the General Regulations with parts relating to

a) general requirements,
b) requirements for food handlers and the handling of food,
c) requirements for markets, stalls and delivery vehicles.

Docks, carriers etc.

Regulation: Food Hygiene (Docks, Carriers, etc.) Regulations 1960 (1960/1602)
Amendments: Food Hygiene (Amendment) Regulations 1990 (1990/1431)
Food Safety (Fishery Products) Regulations 1992 (1992/3163)

Definition

Docks includes any harbour, moorings, wharf, pier, jetty or other works in or at which food can be shipped or unshipped, any warehouse, transit shed or other premises used in connection therewith for the temporary storage or loading for dispatch of food which is unshipped or to be shipped.

These Regulations control the hygiene standards of any

a) docks, public warehouse, public cold store,
b) any place occupied by a carrier of food (except as regulated by the Food Hygiene (General) Regulations),
c) any premises used for the storage of food (except as regulated by the Food Hygiene (General) Regulations).

Only certain of the provisions apply to establishments and factory vessels subject to the Food Safety (Fishery Products) Regulations 1992 (1992/3163)

The Regulations are similar to the General Regulations with parts relating to

4.6

a) general requirements,
b) requirements of dock workers and food handlers,
c) requirements of premises.

Ships

Regulation: Food Hygiene (Ships) Regulations 1979 (1979/27)

These Regulations provide for a 'closure order' or an 'emergency order' to prevent catering or other retail food business on ships from continuing in business when the appropriate authority considers that there is 'danger to health' or 'imminent risk of danger to health' respectively.

The Regulations are similar to the powers in Sections 21 and 22 of the former Food Act 1984 relating to food premises. See also Sections 31–32 of the Food Hygiene (General) Regulations.

Temperature controls

The following information relates to the temperature at which food can be kept for the purposes of the Food Hygiene (General) Regulations 1970 (the '1970 Regs') and the Food Hygiene (Market, Stalls and Delivery Vehicles) Regulations 1966 (the '1966 Regs'). Full details are in the Food Hygiene (Amendment) Regulations 1990 (1990/1431) as amended by the Food Hygiene (Amendment) Regulations 1991 (1991/1343) and the Food Safety (Fishery Products) Regulations 1992 (1992/3163). Guidance on the Regulations has been published by the Department of Health: 'Guidelines on the Food Hygiene (Amendment) Regulations 1990' and 'Guidelines for the Catering Industry on the Food Hygiene (Amendment) Regulations 1990'.

Definitions

Relevant food unless exempt food (see definition), the following food:

a) soft cheese (cut or whole) ripened by the action of moulds or other micro-organisms;
b) cooked products (whether prepared or requiring further heating or cooking) containing (the 1970 Regs) or comprising or containing (the 1966 Regs) (whether or not the food also includes other raw or partially cooked ingredients):
   meat, fish, eggs (or substitutes for meat, fish or eggs), cheese, cereals, pulses or vegetables;
   cooked and chilled crustaceans or molluscan shellfish products;
c) smoked or cured fish;
d) smoked or cured meat which has been cut or sliced after smoking/curing;
e) desserts containing milk (or milk substitute) with a pH of 4.5 or more;
f) prepared vegetable salads (including those containing fruit)

g) cooked pies and pasties containing meat, fish (or meat/fish substitute) or vegetables and encased in pastry (except where nothing is added after cooking and it is intended for consumption (the 1970 Regs) or sale (1966 Regs) by the day following preparation);
h) cooked sausage rolls (except where it is intended for consumption (the 1970 Regs) or sale (the 1966 Regs) by the day following preparation);
i) uncooked or partly cooked pastry products containing meat or fish (or meat/fish substitute);
j) sandwiches, filled rolls and similar bread products containing: meat, fish, eggs (or substitutes for meat, fish or eggs), soft cheese as in (a) above, or vegetables;
k) cream cakes.

Exempt food   food of the following description:

a) bread, biscuits, cake or pastry which would only otherwise be relevant food because they contain egg or milk introduced into the products before they are baked;
b) ice-cream subject to the Ice-Cream (Heat Treatment, etc.) Regulations;
c) food subjected to processes (including dehydration) which prevents the growth of pathogenic micro-organisms at ambient temperatures;
d) food in hermetically sealed containers and heated so as to prevent the growth of pathogenic micro-organisms at ambient temperatures;
e) uncooked bacon, uncooked ham, dry pasta, dry pudding mixes or dry mixes for making beverages;
f) chocolate or sugar confectionery;
g) milk, and, for the 1966 Regs only, cream, which is not combined with other ingredients.

Specified temperature

a) before 1.4.1993, 8 °C for all relevant food;
b) from 1.4.1993 -
   i) for the high-risk food given below   5 °C
   ii) for all other relevant food   8 °C

'High risk' food

a) cheeses which have been cut or otherwise separated from the whole cheese from which they were removed;
b) relevant food in (b) in the definition above which is ready for consumption (i.e. no cooking or reheating is necessary);
c) smoked or cured fish;
d) smoked or cured meat which has been cut or sliced after smoking/curing;
e) sandwiches, filled rolls and similar bread products containing any of the foods in (a)–(d) (unless to be sold within 24 hours of preparation).

4.6

General points - the 1970 Regs

1) The following specific exemptions are listed:
   a) food for sale within 2 hours of preparation which is either heated and maintained at between the relevant temperature and 63 °C or is reheated to at least 63 °C at any time prior to sale
   b) food for sale within 4 hours of preparation and not subject to any heating
   c) a reasonably necessary quantity of food displayed (for a maximum of 4 hours) on catering premises for
   – indicating to prospective purchasers nature of food for sale and consumption on the premises, or
   – service to a purchaser for consumption on the premises
2) More specific exemptions provide for food which is in the process of service or which is between 63 °C and the specified temperature and is being heated or cooled without any unavoidable delay to bring it to the right temperature.
3) A tolerance of 2 °C (for up to 2 hours) is permitted above the specified temperature where this is due to: a process of preparation, defrosting of equipment, temporary breakdown of equipment, movement of the food from one part of the premises to another, or, some other unavoidable reason.

General points - the 1966 Regs

1) For food in any stall or market premises, the following exemptions apply:
   a) if it is not below the specified temperature or above 63 °C, it shall be cooled or heated without delay after arrival or completion of preparation;
   b) kept below the specified temperature or above 63 °C unless it is being cooled or heated (without delay) from one of these temperatures to the other.
2) For food in a delivery vehicle used for making local deliveries, it must be kept below the specified temperature or above 63 °C (except if it is in a goods vehicle of max 7.5 tonnes gross weight and if the specified temperature is 5 °C, it may be kept in the vehicle at max 8 °C for up to 12 hours).
3) The requirements of 1) and 2) do not apply where the food is exempted. Exemptions are the same as those in 1) of 'General Points - the 1970 Regs' given above.
4) A tolerance of 2 °C (for up to 2 hours) is permitted above the specified temperature where this is due to: a process of preparation, defrosting of equipment, temporary breakdown of equipment, movement of the food from one part of the premises, stall or vehicle to another, or, some other unavoidable reason.

Milk and dairies

4.6

Regulation: Milk and Dairies (General) Regulations 1959 (1959/277)
Amendments: Milk and Dairies (Semi-skimmed and Skimmed Milk) (Heat Treatment and Labelling) Regulations 1973 (1973/1064)
Milk and Dairies (General) (Amendment) Regulations 1977 (1977/171)
Milk and Dairies (General) (Amendment) Regulations 1979 (1979/1567)
Food Safety Act 1990 (Consequential Modifications)(England and Wales) Order 1990 (1990/2486)
Milk and Dairies (Standardisation and Importation) Regulations 1992 (1992/3143)

Note: In these Regulations milk includes cream, skimmed milk, standardised whole milk and non-standardised whole milk. Milk-based drinks are controlled by the Food Hygiene (General) Regulations and the special requirements of the Milk-based Drinks (Hygiene and Heat Treatment) Regulations.

The following are the main Parts of these Regulations:

Part II Requires the registration of all dairy farms or dairy farmers; registration may be withdrawn if the conditions existing do not comply with these Regulations (subject to appeal to a tribunal).

Part III Requires the registration of all dairies (other than dairy farms) and of distributors of milk.

Part IV Inspection and health of cattle. Includes a prohibition on the sale or use of milk from certain diseased cows – diseases are specified in the Regulations and include tuberculosis.

Part V General provision relating to buildings and water supplies.

Part VI Provisions relating to the production, treatment, handling and storage of milk. Includes the requirements that, after milking, milk should be rapidly cooled to a maximum of 10 °C, or if the water supply is above 7 °C, then to a maximum of 3 °C above water supply temperature (subject to exemptions for heat treatment, rapid use, rapid delivery to a distributor, etc.).

Part VII Provisions relating to the infection of milk. If anyone having access to milk has a notifiable disease, the medical officer of health is to be informed who then has power to prevent that person having access to milk. If a medical officer of health suspects that a milk supply has caused a disease or is infected, he can prevent its use.

Part VIII General provisions for protecting milk against contamination or infection. These provisions cover:

a) rooms in which milk is handled
   position, drainage, articles in a milk room, protection from contamination, use of milk room,
b) people having access to milk
   clothing, all cuts to be covered, no smoking or spitting, access to personal cleaning facilities and first aid,

4.6 c) no swine or poultry to have access to milk rooms,
d) use of milk churns.

Part IX Provisions relating to cleansing and storage of vessels, utensils and appliances. All vessels to be thoroughly cleaned after use. In particular, any milk tanker, vessel or appliance should be rinsed and washed (with or without detergents) and shall be scalded with boiling water or steam or otherwise effectively cleansed with an approved cleansing agent.

Part X Conveyance and distribution of milk. Controls on the handling of milk during distribution. These provisions include:

a) No vessel containing milk may be opened and no milk may be transferred between vessels except at registered premises (except under certain specified conditions including final retail sale when not in a bottle or carton), and
b) Every bottle or carton of milk (except imported cream) must be filled and closed on registered premises (but see also exception under Imported Milk).

Meat

Regulation: Fresh Meat (Hygiene and Inspection) Regulations 1992 (1992/2037)

The following are the main Parts of these Regulations:

Part II Licensing. Every slaughterhouse, cutting premises, cold store, farmed game handling facility or a farmed game processing facility has to be licensed by the Minister. Licences are only issued subject to various detailed standards being met (set out in detail in the Schedules to the Regulations). These are assessed by the local authority who make a recommendation to the Minister.

Part III Supervision and control of premises. All local authorities must appoint an official veterinary surgeon to act in the examination and seizure of meat, to provide the health certification and to act in various other matters. Inspectors may be appointed as required

Part IV Conditions for the marketing of fresh meat. Places restrictions on the sale of fresh meat including requirements that it comes from licensed premises, that it has been subjected to specified inspection, it has been given a health mark, etc..

Part V Admission to and detention in slaughterhouses and farmed game processing facilities of animals and carcases. Covers requirements when (a) an animal is known to be, or suspected of being, diseased or injured, and
(b) the dressing of any slaughtered and bled animal brought to a slaughterhouse.

Part VI Administration, penalties and enforcement. Specifies the duties of occupiers of licensed premises including the need to keep specified records.

Poultry

4.6

Regulation: Poultry Meat (Hygiene) Regulations 1976 (1976/1209)
Amendments: Poultry Meat (Hygiene) (Amendment) Regulations 1979 (1979/693)
Poultry Meat (Hygiene) (Amendment) Regulations 1981 (1981/1168)
Poultry Meat (Hygiene) (Amendment) Regulations 1992 (1992/2036)

1) Unless imported in accordance with the Imported Food Regulations, no person shall sell for human consumption any poultry meat (from domestic fowls, turkeys, guinea fowls, ducks or geese) unless the relevant part of 2) or 3) apply.
2) For carcases and offal:
   a) obtained from a licensed slaughterhouse,
   b) the poultry has been subject to specified ante-mortem health inspection,
   c) prepared under specified hygienic conditions (including specified requirements relating to immersion chilling),
   d) it has been subject to specified post-mortem health inspection,
   e) it has been given a specified health marking,
   f) it has been stored, packed and transported under specified conditions (which includes a maximum temperature of 4 °C), unless (subject to specified limitations) it is sold direct from the producer to the consumer.
3) For parts of carcase or boned poultry meat:
   a) obtained from licensed cutting premises,
   b) cut under specified hygienic conditions,
   c) obtained from poultry slaughtered in UK in accordance with these Regulations or from EC or from a third country in accordance with Community requirements,
   d) stored and supervised under specified conditions,
   e) health marked as specified,
   f) packed and transported under specified conditions (which includes a maximum temperature of 4 °C).
4) No person shall sell as fresh poultry meat, meat which has been treated with: hydrogen peroxide or other bleaching substance, natural or artificial colouring matter, antibiotics, preservatives or tenderisers.
5) Details are given of those diseases and medical conditions which would render poultry or poultry meat unfit for human consumption.
6) The following are not to be used for human consumption: head (except tongue), trachea, lungs, oesophagus, crop, intestine, gall-bladder.
7) Licences are issued by the Minister after considering any representations by the local authority.
8) The local authority appoints the official veterinary surgeon (who supervises the plant) and any necessary additional inspectors (who

4.6 work under the official veterinary surgeon) or suitably qualified officer (to assist the official veterinary surgeon).

Fishery Products

Regulations: Food Safety (Fishery Products) Regulations 1992 (1992/3163)
Food Safety (Fishery Products)(Derogations) Regulations 1992 (1992/1507)
Food Safety (Fishery Products on Fishing Vessels) Regulations 1992 (1992/3165)

Definitions

Fishery products all seawater or freshwater animals or parts thereof, including their roes but excluding aquatic mammals, frogs and aquatic animals covered by Community Acts other than the Council Directive relating to fishery products.

Aquaculture products

a) all fishery products born or raised in controlled conditions until placed on the market as a foodstuff, and
b) all seawater fish, freshwater fish or crustaceans caught in their natural environment when juvenile and kept until they reach the desired commercial size for human consumption, other than fish or crustaceans of commercial size caught in their natural environment and kept alive to be sold at a later date, if they are merely kept alive without any attempt being made to increase their size or weight.

Place on the market (in relation to fishery products for human consumption) the holding for sale, exposing for sale, displaying for sale, offering for sale, selling, consigning, delivering or any other associated activity of marketing but not either a sale to a final consumer or a sale by a fisherman of a small quantity within a local market under specified circumstances (see Regulations).

General

1) Any fishery product caught in their natural environment may only be placed on the market if specified conditions are met (but see 6 below). These include (see Regulations for details):
   a) caught and subject to certain operations in a way which meets EC fishing vessel requirements;
   b) if handled in a factory vessel, it meets specified conditions;
   c) on landing, handling meets specified conditions;
   d) handled, packaged, prepared, processed, frozen, defrosted or stored hygienically in approved establishments;
   e) subject to specified health control and monitoring;
   f) appropriately packaged;
   g) given an identification mark;
   h) stored and transported under specified conditions.
2) Any aquaculture product may only be placed on the market if specified conditions are met. These include slaughtering under appropriate

conditions of hygiene (including preventing soiling with earth, slime or faeces), chilling if not processed immediately, and the provisions of 1) e) – g) above.

3) Any processed bivalve mollusc or other shellfish may only be placed on the market if, prior to processing, they meet the requirements of the Food Safety (Live Bivalve Molluscs and Other Shellfish) Regulations and they satisfy the requirements of 1) e) – g) above.
4) Any fishery product to be placed on the market live must be kept under conditions most suitable for its survival.
5) The following may not be placed on the market:
   a) poisonous fish of the following species: *Tetraodontidae*, *Molidae*, *Diodontidae* or *Canthigasteridae*;
   b) fishery products containing biotoxins including ciguatera or muscle-paralysing toxins.
6) Certain factory vessels, establishments, auction markets or wholesale markets which were operating before 31.12.1991, could apply for limited derogations from the requirements relating to equipment and structures. Full details are given in the Regulations relating to derogations. Such derogations are only permitted until 31.12.1995.
7) Hygiene conditions are also specified for fishing vessels which are designed and equipped to preserve fishery products on board for more than 24 hours. Full details are given in the Regulations relating to fishing vessels.

Bivalve molluscs/shellfish

Regulations: Food Safety (Live Bivalve Molluscs and Other Shellfish) Regulations 1992 (1992/3164)
Food Safety (Live Bivalve Molluscs)(Derogations) Regulations 1992 (1992/1508)

Definitions

Bivalve molluscs   filter-feeding lamellibranch molluscs.

Other shellfish   live echinoderms, tunicates and marine gastropods.

Production area   any sea, esturine or lagoon area containing either natural deposits of bivalve molluscs or, sites used for the cultivation of bivalve molluscs, including relaying areas, from which live bivalve molluscs are taken.

Relaying area   any area of sea, estuary or lagoon within boundaries clearly marked and indicated by buoys, posts or any other fixed means and which is used exclusively for the natural purification of live bivalve molluscs.

Purification centre   an establishment with tanks fed by naturally clean sea water or sea water that has been cleaned by appropriate treatment, in which live bivalve molluscs are placed for the time necessary to remove microbiological contamination, so making them fit for human consumption.

4.6 Dispatch centre any on-shore or off-shore installation for the reception, conditioning, washing, cleaning, grading or wrapping of either live bivalve molluscs or other shellfish, or both, for human consumption.

General points

1) No live bivalve molluscs shall be placed on the market for human consumption unless specified conditions are met (but see 5) and 6) below). These include (see Regulations for details):
a) they originate from a designated bivalve production area (see 4) below);
b) they have been harvested from such a production area, kept and transported to an approved dispatch centre, approved purification centre, approved relaying area or approved processing plant in accordance with specified requirements;
c) they have, where necessary, been relaid;
d) they have been handled hygienically and where appropriate they have been purified or been subject to intensive purification at an approved purification centre;
e) they meet specified criteria making them fit for human consumption (see 3));
f) any wrapping is as specified;
g) they have been stored and transported under satisfactory conditions of hygiene and in particular certain specified requirements;
h) they have a specified healthmark.
2) No other shellfish shall be placed on the market for human consumption unless specified conditions are met (but see 5) and 6) below). These include (see Regulations for details):
a) after harvesting they have been transported to an approved dispatch centre or approved processing plant;
b) they have been handled hygienically;
c) they meet the same criteria as in 1) e) to h) above.
3) Bivalve molluscs and other shellfish are considered as acceptable for human consumption if they meet the following standards:
a) possession of visual characteristics associated with freshness and viability;
b) less than 300 faecal coliforms or 230 *E. coli* per 100 g of mollusc flesh and intravalvular fluid;
c) salmonella free in 25 g of mollusc flesh;
d) no toxic or objectionable compounds in quantities such that the calculated dietary intake exceeds the permissible daily intake or that impairs the taste;
e) total Paralytic Shellfish Poison (in edible parts) not to exceed 80 micrograms per 100 g of mollusc flesh;
f) absence of Diarrhetic-Shellfish Poison.

4) Bivalve mollusc production areas, when designated, are classified as follows:
   Class A live bivalve molluscs meet the standards in 2).
   Class B prior to relaying or treatment, 90% of live bivalve molluscs have either a) max 6000 faecal coliforms per 100 g flesh, or b) max 4600 *E. coli* per 100 g flesh.
   Class C max 60 000 faecal coliforms per 100 g flesh.
   Live bivalve molluscs from Class B or C areas must be subject to specified treatment or processing before consumption.
5) Certain dispatch centres or purification centres which were operating before 31.12.1991, could apply for limited derogations from the requirements relating to equipment and structures. Full details are given in the Regulations relating to derogations. Such derogations are only permitted until 31.12.1995.
6) Provision is made for the exception from certain controls of coastal fishermen selling specified small quantities of any live bivalve molluscs or other shellfish to a retailer or final consumer (see Regulations).

Imported food

A General

Regulation: Imported Food Regulations 1984 (1984/1918)

The following are the main Parts of these Regulations:

1) No person shall import any food (or food containing such food) intended for sale for human consumption which:
   a) has been rendered injurious to health,
   b) has been examined and found not to be fit for human consumption, or
   c) is otherwise unfit, unsound or unwholesome.
2) If food is found on examination not to comply with the standards in 1), action may be taken as if the food was failing to comply with food safety requirements and appropriate action taken (as provided for in Section 9 of the Food Safety Act 1990).
3) For fresh meat or a meat product (i.e. products prepared from fresh meat but excluding: vitamin concentrates containing meat, pharmaceutical products containing meat, gelatin, rennet, meat products of which meat is not a principal ingredient and which do not contain fragments of meat) additional provisions apply including:
   a) procedures for obtaining examination by an independent veterinary expert when an authorised officer believes the food does not comply (only where relevant EC Directives apply);
   b) a requirement that any fresh meat, meat product (as defined above) or bulk lard bears a specified and recognised health mark (as detailed in the Regulations);

4.6

c) specified wrapping, packing and transporting requirements which include the following maximum temperatures:
i) rabbit meat, hare meat, poultry meat, rabbit offals, hare offals and poultry offals +4 °C
ii) carcasses and cuts not listed in i) +7 °C (chilled) −12 °C (frozen)
iii) offals not listed in i) +3 °C
iv) meat products temperature as specified on label;
d) a requirement that any fresh meat which is derived from domestic bovine animals (including buffalo), swine, sheep, goats, solipeds or poultry or any meat product incorporating such meat must be accompanied by a valid health certificate as defined by the Regulations except that the following meat products are exempt:

meat extract, meat consommé and stock, meat sauces and similar products not containing fragments of meat; whole, broken or crushed bones, meat peptones, meat powder, pork-rind powder, blood plasma, dried blood, dried blood plasma; cellular proteins, bone extracts and similar products; fats melted down from animal tissues; stomachs, bladders and intestines, cleaned and bleached, salted or dried; products containing fragments of meat or meat product not exceeding 10% of the total weight of the final product ready for use.

B Animal and poultry products

Regulation: Importation of Animal Products and Poultry Products Order 1980 (1980/14)
Amendments: Importation of Animal Products and Poultry Products (Amendment) Order 1980 (1980/1934)
Importation of Animal Products and Poultry Products (Amendment) Order 1981 (1981/1238)
Importation of Animal Products and Poultry Products (Amendment) Order 1982 (1982/948)

The landing of any animal product or poultry product from a place outside Great Britain is prohibited except under the authority of a licence. The licence may be general or specific and may contain conditions which are considered necessary to prevent the spreading of disease into or within Great Britain.

The following food products are excluded from these requirements: butter, cheese, condensed milk, evaporated milk, gelatin, meat extract, oils and waxes of animal origin, soup stock, sterilised cream, yogurt.

Imported milk

Regulation: Importation of Milk Regulations 1988 (1988/1803)
Amendment: Milk and Dairies (Standardisation and Importation) Regulations 1992 (1992/3143)

Definitions

Milk means cows' milk and includes cream but not dried or condensed milk.

Raw milk/cream milk/cream which has not been heated beyond 40°C or undergone any treatment that has an equivalent effect.

Thermised milk raw milk which has been heated for at least 15 seconds at a temperature between 57°C and 68°C and shows a positive reaction to the phosphatase test.

Specified drinking milk the following categories of drinking milk: semi-skimmed milk, skimmed milk, standardised whole milk and non-standardised whole milk.

No person shall import milk intended for human consumption unless all the following apply:

a) it is specified drinking milk, raw milk, thermised milk, cream, milk-based drink or bulk milk;
b) unless it is raw milk, thermised milk or raw cream, it has been pasteurised, sterilised or heat treated by the UHT method (see Table below);
c) it has been produced in and imported from an EC Member State,
d) it is accompanied by a certificate (of the form published in *The London Gazette*),
e) it is fit for human consumption and is not injurious to human health,
f) in the case of pasteurised milk, it is imported as pre-packaged milk or in a sealed tanker with a water-tight closure; in the case of sterilised milk, it is imported in the hermetically sealed container in which it was sterilised; in the case of UHT milk, it is imported in opaque containers in which it was packaged aseptically immediately after heat-treatment.

	Heat Treatment	
	Temperature (°C)	*Time*
Pasteurised (1)		
specified drinking milk or bulk milk (2)	min 71.7	min 15 seconds
cream or milk-based drink	min 72	min 15 seconds
Ultra Heat Treated (UHT) (3)		
specified drinking milk or bulk milk	min 135	min 1 second
cream or milk-based drink (1)	min 140	min 2 seconds
Sterilised (4)	min 108	min 45 minutes

Notes:

(1) Other time/temperature combinations are allowed if they have equivalent effect
(2) Product to be immediately cooled to a maximum of 6°C
(3) Product to be packaged aseptically in opaque containers
(4) Product to be cooled as soon as practicable

4.6 *General points*

1) Permitted imported cream and milk-based drinks are exempt from domestic heat treatment requirements.
2) Containers of permitted imported pre-packaged milk do not have to be filled and closed on registered premises.
3) Permitted imported milk is exempt from the requirements of the Imported Food Regulations.
4) Labelling is controlled by reference to certain provisions applied by the Milk and Dairies (Semi-skimmed and Skimmed Milk): (Heat Treatment and Labelling Regulations 1988) by extending them, for the purposes of permitted imported milk, to apply to 'milk' rather than 'semi-skimmed milk and skimmed milk'.

Perishable foods (international)

Regulation: International Carriage of Perishable Foodstuffs Regulations 1985 (1985/1071)
Amendments: International Carriage of Perishable Foodstuffs (Amendment) Regulations 1987 (1987/1066)
International Carriage of Perishable Foodstuffs (Amendment) Regulations 1989 (1989/1185)
International Carriage of Perishable Foodstuffs (Amendment) Regulations 1992 (1992/2682)

The Regulations govern the international transport of perishable foodstuffs by sea crossings of less than 150 kilometres.

The following, taken from the Annexes 2 and 3 of 'ATP' (see page 20), are the maximum temperatures permitted during carriage or unloading:

1) Quick (deep)-frozen food	
Concentrated fruit juice	−20 °C
All other quick (deep)-frozen food	−18 °C
2) Frozen food	
Ice-cream, concentrated fruit juice	−20 °C
Fish	−18 °C
Butter and other fats	−14 °C
Red offal, egg yolks, poultry and game	−12 °C
All other frozen food	−10 °C
3) Chilled foods	
Red offal	3 °C (1)
Butter	6 °C
Game	4 °C
Milk (raw or pasteurised) in tanks for immediate consumption	4 °C (1)
Industrial milk	6 °C (1)
Dairy products (yogurt, kefir, cream and fresh cheese) (2)	4 °C (1)

(*continued*)

Fish, molluscs and crustaceans (3)	(4)
Meat products (5)	6 °C
Meat (other than red offal)	7 °C
Poultry and rabbits	4 °C

Notes:
(1) Carriage should not exceed 48 hours
(2) Fresh cheese means a non-ripened (non-matured) cheese which is ready for consumption shortly after manufacture and which has a limited conservation period
(3) Other than smoked, salted, dried or live fish, live molluscs and live crustaceans
(4) Must always be carried in melting ice
(5) Except for products stabilised by salting, smoking, drying or sterilisation

4.7

4.7 Weights and measures

Prescribed weights and quantities

Order: Weights and Measures Act 1963 (Miscellaneous Foods) Order 1988 (1988/2040)
Amendments: Weights and Measures Act 1963 (Various Foods) (Amendment) Order 1990 (1990/1550)

Given below are details of the prescribed weights and quantities for pre-packed food and drink (for beer, cider, wine and intoxicating liquor, see Order for details). Certain exemptions may be allowed for certain packages (e.g. several small packets in an outer wrapping). The Orders should be consulted for full details.

The Order also provides details of foods which

a) should be prepacked only if marked with an indication of quantity either by net weight or by capacity measurement,
b) shall be pre-packed only if the container is marked with an indication of quantity by number, and,
c) exemptions to these requirements. Check Order for details.

Biscuits and shortbread:
includes wafers (except when not cream-filled), rusks, crispbreads, extruded flatbread, oatcakes and matzos (except when produced and packed on premises where sold), except when 85 g or less, more than 10 kg
100 g, 125 g, 150 g, 200 g, 250 g, 300 g or a multiple of 100 g
Grain and farinaceous products:
barley kernels, pearl barley, rice (including ground rice and rice flakes), sago, semolina, and tapioca, except when 75 g or less, more than 10 kg
125 g, 250 g, 375 g, 500 g or a multiple of 500 g.
Bread:
whole loaves of bread in any form (except breadcrumbs) including fancy loaves, milk loaves, rolls and baps and sliced pre-packed bread, except when 300 g or less
400 g or a multiple of 400 g.
Cereal breakfast foods:
in flake form, (but not cereal biscuit breakfast foods) except when 50 g or less, more than 10 kg
125 g, 250 g, 375 g, 500 g, 750 g, 1 kg, 1.5 kg, or a multiple of 1 kg.
Cocoa and chocolate products:

a) all cocoa products (including drinking chocolate) except when less than 50 g, more than 1 kg
50 g, 75 g, 125 g, 250 g, 500 g, 750 g, 1 kg.
b) the following chocolate in bar or tablet form: plain, gianduja nut, milk, gianduja nut milk, white, filled, cream, skimmed milk, except when less than 50 g, more than 500 g
85 g, 100 g, 125 g, 150 g, 200 g, 250 g, 300 g, 400 g, 500 g.

Coffee, coffee mixtures and coffee bags:
(for coffee bags, the weight relates to the contents) except when less than 25 g, more than 5 kg
2 oz, 4 oz, 8 oz, 12 oz, 1 lb, $1\frac{1}{2}$ lb or a multiple of 1 lb,
or 75 g, 125 g, 250 g, 500 g, 750 g, 1 kg or a multiple of 500 g.

Coffee extracts and chicory extracts:
consisting of solid and paste coffee and chicory products except when 25 g or less, more than 10 kg
50 g, 100 g, 200 g, 250 g (for mixtures of coffee extracts and chicory extracts only), 300 g (for coffee extracts only), 500 g, 750 g, 1 kg, 1.5 kg, 2 kg, 2.5 kg, 3 kg or a multiple of 1 kg.

Dried fruits:
apples (and apple rings), apricots, currants, dates, figs, muscatels, nectarines, peaches, pears (and pear rings), prunes, raisins, sultanas and dried fruit salad except when 75 g or less, more than 10 kg
125 g, 250 g, 375 g, 500 g, 1 kg, 1.5 kg, 7.5 kg or a multiple of 1 kg.

Dried vegetables:
beans, lentils, peas (includes split peas) except when 100 g or less, more than 10 kg
125 g, 250 g, 375 g, 500 g, 1 kg, 1.5 kg, 7.5 kg or a multiple of 1 kg.

Edible fats:
a) butter, margarine, butter/margarine mixtures and low fat spreads except when 25 g or less, more than 10 kg, and
b) dripping and shredded suet, lard and compound cooking fats (and substitutes therefor), and solidified edible oil (except in gel form) except when less than 5 g, more than 10 kg,

50 g, 125 g, 250 g, 500 g or a multiple of 500 g up to 4 kg, or a multiple of 1 kg from 4 kg to 10 kg.

Flour and flour products:
flour of bean, maize, pea, rice, rye, soya bean, wheat, and cake flour (except cake or sponge mixtures), cornflour (except blancmange or custard powders) and self-raising flour except when 50 g or less, more than 10 kg
125 g, 250 g, 500 g or a multiple of 500 g (except for cornflour add 375 g, 750 g).

Honey:
all honey (except chunk honey and comb honey) except when less than 50 g
2 oz, 4 oz, 8 oz, 12 oz, 1 lb, $1\frac{1}{2}$ lb or a multiple of 1 lb.

Jam, marmalade and jelly preserves:
(except diabetic jam and marmalade) except when less than 50 g
2 oz, 4 oz, 8 oz, 12 oz, 1 lb, $1\frac{1}{2}$ lb or a multiple of 1 lb.

Milk:
except when 50 ml or less (except for vending machine sales satisfying specified conditions – $\frac{1}{2}$ pt),

$\frac{1}{3}$ pt, $\frac{1}{2}$ pt and multiples of $\frac{1}{2}$ pt,
or 200 ml, 250 ml, 500 ml, 750 ml, 1 l, 2 l or thereafter a multiple of 500 ml.

Molasses, syrup and treacle:
except when less than 50 g
2 oz, 4 oz, 8 oz, 12 oz, 1 lb, 1½ lb or a multiple of 1 lb.

Oat products:
namely flour of oats, oatflakes and oatmeal except when 50 g or less, more than 10 kg
125 g, 250 g, 375 g, 500 g, 750 g, 1 kg, 1.5 kg or a multiple of 1 kg

Pasta:
except when 50 g or less
125 g, 250 g, 375 g, 500 g or a multiple of 500 g.

Potatoes:
a) for prepacked potatoes except when less than 5 g, more than 25 kg
8 oz, 12 oz, 1 lb, 1½ lb or a multiple of 1 lb,
or 500 g, 1 kg, 1.5 kg, 2 kg, 2.5 kg or a multiple of 2.5 kg up to 15 kg and then 20 kg, 25 kg,
b) for potatoes 175 g or over each, they may be sold by number (with a statement of the minimum weight of each potato).

Salt:
except when 100 g or less
125 g, 250 g, 500 g, 750 g, 1 kg, 1.5 kg or a multiple of 1 kg up to 10 kg, 12.5 kg, 25 kg, 50 kg.

Sugar:
except when 100 g or less, more than 5 kg
125 g, 250 g, 500 g, 750 g, 1 kg, 1.5 kg, 2 kg, 2.5 kg, 3 kg, 4 kg, 5 kg.

Tea:
includes tea sold in tea bags but excludes instant tea except when 25 g or less, more than 5 kg
50 g, 125 g, 250 g, 500 g, 750 g, 1 kg, 1.5 kg, 2 kg, 2.5 kg, 3 kg, 4 kg, 5 kg
(except for tea, other than tea in a tea bag, packed in tins or glass or wooden containers, add 100 g, 200 g, 300 g)

Average weights

Regulation: Weights and Measures (Packaged Goods) Regulations 1986 (1986/2049)
Amendments: Weights and Measures (Quantity Marking and Abbreviations of Units) Regulations 1987 (1987/1538)
Weights and Measures (Packaged Goods)(Amendment) Regulations 1992 (1992/1580)

These Regulations provide the full details of the procedures to be followed to satisfy the requirements contained in Part V of the Weights and Measures Act 1985. It is impossible to summarise all aspects of the detailed

Regulations and packers and importers are advised to consult the Regulations or the 'Code of Practical Guidance for Packers and Importers' published by HMSO and issued under the Act.

Products covered by the average system

The Regulations specify that for most food products (including natural mineral waters) packed to a predetermined constant quantity with a declared weight of between 5 g–10 kg (5 ml–10 l) the average weight system will be used and that the products should conform to the Regulations. Outside these specified limits products should be packed to a minimum weight system.

The following products have prescribed limits different from those given above except when marked with the 'e' mark and packed to satisfy the requirements of 'e' marked goods:

Biscuits (includes wafers, rusks, crispbreads, extruded flatbread, oatcakes and matzos) and shortbread (except as specified below) 50 g–10 kg

Bread (as defined under Prescribed Weights) in single loaf form 300 g–10 kg (per loaf)

Cheese of the following types: processed cheese, cheese spread, cottage cheese and the following natural cheese types – Caerphilly, Cheddar, Cheshire, Derby, Double Gloucester, Dunlop, Edam, Gouda, Lancashire, Leicestershire and Wensleydale 25 g–10 kg

Cocoa products and chocolate products 50 g–10 kg

Edible fats as follows: butter, margarine, butter/margarine mixtures and low fat spreads, dripping or shredded suet, lard and compound cooking fat and substitutes, solidified edible oil (except in gel form) 5 g–20 kg

Herbs and spices 25 g–4 kg

Potato crisps and other similar snack foods 25 g–10 kg

Poultry (or any part of poultry) of any description or food consisting substantially of poultry 5 g–20 kg

Sugar 50 g–10 kg

Sugar confectionery and chocolate confectionery (except as specified below) 50 g–10 kg

Alcoholic beverages 5 ml–5 l

Edible oil in liquid or gel form 5 ml–20 l

Single portion vending machine beverage packs (to include any beverage mentioned below) 25 g–10 kg or 25 ml–10 l

Single portion catering packs (to include any foods mentioned below) 25 g–10 kg or 25 ml–10 l

The following products are excluded from the average weight system:

Bath chaps, meat pies, meat puddings and sausage rolls

Single cooked sausages in natural casings weighing less than 500 g

Sausage meat products other than in sausage form weighing less than 500 g

Poultry pies, fish pies

4.7 Cheese (except as specified above)
Flour confectionery (except when consisting of or including uncooked pastry or shortbread) including bun loaves, fruit loaves, malt loaves and fruited malt loaves
Fresh fruit and vegetables
Ice lollies, water ices and freeze drinks, ice-cream
Single toffee apples
Soft drinks in a syphon
Sugar confectionery and chocolate confectionery of the following types: Easter eggs, figurines of sugar or of chocolate, rock or barley sugar in stick or novelty form, or a collection of these articles
Shortbread in a piece or pieces each weighing 200 g or more
Biscuits in packs weighing less than 100 g sold on the premises on which they are packed.

Three rules for packers

The primary duty of a packer or importer is to ensure that an Inspector's reference test is passed. He can do this by ensuring that his packages comply with three rules:

1) The actual contents of the packages shall be not less, on average, than the nominal quantity (i.e. the weight or volume declared).
2) Not more than 2.5% of the packages may be below the nominal quantity (a negative error) by an amount larger than the Tolerable Negative Error (TNE) specified for the nominal quantity. Packages below this weight are known as 'non-standard'.
3) No package may have a negative error larger than twice the TNE specified. Packages below this weight are known as 'inadequate'. It is generally accepted in the Code of Guidance that in practice this rule will be satisfied if no more than one package in 10 000 is likely to be inadequate (i.e. 0.01%).

The following table gives the Specified Tolerable Negative Errors for different Nominal Quantities:

Nominal quantity (g or ml)	*Tolerable negative error*	
	As % of nominal quantity (1)	g or ml
5–50	9	–
50–100	–	4.5
100–200	4.5	–
200–300	–	9
300–500	3	–
500-1000	–	1.5
1000–10 000	1.5	–
10 000–15 000	–	150
Above 15 000	1	–

Note: (1) To be rounded up to nearest $\frac{1}{10}$ g or ml

Details and records of checks that are conducted to satisfy the Three Rules for Packers must be kept for 12 months.

Use of the 'e' mark

The 'e' mark (shown in the figure) may only be used when the nominal quantity is in the range 5g–10 kg (or 5 ml–10 l). The mark is not obligatory but when used is a guarantee, recognised throughout the EC, that the goods to which it is applied have been packed in accordance with the relevant EC Directive.

However, when used, packers must notify the relevant authorities of their use of the 'e' mark before the end of the day on which the packages are marked. An inspector may give a notice to a packer relieving him of this requirement where the 'e' mark is used regularly or frequently. The following cases should be considered:

1) Product packed in the UK for internal use only: no benefit is gained by using the 'e' mark unless the product falls outside the range of weight or volume specified in the Regulations for that product, yet is still within the 5 g–10 kg (or 5 ml–10 l) range of the EC Directive. In this special case it would allow the packages to be packed to the average system.
2) Product packed in the UK for export to the EC: guarantees that products meet the EC Directive.
3) Imported goods:
   a) from EC use of the mark relieves the importer from checking the goods on import, or from obtaining certain specified documentation.
   b) from outside the EC use of the mark is still possible but the importer must notify the authorities of the type, nominal quantity and place of import of the goods. Certain checks may then be required.

Weight and capacity marking

Regulation: Weights and Measures (Quantity Marking and Abbreviations of Units) Regulations 1987 (1987/1538)

Amendment: Weights and Measures (Quantity Marking and Abbreviations of Units) (Amendment) Regulations 1988 (1988/627)

These Regulations govern the methods of marking allowed for weights, capacity and other measures.

The following are included in the requirements:

1) Weight/capacity marking and abbreviations

4.7

Weight
Metric:
kilogram (kg), gram (g)
Imperial: pound (lb(s)), ounce (oz(s))
Capacity
Metric: litre (l or L), centilitre (cl or cL), millilitre (ml or mL)
Imperial: gallon (gal(s)), quart (qt(s)), pint (pt(s)), fluid ounce (fl oz(s))
(Note: For the above imperial abbreviations, the use of the 's' is optional for plurals)

2) Weight/capacity may be in words or figures (but if expressed in words, the unit shall also be expressed written in words)
3) If weight is gross weight, then 'gross' or 'including container' to be stated.
4) The words 'net' or 'gross' must not be abbreviated.
5) A metric quantity shall not be expressed as a vulgar fraction.
6) a) Marking shall be in metric units but may in addition include imperial units. For products with specified weights where the specified weight is either metric or imperial or imperial only, both metric and imperial weights shall be given.
b) For products with both imperial and metric specified weights both units shall be used with the weight of the pack given first in the units of the specified weight used. For all other products, the quantity first may be either imperial or metric.
c) When both metric and imperial units are used, they shall be of equal size and adjacent.
d) For cows' milk (in any liquid form except condensed milk or cream) and goats' milk packed in imperial quantities, marking must be entirely in terms of the pint, quart or gallon.
7) Size of marking
Figures
The minimum size of characters to be used is determined by the mass or capacity of the contents as follows:

Not exceeding 50 g/5 cl	2 mm
Over 50 g/5 cl but not over 200 g/20 cl	3 mm
Over 200 g/20 cl but not over 1 kg/1 l	4 mm
Over 1 kg/1 l	6 mm

8) Catchweight foods (pre-packed in varying quantities) are exempt from 6) and 7).

Appendix 1

A Regulations for food standards, hygiene, additives and contaminants

Part 1 Listing of Regulations before the Food Safety Act 1990

Notes:

1) This list includes the year and number of the Regulations or Rules which apply in Scotland and Northern Ireland. The requirements are the same although the administrative arrangements may be different. Where an '*' is printed, any Regulations or Rules which do exist, are not directly comparable, and the Regulations or Rules given in the following table should be consulted.
2) This list does not include Regulations which affect only the penalties or enforcement of the listed Regulations. In particular, the following Regulations are not listed:

   Milk and Dairies (Revision of Penalties) Regulations 1982 (1982/1703)
   Foods (Revision of Penalties) Regulations 1982 (1982/1727)
   Food (Revision of Penalties) Regulations 1985 (1985/67)
   Milk and Dairies (Revision of Penalties) Regulations 1985 (1985/68)
   Food (Revision of Penalties and Mode of Trial)(Scotland) Regulations 1985 (1985/1068)
   Food Safety Act 1990 (Consequential Modifications)(England and Wales) Order 1990 (1990/2486)
   Food Safety Act 1990 (Consequential Modifications)(No. 2)(Great Britain) Order 1990 (1990/2487)
   Food Safety Act 1990 (Consequential Modifications)(Scotland) Order 1990 (1990/2625)
   Food Safety (Exports) Regulations 1991 (1991/1476)
   Food (Forces Exemptions)(Revocations) Regulations 1992 (1992/2596)

3) Certain administrative Regulations are not included in this book and the more important are as follows:

Authorised Officers (Meat Inspection) Regulations 1987 (1987/133)
Food Safety (Enforcement Authority)(England and Wales) Order 1990 (1990/2462)
Food Safety (Sampling and Qualifications) Regulations 1990 (1990/2463)
Detention of Food (Prescribed Forms) Regulations 1990 (1990/2614)
Food Safety (Improvement and Prohibition – Prescribed Forms) Regulations 1991 (1991/100)
Food Premises (Registration) Regulations 1991 (1991/2825)

Subject	*England and Wales*		*Scotland*		*Northern Ireland*	
	Regulations	*Amendments*	*Regulations*	*Amendments*	*Rules*	*Amendments*
Infestation of food	1950/416					
Fish cakes	1950/589		1950/589		1960/160	
Milk (Channel Islands, etc.)	1956/919		*		*	
Milk and dairies (general)	1959/277	1973/1064 1977/171 1979/1567 1990/2486 1992/3143	*		*	
Ice-cream (heat treatment)	1959/734	1963/1083	*		*	
Arsenic	1959/831	1960/2261 1963/1435 1972/1391 1973/1052 1973/1340 1975/1486 1984/1304 1992/1971	1959/928	1960/2344 1963/1461 1972/1489 1973/1039 1973/1310 1984/1518 1992/1971	1961/98	1964/172 1972/275 1973/197 1973/466 1984/406 1992/416
Hygiene (docks, etc.)	1960/1602	1990/1431 1992/3136	*		1970/144	1990/301
Skimmed milk (with added fat)	1960/2331	1976/103 1980/1849 1981/1174 1990/607 1992/2597	1960/2437	1976/294 1981/137 1981/1319 1990/816 1992/2597	1961/190	1976/70 1981/305 1982/43 1992/463
Meat (treatment)	1964/19		1964/44		1964/6	
Soft drinks	1964/760	1969/1818 1972/1510 1976/295 1977/927 1980/1849 1983/1211 1992/2597 1993/1240	1964/767	1969/1847 1972/1790 1976/442 1977/1026 1981/137 1983/1497 1992/2597 1993/1240	1976/357	1977/182 1980/28 1981/194 1981/305 1983/265
Hygiene (markets, etc.)	1966/791	1966/1487 1990/1431 1991/1343 1992/3163	*		*	
Mineral hydrocarbons	1966/1073	1992/2597	1966/1263	1992/2597	1966/200	1992/463

(continued)

Subject	*England and Wales*		*Scotland*		*Northern Ireland*	
	Regulations	*Amendments*	*Regulations*	*Amendments*	*Rules*	*Amendments*
Butter	1966/1074	1973/1340 1980/1849	1966/1252	1973/1310 1981/137	1966/205	1973/466 1981/305
Solvents	1967/1582	1967/1939 1980/1832 1983/1211 1984/1304 1992/2597	1968/263	1980/1887 1983/1497 1984/1518 1992/2597	1967/282	1981/192 1983/265 1984/406 1992/463
Ice-cream	1967/1866	1980/1849 1983/1211 1990/607	1970/1285	1981/137 1983/1497 1990/816	1968/13(1)	1981/305 1983/265
Margarine	1967/1867	1980/1849 1990/607 1992/2597	1970/1286	1981/137 1990/816 1992/2597	1968/3	1981/305 1992/463
Cheese	1970/94	1974/1122 1975/1486 1976/2086 1980/1849 1984/649	1970/108	1974/1337 1976/2232 1981/137 1984/847	1970/14	1974/177 1976/382 1981/305 1984/352
Cream	1970/752	1975/1486 1980/1849	1970/1191	1975/1597 1981/137	1970/194	1976/15 1981/305
Hygiene (general)	1970/1172	1990/1431 1991/1343 1991/2825 1992/2597 1992/3163	*		*	
Colours	1973/1340	1974/1119 1975/1488 1976/2086 1978/1787 1979/1254 1987/1987 1992/1978	1973/1310	1974/1340 1975/1595 1979/107 1979/1641 1987/1985 1992/1978	1973/466	1975/283 1976/382 1979/49 1987/471 1992/417
Sugar products	1976/509	1980/1834 1980/1849 1982/255	1976/946	1980/1889 1981/137 1982/410	1976/165	1980/28 1981/193 1981/305 1982/311
Cocoa and chocolate	1976/541	1980/1833 1980/1834 1980/1849 1982/17 1984/1305	1976/914	1980/1888 1980/1889 1981/137 1982/108 1984/1519	1976/183	1981/193 1981/194 1981/305 1982/349 1984/407
Poultry meat (hygiene)	1976/1209	1979/693 1981/1168 1992/2036 1993/209	1976/1221	1979/768 1981/1169 1992/2061 1993/235	*	
Honey	1976/1832	1980/1849	1976/1818	1981/137	1976/387	1981/305
Milk (drinking)	1976/1883	1992/3143	*		*	
Milk (bottle caps)	1976/2186	1992/3143	*		*	
Erucic acid	1977/691	1982/264	1977/1028	1982/18	1977/135	1982/184
Fruit juices and nectars	1977/927	1979/1254 1980/1849 1982/1311 1991/1284	1977/1026	1979/1641 1981/137 1982/1619 1992/1284	1977/182	1980/28 1981/305 1983/48 1991/251
Condensed and dried milk	1977/928	1980/1849 1982/1066 1986/2299 1989/1959	1977/1027	1981/137 1982/1209 1987/26 1989/1975	1977/196	1981/305 1983/26 1987/65 1989/430
Antioxidants	1978/105	1980/1831 1983/1211 1984/1304 1991/2540 1992/1978	1978/492	1980/1886 1983/1497 1984/1518 1991/2540 1992/1978	1978/112	1981/191 1983/265 1984/406 1991/495 1992/417
Coffee and coffee products	1978/1420	1980/1849 1982/254 1987/1986	1979/383	1981/137 1982/409 1987/2014	1979/51	1980/28 1981/305 1982/298 1988/23

Regulations for food standards, hygiene, additives and contaminants (*continued*)

Subject	*England and Wales*		*Scotland*		*Northern Ireland*	
	Regulations	*Amendments*	*Regulations*	*Amendments*	*Rules*	*Amendments*
Hygiene (ships)	1979/27		*		*	
Lead	1979/1254	1985/912 1992/1971	1979/1641	1985/1438 1992/1971	1979/407	1981/194 1985/163 1992/416
Animal product (imports)	1980/14	1980/1934 1981/1238 1982/948	1980/14	1980/1934 1981/1238 1982/948	*	
Chloroform	1980/36		1980/289		1980/75	
Miscellaneous additives	1980/1834	1980/1849 1982/14 1983/1211 1984/1304 1990/399 1992/1978	1980/1889	1981/137 1982/515 1983/1497 1984/1518 1990/395 1992/1978	1981/193	1981/305 1982/258 1983/265 1984/406 1990/78 1992/417
Jam and similar products	1981/1063	1982/1700 1983/1211 1988/2112 1989/533 1990/2085	1981/1320	1982/1779 1983/1497 1988/2084 1989/581 1990/2180	1982/105	1982/398 1983/265 1988/433 1989/152 1990/388 1990/2051
Sweeteners	1983/1211	1988/2112 1992/1978	1983/1497	1988/2084 1992/1978	1983/265	1985/163 1988/433 1989/152 1992/417
Milk-based drinks (hygiene and heat treatment)	1983/1508	1986/720	*		*	
Cream (heat treatment)	1983/1509	1986/721	*		*	
Poultry meat (water content)	1984/1145		1983/1372	1984/1576	1982/386	
Bread and flour	1984/1304	1990/399	1984/1518	1990/395	1984/406	1989/152
Labelling	1984/1305	1984/1566 1985/71 1985/2026 1986/2299 1987/1986 1988/2112 1989/768 1989/2321 1990/607 1990/2488 1990/2489 1992/1971 1992/1978 1992/2597	1984/1519	1984/1714 1985/71 1986/836 1987/26 1987/2014 1988/2084 1989/809 1990/1 1990/816 1990/2505 1990/2506 1992/1971 1992/1978 1992/2597	1984/407	1985/120 1986/40 1988/23 1988/433 1989/229 1990/37 1990/103 1990/440 1991/216 1992/416 1992/417 1992/463
Meat products and spreadable fish products	1984/1566	1986/987	1984/1714	1986/1288	1984/408	
Imported food	1984/1918		1985/913		1984/1917(2)	1991/475
Natural mineral waters	1985/71		1985/71		1985/120	
International carriage	1985/1071	1987/1066 1989/1185 1991/425 1991/969 1992/2682	1985/1071	1987/1066 1989/1185 1991/425 1991/969 1992/2682	1985/1071(2)	1987/1066 1989/1185 1991/425 1991/969 1992/2682
Caseins and caseinates	1985/2026	1989/2321	1986/836	1990/1	1986/40	1990/37
Materials and articles in contact with food	1987/1523		1987/1523		1987/432	
Olive oil	1987/1783	1992/2590	1987/1783	1992/2590	1987/431	1993/9
Hormonal substances	1988/849		1988/849		1990/151	

(*continued*)

Subject	*England and Wales*		*Scotland*		*Northern Ireland*	
	Regulations	*Amendments*	*Regulations*	*Amendments*	*Rules*	*Amendments*
Pesticide residues	1988/1378		1988/1378			
Imported milk	1988/1803	1992/3143	1988/1814	1992/3136	1988/420	
Milk (semi-/skimmed, heat treatment/ labelling)	1988/2206	1989/2382 1990/2491	1988/2190		*	
Preservatives	1989/533	1989/2287 1992/1978	1989/581	1989/2216 1992/1978	1989/152	1989/460 1992/417
Emulsifiers and stabilisers	1989/876	1992/165 1992/1978	1989/945	1992/165 1992/1978	1989/308	1992/67 1992/417
Olive oil (tetrachloroethylene)	1989/910		1989/837		1989/261	
Bovine offal	1989/2061	1992/306	1990/112	1992/158	1990/30	
Milk (special designation)	1989/2383	1990/2492 1992/1208 1992/3143	1988/2191	1990/2656 1992/1896 1992/3136	*	
Milk (protection of designations)	1990/607		1990/816		1990/103	
Preserved sardines	1990/1084		1990/1139		1990/194	
Tryptophan	1990/1728		1990/1792		1990/329	

Notes:
(1) Includes heat treatment
(2) Statutory Instrument

Part 2 Listing of Regulations after the Food Safety Act 1990

Subject	*England, Wales and Scotland*		*Northern Ireland*	
	Regulations	*Amendments*	*Rules*	*Amendments*
Food irradiation	1990/2490		1992/172	
Quick-frozen foods	1990/2615		1990/455	
Meat (residue limits)	1991/2843		1992/39	
Tin	1992/496		1992/166	
Lot marking	1992/1357		1992/281	
Fishery products (derogations)	1992/1507		1992/296	
Live bivalve molluscs (derogrations)	1992/1508		1992/295	
Flavourings	1992/1971		1992/416	
Additives (labelling)	1992/1978		1992/417	
Fresh meat (hygiene and inspection)	1992/2037			
Organic products	1992/2111	1993/405		
Plastic materials	1992/3145		1993/173	
Fishery products (general)	1992/3163		1993/51	
Live bivalve molluscs (general)	1992/3164		1993/52	
Fishery products (on fishing vessels)	1992/3165		1993/53	
Aflatoxin	1992/3236		1993/31	
Animal products (import/ export)	1992/3296			
Egg products	1993/1520			
Extraction solvents	1993/1658			

Part 3 Regulations specific to Scotland

These Regulations are specific to Scotland and are not directly comparable to Regulations in force in England and Wales. Full details of these Regulations are not given in this guide.

	Regulations	*Amendments*
Milk (sale of)	1914/175	
Ice-cream (heat treatment)	1948/960	1948/2271
		1960/2108
		1963/1101
Food hygiene	1959/413	1959/1153
		1961/622
		1966/967
		1978/173
Meat (prep. and distrib.)	1963/2001	1967/1507
Milk (Channel Islands, etc.)	1967/81	
Milk (bottle caps)	1976/875	1992/3136
Drinking milk	1976/1888	1992/3136
Milk (special designations)	1980/1866	1983/939
		1983/1527
Milk (labelling)	1983/938	1990/2508
		1992/3136
Milk based drinks	1983/1514	1986/790
Cream (heat treatment)	1983/1515	1985/1222
		1986/789
		1990/2392
Imported milk	1988/1814	1992/3136
Milk and dairies	1990/2507	1992/3136

Part 4 Regulations specific to Northern Ireland

These Regulations (usually published as Statutory Rules) are specific to Northern Ireland and are not directly comparable to Regulations in force in England and Wales. Full details of these Rules are not given in this guide.

	Regulations	*Amendments*
Food hygiene	1964/129	1990/301
		1991/383
		1992/463
Import of poultry or products	1965/175	1968/106
Marketing of milk products	1966/204	1983/336
		1991/526
Landing of animal products	1970/145	1972/113
		1976/324
Shell fish (public health)	1973/453	
Imported animals (diseases)	1981/1115 (1)	
Milk	1987/229	1988/436
		1990/13
		1991/151
		1992/302
Meat inspection	1991/5	

Note: (1) Statutory Instrument

B Regulations for trade descriptions and weights

Subject	*England, Wales and Scotland*		*Northern Ireland*	
	Regulations	*Amendments*	*Rules*	*Amendments*
Trade descriptions (Exemption 1)	1972/1886		1972/1886(1)	
Trade descriptions (Exemption 10)	1976/260		1976/260(1)	
Prescribed weights (miscellaneous foods)	1988/2040	1990/1550	1989/69	1990/395
Average weight controls	1986/2049	1986/2049 1987/1538 1992/1580	1990/410	1991/320 1992/485
Weight marking and abbreviations	1987/1538	1988/627	1991/320	

Appendix 2

A Reports of the Food Standards Committee (FSC)

1 Foods and additives

Antioxidants	1953, 1954, 1963
Beer	1977
Bread and flour	1960, 1974
Bread, milk	1959
Cheese	1982
Cheese, (processed cheese and cheese spread)	1949, 1956
Cheese (processed cheese)	1949
Cheese (hard, soft and cream cheeses)	1962
Coffee mixtures	1951
Colouring matters	1954, 1955, 1964
Cream	1950, 1967, 1982
Cream (artificial and synthetic)	1951
Curry powder	1948
Emulsifying and stabilising agents	1956
Fish cakes	1951
Fish paste	1950
Fish and meat pastes	1965
Flavouring agents	1965
Gelatine	1950
Ice-cream	1957
Infant formulae (artificial feeds for young infants)	1981
Jams and marmalade	1952
Jams and other preserves	1968
Margarine and other table spreads	1981
Margarine, vitaminisation of	1954
Meat pies	1963
Meat, canned	1962
Meat products	1980
Meat products, offals in	1972
Milk, condensed	1969, 1973
Milk, dried	1962
Mince	1983
Mineral oil	1962
Novel protein foods	1974
Preservatives	1959, 1960
Saccharin tablets	1952
Salt, iodisation of	1950
Sausages	1956
Soft drinks	1959
Part I: fruit juices and nectars	1975
Part II: soft drinks	1976
Soups	1968
Suet	1952
Tomato ketchup	1948
Vinegars	1971
Water in food	1978
Yogurt	1975

2 Miscellaneous

Claims and misleading descriptions	1966, 1980
Date marking of food	1972
Food labelling	1964, 1980
Pre-1955 compositional orders	1970

3 Trace elements

Arsenic	1950, 1951, 1955
Copper	1951, 1956
Flourine	1954, 1957
Lead	1951, 1954
Tin	1954
Zinc	1954

B Reports of the Food Additives and Contaminants Committee (FACC)

Aldrin and dieldrin	1967
Antioxidants	1965, 1966, 1971, 1974
Arsenic	1984
Asbestos	1979
Azodicarbonamide	1968
Beer, additives and processing aids used in the production of	1978
Bread and flour, additives to	1971 (See FSC Report)
Bulking aids	1980
Cheese	1982 (See FSC Report)
Colouring matter in food	1979
Cream	1982 (See FSC Report)
Cyclamates	1966, 1967
Emulsifiers and stabilisers	1970, 1972
Enzyme preparations	1982
Flavourings in food	1976
Flavour modifiers	1978
Further classes of food additives	1968
Infant formulae	1981 (See FSC Report)
Leaching of substances from packaging materials into food	1970
Lead in food	1975
Liquid freezants	1972, 1974
Metals in canned food	1983
Mineral hydrocarbons in food	1975
Modified starches	1980
Nitrites and nitrates in cured meats and cheese	1978
Packaging	1970
Preservatives	1972
Solvents	1966, 1974, 1978
Sorbic acid	1977
Sulphur dioxide in canned peas	1977
Sweeteners	1982

A2 C Reports of the Food Advisory Committee (FdAC)

1)	Skimmed milk with non-milk fat	1984
2)	Additives to cloud soft drinks	1985
3)	Coated and ice-glazed fish products	1987
4)	Colouring matter	1987
5)	Old compositional orders (includes mustard, curry powder, tomato ketchup, suet, salad cream and ice-cream)	1989
6)	Response to comments on the review of colouring matter	1989
7)	Potassium bromate	1990
8)	Mineral hydrocarbons	1990
9)	Saccharin	1990
10)	Food labelling and advertising	1990
11)	Emulsifiers and stabilisers	1992
12)	Use of additives in food specially prepared for infants and young children	1992

Appendix 3

Codes of practice

Codes of practice often provide additional guidance as to the interpretation of legislation. This Appendix lists those which have significant legal authority. For a more complete listing of about 400 codes, readers are advised to consult the 'Listing of Codes of Practice Applicable to Foods' published by the Institute of Food Science and Technology, 1993.

A Food hygiene

1)	Hygiene in the retail meat trade	1959
2)	Hygiene transport and handling of meat	1959
3)	Hygiene in the retail fish trade	1960
4)	Hygiene transport and handling of fish	1960
5)	Poultry dressing and handling	1961
6)	Hygiene in the bakery trade and industry	1966
7)	Hygiene in the operation of coin operated vending machines	1967
8)	Hygiene in the meat trades	1969
9)	Hygiene in microwave cooking	1972
10)	The canning of low acid foods. A guide to good manufacturing practice	1981

B LAJAC

For full details of these codes, see the *Journal of the Association of Public Analysts* in the issues stated below. For the terms of reference of the LAJAC, see the *Journal* (1963, vol **1**(2), p. 50).

1) Use of the word 'chocolate' in flour confectionery (1963, vol **1**(2), p. 49)
   Min 3% dry non-fat cocoa solids in the moist crumb (does not apply if called 'chocolate flavoured').
2) Labelling of Brandy (1963, vol **1**(4), p. 101)
   Brandy must come from grapes; 'Cognac' and 'Armagnac' must come from those regions.

3) Crab meat content in Norwegian canned crab products (1963, vol 1(4), p. 105).
4) Canned fruit and vegetables. (Now replaced by new Code of Practice; see LACOTS below).
5) Canned beans in tomato sauce (1965, vol 3(4), p. 111)
   Covers beans and sauce; standards for total solids, tomato solids and sugar (according to can size).
6) Marzipan, almond paste and almond icing (1969, vol 7(2), p. 40)
   Min 23.5% almond substance (no other nut ingredient) and min 75% of remainder to be solid carbohydrate sweetening matter.
7) Bun loaves, chollas and buttercream (1971, vol 9(4), p. 107)
   Bun loaf: min 5% liquid whole egg and/or fat
   min 10% egg and or fat and/or sugar
   Chollas: normally same as for bun loaf
   Buttercream (not 'butter cream' or 'butter-cream'):
   min 22.5% butter-fat and no other added fat.

C LACOTS

The following codes have been prepared and adopted by the relevant industrial associations in consultation with LACOTS:

1) UK Association of Frozen Food Producers: 'Code of Practice for the Breadcrumb Covering of Scampi'; 1980.
2) Dairy Trade Federation: 'Code of Practice for the Composition and Labelling of Yogurt'; 1983.
3) British Meat Manufacturers Association: 'Code of Practice on the Labelling of Re-formed Cured Meat Products'; 1985.
4) Honey Importers and Packers Association: 'Code of Practice for the Importation, Blending, Packaging and Marketing of Honey'; 1986.
5) British Fruit and Vegetable Canners' Association: 'Code of Practice on Canned Fruit and Vegetables'; 1986 (replaced LAJAC Code No 4).
6) Fish and Meat Spreadable Products Association: 'Code of Practice for the Composition of Meat and Fish Pastes and Pâtés'; 1986.
7) Grain and Feed Trade Association: 'Rice Standards Section Code of Practice for Rice'; 1992.

D NMCU

The following codes have been prepared to help manufacturers meet the requirements of the average weight system. They were prepared in consultation with the NMCU and have been approved by the Secretary of State for Trade and Industry:

1) National Association of Master Bakers, Confectioners and Caterers and the Scottish Association of Master Bakers: 'Code of Practical Guidance of Small Bakers'; 1982.
2) Federation of Bakers: 'Code of Practice on Bread Weight Checking for Plant Bakers'; amended version 1985.
3) British Soft Drinks Council: 'The Average System of Quantity Controls on Packages: Code of Practice for the Soft Drinks Industry'; 1983.
4) Brewers' Society: 'The Average System of Quantity Control: Code of Practice for Beer Packaging'; 1983.
5) Cake and Biscuit Alliance: 'Code of Practical Guidance for the Biscuit Industry'; 1983.
6) British Poultry Federation: 'Code of Practice for the Average Weighing of Whole Poultry and Poultry Portions'; 1985.

E Enforcement codes

The following codes have been issued under Section 40 of the Food Safety Act 1990 and are available from HMSO:

1) 'Responsibility for Enforcement of the Food Safety Act 1990', 1991.
2) 'Legal Matters', 1991.
3) 'Inspection Procedures – General', 1991.
4) 'Inspection, Detention and Seizure of Suspect Food', 1991.
5) 'The Use of Improvement Notices', 1991.
6) 'Prohibition Procedures', 1991.
7) 'Sampling for Analysis or Examination', 1991.
8) 'Food Standards Inspections', 1991.
9) 'Food Hygiene Inspections', 1991.
10) 'Enforcement of the Temperature Control Requirements of Food Hygiene Regulations', 1991.
11) 'Enforcement of the Food Premises (Registration) Regulations', 1991.
12) 'Division of Enforcement for the Quick Frozen Foodstuffs Regulations 1990', 1991.
13) 'Enforcement of the Food Safety Act 1990 in Relation to Crown Premises', 1992.
14) (Publication pending).
15) (Publication pending).
16) 'Enforcement of the Food Safety Act 1990 in Relation to the Food Hazard Warning System', 1993.

Appendix 4

EC food legislation

A Regulations

These are directly applicable to all member states and do not require national enactment. Certain measures may be adopted nationally to aid the enforcement or interpretation of the Regulations

Subject	*Regulation*	*Amendments/additional requirements*					
Oils and fats							
a) general	136/66	1547/72	1707/73	2560/77	1562/78	1585/80	3454/80
		1413/82	1416/82	1726/82	1097/84	1101/84	1556/84
		2260/84	231/85	3768/85	1454/86	1915/87	3994/87
		1098/88	2210/88	2902/89	3499/90	3577/90	1720/91
		356/92	2046/92				
b) characteristics, analysis	2568/91	2988/91	1683/92	1996/92	3288/92	183/93	620/93
Milk and milk products	1411/71	3358/75	556/76	222/88	2138/92	323/93	
Water content of frozen poultry							
a) standards	2967/76	1691/77	361/78	2238/78	641/79	2632/80	2785/80
		2835/80	3204/83				
b) rules	2785/80	3134/81	3759/85				
Protection of dairy designations	1898/87	222/88					
Spirit drinks	1576/89	3773/89	1014/90	1759/90	3207/90	3750/90	1180/91
		1781/91	3280/92	3458/92			
Preserved sardines	2136/89						
Poultrymeat	1906/90	1538/91	2988/91	315/92	1980/92	317/93	
Organic products							
a) general	2092/91	1535/92	2083/92				
b) imports	94/92						
	3457/92						
Designations							
a) geographical	2081/92						
b) specific character	2082/92						
Contaminants	315/93						

B Directives

These require enactment by national regulations for implementation. Given below are details of the Directives relating to the harmonisation of laws for foodstuffs. Many of the Regulations listed in this guide implement the Directives listed.

Subject	*Directive*	*Amendments/additional requirements*					
Colour							
a) general	2645/62	65/469	67/653	68/419	70/358	73/101	76/399
		78/144	81/20	85/7			
b) analysis	81/712						
Preservatives							
a) general	64/54	65/569	66/722	67/427	68/420	70/359	71/160
		72/2	72/444	73/101	74/62	74/394	76/462
		78/145	81/214	85/7	85/172	85/585	
b) purity criteria	65/66	67/428	76/463	86/604			
c) analysis	81/712						
Fresh meat (health)							
a) inspection, etc.	64/433	66/601	69/349	75/379	81/476	83/90	85/323
		85/325	91/497	93/120			
b) diseases	72/461	75/379	77/98	80/213	80/1099	81/476	82/893
		83/646	84/336	84/643	3768/85	85/322	87/64
		87/231	87/489	89/662	91/226	91/687	
c) third countries	72/462	75/379	77/96	77/98	78/685	81/476	83/91
		3768/85	86/469	87/64	88/289	88/657	89/227
		90/423	90/425	90/675	91/69	91/266	91/496
		91/497					
d) extension	91/497						
e) BSE	90/200						
Antioxidants							
a) general	70/357	73/101	74/412	78/143	81/962	85/7	87/55
b) purity criteria	78/664	82/712					
c) analysis	81/712						
Poultry meat (health)							
a) general	71/118	73/101	75/379	75/431	78/50	80/216	80/879
		81/476	81/578	82/532	84/186	84/335	84/642
		3768/85	85/324	85/326	88/657	89/662	90/484
		90/654	92/116				
b) third countries	91/494						
c) health marking (large packs)	80/879						
Cocoa and chocolate	73/241	74/411	74/644	75/155	76/628	78/609	78/842
		80/608	85/7	89/344			
Sugars							
a) general	73/437						
b) purity criteria	79/796						
Emulsifiers, stabilisers, thickeners and gelling agents							
a) general	74/329	78/612	80/597	85/6	85/7	86/102	89/393
b) purity criteria	78/663	82/504	90/612				
Honey	74/409						
Volumes of pre-packaged liquids	75/106	78/891	79/1005	85/10	88/316	89/676	
Fruit juices, etc.	75/726	79/168	81/487	89/394			
Dehydrated preserved milk							
a) general	76/118	78/630	83/635				
b) analysis	79/1067						
	87/524						
Weights of pre-packaged products	76/211	78/891					

A4 (*continued*)

Subject	*Directive*	*Amendments/additional requirements*					
Erucic acid in oils and fats							
a) general	76/621						
b) analysis	80/891						
Pesticide residues							
a) fruit and vegetables	76/895	80/428	80/36	80/528	85/3768	88/298	89/186
b) cereals	86/362	88/298	90/654				
c) animal origin	86/363						
d) general	90/642						
Meat products (health)							
a) general	77/99	80/214	81/476	85/327	85/328	92/5	93/120
b) exceptions	83/201						
Coffee and chicory extracts							
a) general	77/436	85/7	85/573				
b) analysis	79/1066						
Vinyl chloride monomer							
a) general	78/142						
b) analysis	80/766						
Labelling, presentation and advertising	79/112	85/7	86/197	89/395	91/72		
Jam, jellies, etc.	79/693	80/1276	88/593				
Prescribed weights	80/232	86/96	87/356				
Packaging symbol	80/590						
Natural mineral waters	80/777	80/1276	85/7				
Hormonal substances	81/602 85/358						
Migration of constituents of plastic materials	82/711 85/572	93/8					
Regenerated cellulose film	83/229	86/388	92/15	93/10			
Caseins and caseinates							
a) general	83/417						
b) analysis	85/503 86/424						
Ingredients' labelling	83/463						
Ceramic articles	84/500						
Heat-treated milk							
a) general	85/397	3768/85	382/89	89/159	89/165	89/362	89/662
b) analysis	91/180	92/608					
Methods of sampling and analysis	85/591						
Labelling (alcoholic strength)	87/250						
Extraction solvents	88/344	92/115					
Flavourings (general)	88/388	88/389					
Minced meat, etc.	88/657	89/662	92/110				
Additives (general)	89/107						
Quick-frozen foods							
a) general	89/108						
b) monitoring, etc.	92/1 92/2						
Materials and articles in contact with food	89/109						
Lot marking	89/396	91/238	92/11				
Official control	89/397						
Food for particular nutritional uses	89/398						
Egg products	89/437	89/662	91/684				
Plastic materials	90/128	92/39	93/9				
Nutrition labelling	90/496						
Aquaculture animals and products (health)	91/67	92/528	92/532	92/538			

(*continued*)

Subject	*Directive*	*Amendments/additional requirements*
Live bivalve molluscs (health)	91/492	
Fishery products (health)	91/493	
Rabbit meat and farmed game meat	91/495	
Infant formulae		
a) general	91/321	
b) export	92/52	

Appendix 5

Useful addresses

Government departments

Ministry of Agriculture, Fisheries and Food
Ergon House
c/o Nobel House
17 Smith Square
London
SW1P 3JR

Ministry of Agriculture, Fisheries and Food
(Meat Hygiene Division)
Tolworth Tower
Surbiton
Surrey
KT6 7DX

Department of Health
80 London Road
Elephant and Castle
London
SE1

Scottish Office
(Agriculture and Fisheries Department)
Pentland House
47 Robb's Loan
Edinburgh
EH14 1TY

Department of Health and Social Services
(Food Control Branch)
Castle Buildings

Stormont
Belfast
BT4 3RA

Trade Descriptions (UK)
Department of Trade and Industry
(Consumer Affairs Division)
10–18 Victoria Street
London
SW1H 0NN

EC Commission (London office)

EC Commission
8 Storey's Gate
London
SW1P 3AT

Enforcement

LACOTS
PO Box 6
Token House
1A Robert Street
Croydon
CR9 1LG

Her Majesty's Stationery Office

Copies of the legislation listed in this guide may be obtained from:

Postal application:

HMSO
PO Box 276
London
SW8 5DT

Personal application:

HMSO
49 High Holborn
London
WC1V 6HB

Or through local branches of HMSO or through booksellers.

Appendix 6

Late amendments

This Appendix provides some information concerning the regulations which were published between the date the original manuscript was completed (31 January 1993) and the date when material for the first reprint was required (15 June 1994). The information is given in the order it would appear in the book.

A–Z food standards: Soft Drinks

Regulation: Soft Drinks (Amendment) Regulations 1993 (1993/1240)

These Regulations further amend the Soft Drinks Regulations 1964 (see pages 74–78). Their main effect was to remove the minimum sugar composition requirement. Therefore, in the table on pages 75–76, the two columns headed 'Minimum added sugar' are deleted and, in Note (2) to the table, the two minimum figures for added sugar (2.25 and 11.25) are deleted. There is an additional minor amendment but it did not relate to information given.

A–Z food standards: Drinking Water

Regulation: Drinking Water in Containers 1994 (1994/743)

These Regulations introduce new requirements for drinking water in containers. Previously only water which was classified as natural mineral water was required to meet specified standards (see pages 69–72).

Definitions

Drinking water water intended for sale for human consumption in any bottle.

Bottle (as a noun) a closed container of any kind in which water is sold for human consumption; (as a verb) construed accordingly.

Requirements

1) Detailed requirements are specified for a range of properties, elements, organisms and substances (see Regulations).
2) The Regulations do not apply to a recognised natural mineral water.

Additives: Emulsifiers and stabilisers

Regulation: Emulsifiers and Stabilisers in Food (Amendment) Regulations 1993 (1993/1161)

These Regulations make a minor amendment to the Emulsifiers and Stabilisers in Food Regulations 1989 which does not affect the detail given in Emulsifiers and stabilisers (pages 85–88).

Additives: Flavourings

Regulation: Flavourings in Food (Amendment) Regulations 1994 (1994/1486)

These Regulations amend the Flavouring in Food Regulations 1992 (see pages 88–91) and make related amendments to the Food Labelling Regulations 1984 (page 133).

On page 91, items 4) and 5) refer to 'business sale' – the amendment extends these provisions to include consumer sales.

On page 133, the term flavouring and note (2) are deleted from the table of categories of additives. A new item, d), should be included after the table:

d) Where an ingredient serves the function of a flavouring, it should indicated by the word 'flavouring' or a more specific name or description. The term 'natural' (or similar term) may only be used where the flavouring ingredients are flavouring substances coming within category i) of the definition of flavouring substances on page 88 and/or flavouring preparations. If the name of the ingredient refers to its animal or vegetable source, then the word 'natural' may only be used if the flavouring components have been isolated (either by physical, enzymatic, microbiological or normal food preparation processes) wholly or mainly from that vegetable or animal.

Processing and packaging: Extraction solvents

Regulation: Extraction Solvents in Food Regulations 1993 (1993/1658)

These Regulations, which implement an EC Directive, introduce detailed controls on extraction solvents for the first time.

Definitions

Extraction solvent any solvent which is used or intended to be used in an extraction procedure and includes in any particular case, further to its use in such a procedure, any substance other than such a solvent but deriving exclusively from such a solvent.

Solvent any substance which is capable of dissolving food, or any ingredient or other component part of food, including any contaminant which is in or on a food.

Residue includes any residual substance other than an extraction solvent but deriving exclusively from an extraction solvent.

Permitted extraction solvents

1) The following extraction solvents may be generally used:
   water, any food possessing solvent properties.
2) The following extraction solvents may be generally used so long as its use has resulted in the presence in or on the food only of residues in technically unavoidable quantities that present no danger to human health:
   propane, butane, butyl acetate, ethyl acetate, ethanol, carbon dioxide, acetone (not to be used for olive-pomace oil), nitrous oxide.
3) The following extraction solvents may be generally used so long as its (or their) use results in the presence of a maximum residue (singly or combined) of 10 mg/kg:
   methanol, propan-2-ol.
4) The following extraction solvents may only be used for the purposes listed in the following table and must result in a residue no greater than the maximum specified:
   hexane, methyl acetate, ethylmethylketone, dichloromethane (but note that hexane and ethylmethylketone are not to be used in combination):

Specified foods	*Permitted extraction solvent and purpose for addition*	*Maximum residue of solvent in the food (or as specified)*
Fats	(a) Hexane, for the production or fractionation of the fats, or (b) Ethylmethylketone, for the fractionation of the fats	5 mg/kg

Oils	(a) Hexane, for the production or fractionation of the oils, or (b) Ethylmethylketone, for the fractionation of the oils	5 mg/kg
Cocoa butter	Hexane, for the production of the cocoa butter	5 mg/kg
Protein products	Hexane, for the production of the protein products	10 mg/kg in any food in which the protein products are an ingredient
Defatted flours	Hexane, preparation of the defatted flours	10 mg/kg in any food in which the defatted flours are an ingredient
Defatted cereal germs	Hexane, for the preparation of the defatted cereal germs	5 mg/kg
Defatted soya products	Hexane, for the preparation of the defatted soya products	30 mg/kg in the defatted soya products as sold to the final consumer
Coffee	Methyl acetate, ethylmethylketone or dichloromethane (alone or in combination), for decaffeination and/or removal of irritants and bitterings	(a) methyl acetate or ethylmethylketone, 20 mg/kg (1) (b) dichloromethane, 2 mg/kg
Tea	Methyl acetate, ethylmethylketone or dichloromethane (alone or in combination), for decaffeination and/or removal of irritants and bitterings	(a) methyl acetate or ethylmethylketone, 20 mg/kg (1) (b) dichloromethane, 5 mg/kg
Sugar from molasses	Methyl acetate, for the production of sugar from molasses	1 mg/kg

Note: (1) If used in combination, the combined total residue shall not exceed 20 mg/kg

5) The following extraction solvents may be used for the preparation of flavourings prepared from natural flavouring materials provided that, as a result of their use, any food containing or consisting of the flavourings has no more residue than indicated:
hexane (1 mg/kg), methyl acetate (2 mg/kg), ethylmethylketone (1 mg/kg), dichloromethane (0.02 mg/kg), diethyl ether (2 mg/kg), butan-1-ol (1 mg/kg), butan-2-ol (1 mg/kg), methyl-propan-1-ol (1 mg/kg), propan-1-ol (1 mg/kg).

General

1) The Regulations do not apply to extraction solvents used in the production of any food additive, vitamin, or any other nutritional additive except where specified above.
2) The Regulations also contain requirements for the labelling of permitted extraction solvents.

Processing and packaging: Frozen foods

Regulation: Quick-frozen Foodstuffs (Amendment) Regulations 1994 (1994/298)

These amendment Regulations place additional requirements on manufacturers, storers, transporters, local distributors and retailers of quick-frozen foods to ensure that means of storage and transport are fitted with appropriate instruments for monitoring and measuring air temperatures and that records are taken and kept for at least one year. Instruments must meet specified standards (see Regulations). No changes are made to the details given on pages 123–124.

Processing and packaging: Materials and articles in contact with food

Regulation: Materials and Articles in Contact with Food (Amendment) Regulations 1994 (1994/979)

These Regulations make a number of minor technical amendments to the details on page 126 relating to regenerated cellulose film. In the summary given on page 126, the only detail to have been changed is item 3) c) where the figure of 50 mg/kg food has been reduced to 30 mg/kg food. Other changes relate to the list of specified substances (see Regulations).

Labelling: General labelling requirements

Regulations: Food Labelling (Amendment) Regulations 1993 (1993/2759). Food Labelling (Amendment) Regulations 1994 (1994/804)

(Note: see also the amendment listed above under 'Additives: Flavourings'.)

The 1993 amendment Regulations delete from the table of words and descriptions on page 144 the entries relating to 'shandy', 'ginger beer shandy', 'shandygaff', 'cider shandy', 'cider and ginger beer shandy' and 'cider shandygaff'.

The 1994 amendment Regulations implement the EC Nutrition Labelling Directive with effect from 1 March 1995. Food complying with the new requirements may however be sold before that date. The amendments make significant changes to the various restrictions specified on pages 138–142 (under the heading 'Claims') and minor consequential changes on pages 130 and 143. In particular, among the changes, the following should be noted (see the amendment Regulations for full details):

1) A revised table of recommended daily allowances has been incorporated (replacing the table on page 141) as follows:

	Recommended daily allowance (RDA)
Vitamins:	
Vitamin A	800 μg
Vitamin D	5 μg
Vitamin E	10 mg
Vitamin C	60 mg
Thiamin	1.4 mg
Riboflavin	1.6 mg
Niacin	18 mg
Vitamin B_6	2 mg
Folacin (Folic acid)	200 μg
Vitamin B_{12}	1 μg
Biotin	0.15 mg
Pantothenic acid	6 mg
Minerals:	
Calcium	800 mg
Phosphorus	800 mg
Iron	14 mg
Magnesium	300 mg
Zinc	15 mg
Iodine	150 μg

2) Revised conversion factors should be used in calculating the energy value (replacing those on page 142) as follows:

1 g carbohydrate (excluding polyols) = 17 kJ (4 kcal)
1 g polyols = 10 kJ (2.4 kcals)
1 g protein = 17 kJ (4 kcal)
1 g fat = 37 kJ (9 kcal)
1 g ethanol = 29 kJ (7 kcal)
1 g organic acid = 13 kJ (3 kcal)

3) Protein is now defined as total Kjeldahl nitrogen x 6.25

4) In item 1 on page 130 and in the table on page 143 (in the term relating to 'vitamin') the references to vitamin B_6, pantothenic acid, biotin and vitamin E are deleted (leaving only the references to vitamin K).
5) Nutrition labelling must now be presented in a specified way and contain specified information. A transitional provision (available until 5 October 1995) allows for a reduced content in certain situations.

Labelling: Organic foods

Regulation: Organic Products (Amendment) Regulations 1993 (1993/405)

These Regulations make a minor amendment to the Organic Products Regulations 1992 which does not affect the detail given in Organic Foods (pages 148–149).

Hygiene and health: Imported food – animal products

Regulation: Products of Animal Origin (Import and Export) Regulations 1992 (1992/3296)

Note: Although 1992 Regulations, these were not published until February 1993

The Regulations provide for the application of a number of EC Internal Market Directives which provide for veterinary checks on products of animal origin for intra-Community trade and for trade with third countries. The Directives concerned are:

64/433 – on health problems affecting intra-Community trade in fresh meat
71/118 – on health problems affecting trade in fresh poultry meat
72/461 – on health problems affecting intra-Community trade in fresh meat
77/99 – on health problems affecting intra-Community trade in meat products
80/215 – on animal health problems affecting intra-Community trade in meat products
85/397 – on health and animal health problems affecting intra-Community trade in heat-treated milk
88/657 – laying down the requirements for the production of, and trade in, minced meat, meat in pieces of less than 100 gram and meat preparations

89/437 – on hygiene and health problems affecting the production and the placing on the market of egg products
91/67 – concerning the animal health conditions governing the placing on the market of aquaculture animals and products
91/492 – laying down the health conditions for the production and the placing on the market of live bivalve molluscs
91/493 – laying down the health conditions for the production and the placing on the market of fishery products
91/494 – on animal health conditions governing intra-Community trade in and imports from third countries of fresh poultry meat
91/495 – concerning public health and animal health problems affecting the production and placing on the market of rabbit meat and farmed game meat

Where the above Directives affect the import and export of products of animal origin their provisions must be complied with. In such cases, the Regulations disapply the provisions of other Regulations which would otherwise specify other requirements. This relates in particular to the Importation of Animal Products and Poultry Products Order 1980 (1980/14), the Imported Food Regulations 1984 (1984/1918) and the Importation of Milk Regulations 1988 (1988/1803).

Hygiene and health: Poultry meat, farmed game bird meat and rabbit meat

Regulation: Poultry Meat, Farmed Game Bird Meat and Rabbit Meat (Hygiene and Inspection) Regulations 1994 (1994/1029)

These Regulations replace the Poultry Meat (Hygiene) Regulations 1976 (as amended) (see pages 159–160) and extend their scope to cover farmed game bird meat and rabbit meat.

Definitions
Poultry means domestic fowls, turkeys, guinea fowls, ducks and geese.
Farmed game birds birds, other than poultry, which are not generally considered domestic but which are bred, reared and slaughtered in captivity.
Rabbit a domestic rabbit.

Requirements

1) Subject to a number of exceptions, no person shall sell any poultry meat, farmed game meat or rabbit meat unless:

a) it has been obtained from licensed premises (meeting specified conditions);
b) it has been subject to specified pre-slaughter health inspection;
c) it has been chilled and prepared under specified hygienic conditions;
d) it comes from a body of a bird or rabbit which has been subject to specified post-mortem health inspection;
e) it has been given a specified health mark;
f) it is accompanied during transport by specified documents;
g) if it has been stored, the conditions met specified conditions;
h) if wrapped or packaged, the conditions met specified conditions;
i) if transported, the conditions met specified conditions.

2) Subject to a number of limited exceptions, no person shall sell any poultry meat, farmed game meat or rabbit meat which:

a) has been treated with an antibiotic or tenderiser;
b) has been marked with a colourant (except as required by the Regulations);
c) has not been eviscerated;
d) has been treated with a preservative other than a permitted preservative;
e) has been chilled by an immersion technique which does not meet the specified conditions;
f) in the case of rabbit meat or farmed game meat, has been treated with ionizing or ultra-violet radiation

3) Fresh meat, after chilling, shall be kept at or below 4°C, or, after freezing, at or below −12°C.

Hygiene and health: Egg products

Regulation: Egg Products Regulations 1993 (1993/1520)

These Regulations implement EC Directives. They contain some detailed new provisions summarised below and replaced the Liquid Egg (Pasteurisation) Regulations 1963.

Definitions

Egg an egg laid by a hen, duck, goose, turkey, guinea fowl or quail.

Egg products   products obtained from eggs, their various components or mixtures thereof, after removal of the shell and outer membranes, intended for human consumption, and includes such products when partially supplemented by other foodstuffs and additives and such products when liquid, concentrated, crystallised, frozen, quick-frozen or dried but does not include foodstuffs.

Whole egg   a mixture of yolk and albumen.

Cracked eggs   eggs with a damaged but unbroken shell, with intact membranes.

General

1) Egg products which are a mixture of egg products obtained from more than one species cannot be sold except certain egg products may be used at the establishment where they were obtained if they comply with certain hygiene requirements (*see* Regulations).
2) Egg products must comply with specified hygiene and processing requirements (*see* below).
3) Egg products prepared in Great Britain must have been prepared in an approved establishment, approval being given by the local authority. Egg products from other EC countries must have been prepared in establishments which meet the equivalent EC standards.

Hygiene and processing

1) Only non-incubated eggs which are fit for human consumption may be used, and their shells must be fully developed and contain no breaks. Cracked eggs may be used if delivered direct from the packing centre or farm to the heat treatment establishment and broken there as quickly as possible.
2) Pasteurisation conditions are specified as follows:

   Whole egg or yolk   min 64.4°C for min 2 minutes 30 seconds (or an equivalent process) followed by cooling as quickly as possible to below 4°C. Pasteurised product should pass a specified alpha-amylase test.

   Albumen   heat treated by a process designed to take account of the likely microbiological contamination levels in the untreated albumen so as to meet microbiological criteria (*see* 3).
3) For each batch of heat treated egg products the following microbiological criteria shall be met:

   salmonellae   absence in 25 g or 25 ml of egg products
   mesophilic aerobic bacteria $M = 10^5$ in 1 g or 1 ml
   enterobacteriaceae $M = 10^2$ in 1 g or 1 ml
   Staphylococcus aureus   absence in 1 g of egg products
   where M = maximum value for the number of bacteria; the result is

A6

considered unsatisfactory if the number of bacteria in one or more sample units is M or more.

4) Samples of egg products shall meet the following criteria:

   3-hydroxybutyric acid max 10 mg/kg in the dry matter of the unmodified egg product
   lactic acid max 1000 mg/kg of egg product dry matter (applicable only to the untreated egg product)
   succinic acid max 25 mg/kg of egg product dry matter

5) If heat treatment is not carried out immediately after breaking, egg product shall be stored frozen or at a temperature of not more than 4°C (for up to 48 hours maximum).
6) The quantity of egg shell remains, egg membrane and any other particles in the egg product shall not exceed 100 mg/kg of egg product.
7) Maximum storage temperatures are specified:

   deep frozen egg products −18°C
   other frozen products −12°C
   chilled products +4°C

8) Additional detailed requirements are specified for the handling of the eggs and egg products and for the transport, supervision, general conditions for approved establishments, hygiene requirements, packaging of egg products and the marking of egg products (*see* Regulations).

Hygiene and health: Perishable foods (international)

Regulation: International Carriage of Perishable Foodstuffs (Amendment) Regulations 1993 (1993/1589)

These Regulations make a minor amendment to the International Carriage of Perishable Foodstuffs Regulations 1985 which does not affect the detail given perishable foods (international) (pages 166–167).

Weights and measures: Average weights

Regulation: Weights and Measures (Packaged Goods) (Amendment) Regulations 1994 (1994/1258)

A minor amendment is made to the details given on page 171. After the words ‘Alcoholic beverages’, there should be inserted: (except certain wines, grape musts, sparkling wines, spirits, liqueurs and other spiritous beverages and compound alcoholic preparations).

Index

Note: Entries in bold have their own sub-section in the book